Res
i

Research and Writing in the Seminary

Practical Strategies and Tools

DIANE CAPITANI *and*
MELANIE BAFFES

McFarland & Company, Inc., Publishers
Jefferson, North Carolina

The following papers are reprinted by permission of the publishers: "Jesus Grants Honor, Equality, and Voice to the Canaanite Woman," Melanie S. Baffes, originally published as "Jesus and the Canaanite Woman: A Story of Reversal." *Journal of Theta Alpha Kappa* 35, no. 2 (Fall 2011): 12–23. (In Chapter 2.) "Thin Places," Melanie S. Baffes, originally published in *Your Turn! Stories of Renewal*, edited by Carol S. Lawson and Robert F. Lawson, 15–19. West Chester, PA: Chrysalis/Swedenborg Foundation, 2008. (In Chapter 4.) "Reflections on the Border," Alicia M. Van Riggs, originally published in *Pacific School of Religion (PSR) Bulletin* 87, no. 1 (Spring 2008), www.psr.edu/reflections-border. (In Chapter 4.) "Imagining God in Our Ways: The Journals of Frances E. Willard," Diane N. Capitani, originally published by Sage Publications in *Feminist Theology* 12, no. 1 (Sept. 2003): 75–88. (In Chapter 7.) "Does Suicide Exempt the Deceased from the Hope of Future Redemption?" Michele Watkins-Branch, originally published in *Testamentum Imperium: An International Theological Journal Focusing on the Eternal Security of the Christian*, Vol. 3 (2011), *Constructing a Practical Theology on the Doctrine of the Irrevocable Nature of Salvation*, www. preciousheart.net/ti/2011/index.htm, founded by director Kevaughn C.A. Mattis and published by managing editor Michael G. Maness and Kevaughn C.A. Mattis. (In Chapter 7.)

LIBRARY OF CONGRESS CATALOGUING-IN-PUBLICATION DATA

Capitani, Diane N.
 Research and writing in the seminary : practical strategies and tools / Diane Capitani and Melanie Baffes.
  p.   cm.
 Includes bibliographical references and index.

 ISBN 978-0-7864-7864-4 (softcover : acid free paper) ∞

 1. Theology—Research. 2. Theology—Authorship.
3. Academic writing.   I. Title.
BR118.C235 2014
808.06'623—dc23   2014016139

BRITISH LIBRARY CATALOGUING DATA ARE AVAILABLE

© 2014 Diane Capitani and Melanie Baffes. All rights reserved

No part of this book may be reproduced or transmitted in any form or by any means, electronic or mechanical, including photocopying or recording, or by any information storage and retrieval system, without permission in writing from the publisher.

On the cover: Victorian stained glass window, St. John the Evangelist (Sybille Yates/Dreamstime.com)

Printed in the United States of America

McFarland & Company, Inc., Publishers
 Box 611, Jefferson, North Carolina 28640
 www.mcfarlandpub.com

To Kelsey and Matt,
in gratitude for all the joy
they have brought to so many lives.
—*Diane*

To all the wonderful teachers who have mentored me,
with gratitude for your wisdom and guidance.
—*Melanie*

Acknowledgments

The authors wish to thank the following students for granting us permission to reproduce their papers in this volume: Jean Engel, Laura Harris-Adam, Nathan B. Hollifield, Mary Jane Huber, Sarah Lee, Krista J. McNeil, Fernando Rivera, Alicia M. Van Riggs, Michele Watkins-Branch, Rebecca Wilson and Thomas Yang.

Table of Contents

Acknowledgments	vii
Introduction	1
One. Theological Book Reviews	7
Two. Exegetical Papers	20
Three. Theological Essays or Summaries	59
Four. Reflection Papers	83
Five. Research Papers	102
Six. Sermons	163
Seven. Journal Articles	181
Appendix A. Theological Terms	225
Appendix B. Research Sources	229
Appendix C. Style Guides	239
Appendix D. Recommended Reading for Beginning Seminary Students	241
Chapter Notes	245
Bibliography	247
Index	249

Introduction

Both of us entered the seminary with many years experience in writing, either as a teacher/professor of writing at the college and university level (Diane) or as an editor (both Diane and Melanie). Both of us had published work. But what we both discovered was that research and writing in and for the seminary was an entirely different thing altogether and required different skills, as well as a different vocabulary. As I (Diane) write this introduction, I remember my first day in seminary, thinking that research and writing were certainly not going to be areas that would cause me *any* trouble at all. And vocabulary had *always* been my strong suit. How surprised I was when professors began throwing around words that I had not really heard much or at all, words like "pericope"; I certainly was not going to raise my hand and ask what it meant. There didn't seem to be any vocabulary books out there that had a list of "words to know in seminary" so I spent considerable time looking up any word that I jotted down in class, feeling as if having a master's degree in English from a significant institution wasn't serving me very well at all.

Research was another stumbling block. Doing theological research was quite different from the academic research I had done for the master's degrees I held in French, English and comparative literature. Who knew? In my (I hate to admit this) arrogance, I wasn't expecting to have to ask so many questions about the best way to approach theological research and writing, but I swallowed my pride and found that the librarians at my particular seminary were wonderful and very willing to help at all times—an important fact to remember. However, what I also wished for was a book about research and writing in the seminary, with a vocabulary list in one place and instructions on how to write certain types of papers particular to seminary work.

As I finished a master's degree in theological and historical studies and continued on for a Ph.D. in the same areas of study—and because I had been teaching English composition and writing for years at the college level—the academic dean at my institution asked me to develop a course on research and writing for incoming master's students at the seminary that I would then teach. I was excited to do so and pleased to have the opportunity. At last, I could put together a course containing the information that I had yearned for as a student and that I had not been able to find. True, there were a very few books that had begun to present themselves on "writing for the seminary," but none really contained all the information that I felt a seminary student needed, nor were they as practical as they needed to be because they didn't contain "how-to" examples.

After a few years of teaching and continually developing my "Theological Research and Writing" course, I was pleased to have Melanie Baffes as one of my students. Melanie was a writer already and a good one; her papers were a joy to behold. But she also had noted that there were requirements of seminary writing that she was not familiar with, terms that needed explanation, types of research that needed clearer guidelines. As Melanie and I became colleagues and friends, we decided to put together a book that would fill in all those blanks for research and writing in the seminary and possibly make life easier for the incoming seminary student. I will let Melanie tell her part of the story before we continue.

It's true that I (Melanie) came to seminary thinking writing would be no problem for me. I'd worked as an editor for years, but I soon began to wonder if "those who *can*, write … and those who *can't*, edit." Not only was the new terminology a challenge (and I didn't always catch it when my spell-check changed "pericope" to "periscope" and "paraclete" to "parakeet"), but there were *forms* of writing I had never heard about. Exegesis? Reflection paper? I had no idea what these were and didn't have a clue where to look to find the answer. I was grateful for Diane's class; it demystified the process of theological writing and taught me the research basics I needed to complete the M.Div. program. I learned strategies that saved me countless hours and made the work much more enjoyable. It occurred to me afterwards that, although most students believe they either *can* or *cannot* write, writing is a skill that *can* be learned … maybe not outstanding writing, but certainly competent and clear writing. In my life before seminary, in addition to editing and publishing, I'd also spent a dozen or so years developing educational curricula and training programs for youth and adults. So, when we considered Diane's expertise in writing, teaching, research, theology, and English literature and my experience in editing, educational publishing, and curriculum development, it seemed like a good starting point for a book like this one. We've put our heads together to offer practical strategies and tools to help new seminary students get started in theological research and writing.

A few general words about writing before we get down to specifics: we do NOT want this to be a wordy book that bores students to death with theories about writing. We've learned from experience in teaching writing that students simply don't read those books. This is a how-to book, a practical handbook for seminary assignments. It's divided into chapters, each focusing on typical seminary assignments like writing the exegetical paper, writing the reflection paper, and others. Of course, a chapter is devoted to writing the seminary research paper. It also contains a short glossary of terms (Appendix A).

General Thoughts on Writing

Before we get into the real meat of this book, here are a few thoughts that apply no matter where you attend seminary:

1. Don't try to get everything you know about a subject into your paper.
2. Know the *difference* between personal opinion and objective viewpoint.
3. Remember that spell-check does not always serve you well, i.e., it is not *reading* your paper and does not know you meant "off" instead of "of." You *must* always proofread carefully, and the best way to do this is to read your paper out loud. You will hear your mistakes.
4. Use active voice, not passive, in your writing. It makes for a dynamic paper: "John ate the cookie." Not "The cookie was eaten by John."

5. Always cite your sources. If you paraphrase an idea from an author, you must still give credit where credit is due and cite that author's work in a footnote. Never let yourself be accused of plagiarism. More on this subject later.

6. Keep a journal. Write down your thoughts, quotations that appeal to you, including clever cartoons or ideas that can be used for sermons or papers. That journal can be a source of inspiration and comfort for you in the future. You can date the journal on the date you begin writing and look back on it a year or two later to see how you have grown or how your thoughts have changed or progressed. Your journey is just beginning.

7. Perhaps your experience with writing has not always been a pleasant one. One thing we have found is that people enter seminary with a variety of backgrounds, unlike that of other fields of advanced study. Do not let yourself be discouraged if you are sitting next to someone with a law degree or an advanced degree in creative writing. Some of you will enter the pulpit, some of you will teach in the Academy. You all have a place here. Don't forget that.

8. Remember that seminary librarians are your friends. They are there to help you and are usually a treasure trove of information. They love to look up things. If anything, they are unhappy when students don't come find them. So make them happy and look for them when you're struggling with databases and online catalogues; they will be delighted to help you.

9. If your seminary has a writing center or writing tutor, and you feel you're getting behind or are struggling a little, don't wait to ask for help. Do so immediately so you don't fall behind. It's not a mark against you and can help get you off to a good start. It is a sign of a good student.

10. Begin your seminary studies by making a calendar of each class and the assignments it requires:
    A. Introduction to New Testament
        1. Six- to eight-page mid-term paper
        2. Two short reflection papers (two pages each)
        3. Final 15-page paper

Make a chart like this for each class, and note the dates each assignment is due. Keep the dates in order on a calendar and prioritize the assignments. Charts like this may keep you from falling behind. While this might seem like a beginning writer's process, you will find that, in the long run, you'll be grateful that you have kept yourself so organized and on track.

With all this in mind, we offer one caveat: remember that various professors in your individual seminaries will give instructions on the ways in which they want you to write each type of paper you are assigned, i.e., there are no hard-and-fast rules for writing the kinds of papers usually required in seminary. What we're attempting to do is give you a handbook of style that presents the most *commonly* used format for many seminary papers. This should give you a good starting point for a successful seminary writing career.

CHAPTER ONE

Theological Book Reviews

Revise, revise, revise—it is the only act of writing that will set you above the norm.—Elizabeth Dipple, English professor, Northwestern University

There are, of course, different reasons for writing a book review. If you are a student in a seminary, your first introduction to this type of writing may come in the form of a class assignment. Later, as an advanced graduate student entering the publishing world, or whether you have chosen a career in the Academy or a career as a pastor, you may find yourself writing professional book reviews for academic journals, so learning the skill of writing a good theological book review will prove a valuable one. One of the most important points to remember from the beginning of this chapter is that a book review is not a summary of a book. This is not a book report, so you should never approach your book review in this way. You will be discussing the main issues the book raises and you will tell the reader of your review whether the author of the book achieves his or her purpose in writing, but remember, there is a striking difference between doing that and summarizing.

With this thought in mind, we realize that most students will be assigned a book review as they proceed through graduate school. It's a good writing exercise, in particular because the usual review is kept to a very specific word count by the journal to which it is being submitted, so the writer is forced to be concise, clear and disciplined in his or her writing. This is not always easy to do. Good preparation for this exercise is reading reviews in scholarly journals. First, this keeps you abreast of what's new in your field and this is always a good thing; by reading about the latest work published in your area of study, you can keep informed of work you may want to read when you have a chance. Secondly, it prepares you to write a good review yourself; good writing comes about, in part, by modeling good writing.

There are, certainly, two types of book reviews. There are book reviews that are summaries of books, "descriptive" book reviews that do not give a critical analysis. This is not the kind of review that we discuss here. You will be spending your time doing critical book reviews, which do give some summary points of the book, but devote more of their time to evaluation along with description. Remember that the length of your review, in the seminary, will be determined by the class assignment. When submitting a review to a professional journal, you will need to consult the individual journal's publication guidelines. Whichever you are writing, however, you MUST be concise.

Beginning the Book Review

1. Read the book carefully. If possible, you will probably need to read the book more than once. Take careful notes. Is the title a good one? Does it catch your interest? Later, you'll comment on whether it's true to the book.

2. Look at the table of contents. You'll see later if it is a good indicator of what's ahead.

3. Pay particular attention to the author's introduction. It is in the introduction that the author will lay out the plan for the book, the purpose for writing, the thesis of the book, the main argument or arguments he or she hopes to prove and how it is hoped to develop them. Who is the expected audience? Are the author's theological biases evident here?

4. See if you can find any background information on the author. Has she or he written anything else? Was it well-regarded?

5. Where does the author fit in the larger picture of the field of study? Does the author represent one perspective in a certain field of study?

As You Read

Be a critical reader. As noted above, take notes, paying particular attention to the author's thesis and how well it is developed. Is there a clear pattern to the writing? Does the author lay out the book in clear sections? Do points flow from one to the other? Does he or she argue the case with well-presented evidence? Remember, you do not have to agree with the argument, necessarily, but you can see that the author has done a thorough job of presenting evidence that is valid. If the author uses research for support, how did she or he do the research? Was there a dependable research method? If the author used material from other writers, were these sources respected members of the Academy? Remember that the author must be accurate in quoting from sources, both ancient and modern, use current and up-to-date materials, show an awareness of new methodology in the field of study, and acknowledge any biases that she or he has.

The following is an example of a short critical review of a well-known book many of you may be familiar with. This is for you to examine before we break down the steps for you to follow in writing a review like it.

* * *

Book Review: The One-Page Version

Wayne C. Booth, Gregory G. Colomb,
Joseph M. Williams, *The Craft of Research*
(Chicago: University of Chicago Press, 1995)
ISBN 0-226-06584-7

From the publisher of *The Chicago Manual of Style* comes this well-put together, concise guide to researching and writing. Booth, Colomb and Williams, combining years of expertise in the field of research writing, guide beginning, immediate and experienced writers through every stage of the process of research and they do it clearly and well. The authors divide the work of research into a series of steps that allow even the novice

| *Note the opening sentence that immediately tells readers what the book is about. The first paragraph is concise and identifies the book as helpful for beginners and experienced writers—which you want to do if your review is to be helpful.* |

to execute a research paper with confidence and, hopefully, some element of skill.

This is not a formalized work, i.e., it does not create fear in the heart of the beginner, and it does present new tips for the more experienced academic writer. The research and writing process is divided into a series of steps with encouraging boxed notes along the way, and begins with finding a topic of interest that the researcher can understand, creating an appropriate question, narrowing it into a reasonable problem for examination, and formulating the argument. In particular, the time spent on locating significant sources is of interest even to the scholar who has done research before.

> *The second paragraph develops the idea of how helpful the book is and then continues with details about precisely how it is useful.*

The book contains useful sections on specific elements of research, both finding and locating them, and specific ways to make claims and provide evidence. Of certain interest is the section on "warrants," which the authors note may be of more interest to more sophisticated writers. One could argue that any professor would hope that even their beginning students would take the time to read it. A warrant, they claim, is "a general principle that creates a bridge between particular evidence and a particular claim" (112). Many in the field, having forged their way through poorly-done student papers, would be pleased to have students who understood this definition and attempted to employ it in their research work. Contained within the early section is a discussion of rebutting and conceding arguments, and why the writer should be prepared to do so, which is of particular interest. Each section ends with "Quick Tips," summarizing each area that was covered, and presenting the important points once again.

> *Each paragraph opens with a good topic sentence, which is then developed with a specific example.*

The usability of the book comes from the fact that the authors treat research and writing as a craft that can be mastered like any other, an important idea and encouraging for the beginner; they do not believe it to be a "mysterious creative process." In particular, they emphasize the importance of good, clear writing, in language the reader can understand, rather than "heavy writing" that masks "sloppy thinking." Complex language, they claim, does not necessarily indicate complex thinking, a claim with which many may concur. "What counts in your research is not just

> *The reviewer continues with additional details about what the book does so well.*

the apparent truth of your conclusions but the quality of reasoning that got you there," they state (115). The question under consideration must be one that will interest the reader; it is the job of the researcher to convince the reader that the question is of enough significance to explore. Using this practical, well-constructed, and readable guide will certainly put the writer on the right road to success. The prologue will tell the reader what is ahead and encourage them to believe that following the step-by-step process carefully laid out will produce a readable, interesting piece of work; the section on drafting and revision will take the writer through that final, all-important stage. In the end, style and clarity, along with precise scholarship, are the key elements in the "craft of research."

The review concludes by reinforcing the points made earlier—the fact that the book is useful for all and why it is useful. A reviewer should give his or her affiliation at the end of the review.

Diane Capitani
Garrett-Evangelical Theological Seminary, Evanston, IL

* * *

Breaking Down the Book Review: What to Look For

1. Note that there are no footnotes in the short book review. A short book review uses internal citations, usually just the page number on which your quotation appears, placed in parentheses after the quote. There is no room for footnotes if you are to keep within the one-page length.

2. The short book review is generally only one page in length. Because of the short length of this type of review, you must be concise and to-the-point. This is not a summary that tells the entire story.

3. In the end, you are telling the reader if this book is worth buying and worth reading. You are fulfilling an important role. Be honest in your writing. Even if this is an assignment, write as if you were doing this for a major publication.

4. Always use active voice.

5. Engage the text with quotations in strategic places. It proves you really have read the book.

Book Review: The Longer Version (#1)

Craig R. Koester, *Symbolism in the Fourth Gospel: Meaning, Mystery, Community* (Minneapolis: Augsburg Fortress, 2003) ISBN 0-8006-3594-9

In this book, Craig Koester, New Testament professor at Luther Seminary, explores the way that people come to know God through the use of symbolic language in the Gospel of John. He claims that the symbolic language of the Gospel points to the eternal union of Jesus and God, while simultaneously pointing toward the cross, grave, and resurrection. Everyday experiences and objects are used symbolically: "The Gospel presents the paradox that the divine is made known through what is earthly, and the universal is disclosed through what is particular" (Koester, 3). Other dualities that are lifted up in the discussion of the various symbols include the tension between those things from above and those from below, as well as the way the symbolic language focuses simultaneously on Jesus and the disciples.

The review starts with a clear identification of the author, his credentials, and his purpose. It also immediately establishes the author's claim. Good use of a quote to illustrate.
It is good to expand further on what the author is going to do in the opening paragraph.
This is a strong statement with which to end the introductory paragraph; it sums up the book as a whole and directs readers to follow along to see if the author does what he claims he will do.

Koester's insights expand the understanding of the multiplicity of the symbolic language so that more light can break through from the Scriptures into the lives of the people of God.

Koester presents his argument in terms of universal application, rather than application for a specific contextual setting. He does not articulate his social location, so I surmise that he believes his position is hegemonic. He does, however, leave room for contemporary contextual application by the reader. Koester divides the symbols into two groups: core symbols that appear in multiple places in the text, and supportive symbols that assist in the revelatory properties of the core symbols (Koester, 5–6). Many of the symbols explored in the book can be perceived by the senses, such as light, bread, water, and wine, along with sym-

An important first sentence—in order to present how the author develops his argument.

bolic actions of healing and restoration, all of which should be understood contextually.

In order to understand the complex nature of these symbols, it is important to understand the context of the first century, since symbols do not function in a void. For Koester, the author of the Fourth Gospel had a particular audience in mind, which consisted of Jewish Christians (Koester, 19). This was not, however, the exclusive audience, as the Greeks and Samaritans are always on the horizon, if not, at least temporarily, front and center (Koester, 20–22). Once the audience and contextual framework is covered in his introductory chapter, Koester structures the remaining seven chapters into two sections. The first section, Chapters 2 to 5, works through a variety of symbols and symbolic actions that are found in John. This includes representative figures such as Nicodemus and the Samaritan Woman, symbolic actions such as healings and feeding the multitudes, as well as an exploration of light and dark, water and the crucifixion.

| *After establishing in the second paragraph what the author is doing—developing the argument around symbols—the reviewer now gets specific in presenting examples of the "meat" of the book. This is always important in a book review.* |

The second section focuses on how the symbolic language functioned in the society. For Koester, the intersection of symbol and community is found by looking at the sociological unity that can be teased out from the symbolic language. Koester states that one should consider "a number of Johannine communities located in different places" (Koester, 254), rather than a single cohesive group.

| *This paragraph continues what the reviewer was doing in the last one. The use of a specific quote adds strength to the review.* |

A common faith in Jesus, and distinguishing themselves from the Jewish synagogues, were uniting factors for the community, which was shaped by the symbols that reinterpret Jewish symbols and practices Christologically (Koester, 260). The final chapter focuses on how the symbolic language points to the unity of Jesus and God, and that through coming to, knowing, and believing in Jesus, one comes to know God. It is this eternal and indivisible unity of Jesus and God that is distinctive in the Gospel of John. The signs, stories, and symbols used in the Gospel are done to one end, to bring people to faith.

The symbolic themes are woven together in Chapter 7 and show how the Gospel writer created a rich symbolic tapestry in the crucifixion story, which was "written for believers but was forged in a context of disputes with the non–Christian world" (Koester, 208). The challenge for the Gospel writer is to articulate how the death of Jesus revealed the power of God's love. Symbolic language is the only way that this could be done. Koester shapes this chapter around four levels of Christological symbolism: "(1) the meaning of his death at the simple human level, (2) its relationship to Jewish scripture and their understanding of sacrifice, (3) the significance of the crucifixion for Jesus' identity as prophet and Messiah, and (4) the cross as the glorification of Jesus and God" (Koester, 209). The incarnation makes the death a real death that, from the Roman perspective, should serve as a deterrent to others who would have politically subversive attitudes. The trial, scourging, the conflict and collusion between Roman and Jewish authorities, and the timing of the actions, bring to a head the ongoing confrontation between Jesus and the Jewish system of sacrifice that begins in John 2:13. The fulfillment of Scriptures allows for the possibility of continuity between the Jewish belief and belief in Jesus, but demands a shift in understanding to ensure, from the Gospel writer's perspective, that believers understand that Jesus carried out the will of God in giving up his life.

> *This is one of Koester's most important points, so it is good to quote it entirely in the review.*

I continue to be challenged by Koester's articulation of atonement. The author of the Fourth Gospel has the ultimate challenge to show how and why a non-sin sacrifice of Passover can be connected to the crucifixion of Jesus. In the Prologue, John the Baptist says "Behold the Lamb of God who takes away the sins of the world (1:29). The connection, therefore, between the Passover observance and the crucifixion is of utmost importance. Koester states that "Sin is lethal estrangement from God, but through the cross the self-sacrificing love of God is revealed, overcoming hostility then it transforms it into faith. This reconciliation is atonement ... in a Johannine sense" (Koester, 221). Koester examines the relationship between the Pascal lamb, the suffering servant, and the binding of Isaac, which he finds tenuous at best, and is incongruous with the rest of his arguments, based on the four Christological symbols listed above.

> *At this point, the reviewer can begin to either agree or disagree, or simply express, as this reviewer does, challenges with the book being reviewed. You must, however, take a position and give examples, expressing a point of view.*

For Koester, the actions of Jesus, and the entire crucifixion narrative, when understood symbolically, reveal the divine nature of Jesus, consistent with the opening words of the Prologue. The glory of God is finally revealed in the symbolic flow of the water of life from Jesus' side, the drawing of all people to God when the glory is revealed as indicated by the representative characters of Joseph of Arimathea and Nicodemus. This revelation of God's glory reflects directly on the oneness of God and the Word. Koester claims that the Johannine community is shaped by the self-giving love of Jesus.

| *The reviewer is summarizing the text, leading to her conclusion.* |

As a pastor and teacher, I find Koester's work to be a helpful resource in exegesis and Bible study. Within the realm of storytelling, the exploration of symbolic language is very important, and Koester's work and model for exploring the power of symbolic language will provide much fodder for my future endeavors. I will be particularly interested to compare and contrast his articulation of the symbolic nature of the crucifixion with others articulations as I continue to explore the atonement in John.

| *As a student, you will want to comment in the conclusion on whether this book will be helpful to you in your future work or whether you do not feel it will.* |

Mary Jane Huber
Garrett-Evangelical Theological Seminary, Evanston, Il

* * *

Book Review: The Longer Version (#2)

Barbara Rossing, *The Rapture Exposed: The Message of Hope in the Book of Revelation*
(New York: Basic Books, 2004) ISBN: 0-8133-4314-3

Rossing gives readers a clear, in-depth look at Rapture theology and dispensationalism, the belief in God's master plan for the history of the world that leads to a warlike "end-times." In this very readable volume, the author outlines Rapture proponents' arguments and shows how believers use proof-texting of Scripture passages (primarily from Daniel and the Book of Revelation) to support their beliefs. As she deconstructs

| *The first paragraph gives a brief overview of what the author of the book intends to do. To do this well, you must take time to really grasp the author's argument.* |

the Rapture interpretation of Scripture, highlighting the distortions and fictionalizations, Rossing places it alongside a thoughtful, balanced, and more accurate reading of the text. Her thesis is that Rapture theology is a dangerous distortion—a complete reversal, in fact—of the primary message of Scripture, a message that culminates in the Book of Revelation.

> *Here, the reviewer outlines the author's thesis statement, which makes more sense after a clear summary of the book's purpose.*

Rossing first guides readers through a summary of Rapture theology and its distinctive claims. In discussing the Rapture emphasis on *escape* from the world, Rossing points out the "appalling ethics" (Rossing, 7) it espouses—a "selfish non-concern for the world" (Rossing, 18)—ethics that are the direct opposite of those mainstream Christians draw from Scripture. But much more damaging than these values, according to Rossing, is the "ethos of righteous Christian violence" that permeates the thinking and rhetoric of Rapture theology (Rossing, 40). Because Rapture believers connect their end-times scenarios to contemporary politics, finding signs of Apocalypse in every conflict and seeing the Antichrist in every aggressor, they justify and welcome violence because they see it as an inevitable component of their dispensationalist script. Most alarming is their steadfast belief that Israel's rebirth and restoration is necessary in order for Jesus to return, a belief that allows them to support Israel's violent takeover of territories from Palestinians, no matter what the human cost. Both Jews and Palestinian Christians are merely players in a story that exists for the sole benefit of Rapture Christians. The most frightening result of Rapture theology is that fictional accounts of the Apocalypse, such as those depicted in the *Left Behind* series, have allowed this kind of thinking to find its way into the popular culture.

> *Subsequent paragraphs go into more detail about the author's argument and the warrants she uses to back up her claim. This paragraph describes the author's deconstruction of Rapture theology and the specific dangers it poses.*

Because believers find the Rapture story so compelling, Rossing sets out to offer another, more powerful and accurate story. She focuses on the Book of Revelation, since it informs so much of Rapture belief, but frames her discussion in a comprehensive theology of Scripture that finds fulfillment in the last book of the Bible. She explains the true meaning of prophecy—not as a prediction of future events as Rapture theology says, but a warning "of the consequences of destructive behavior" (Rossing, 89). She explains that Revelation is not a book that forecasts doom, but is instead a warning combined with a message of hope. It is a *vision*, not a literal vision of future events, but a visionary journey we take in order to see what could happen if we fail to respond to God's word. Through a detailed analysis of Revelation, Rossing argues that God does not snatch us *out* of the world as Rapture theology claims, but instead comes *into* the world to be with us, to dwell with us and to walk with us. God comes not to destroy the world, but to heal the world, and Rossing suggests that the tree of life, which appears both in Genesis and in Revelation, comes full circle to signify a "healing vision for the world" (Rossing, 80). This new vision, Rossing says, "can transform the way we live out God's reign in the world today" (Rossing, 164).

Here, we learn more about the alternative—and more positive— theology the author constructs based on the Book of Revelation.

In reviews of a single work (a book, book chapter, or article), it's usually preferable to cite page numbers in parentheses within the text rather than in footnotes.

Rossing develops her argument skillfully, by highlighting a series of "reversals" that place the true meaning of Revelation over against Rapture theology. The first is the image of the Lamb, an unexpected image of power. Rossing claims that Revelation's vision of the Lamb symbolizes the power of nonviolent love to change the world. Within Revelation, the Lamb reframes the prevailing idea of victory: no longer is Rome's imperial theology the victor, but true victory comes through Jesus' self-giving love. But also, Rossing point outs, the Lamb redefines and reverses the idea of violence itself, as "God's people are called to conquer not by fighting but by remaining faithful" (Rossing, 111). This image is in direct contrast to the Rapture focus on violence and destruction as power.

We've heard the "what" of the author's argument; now this part of the review reveals more about the "how"—specifically how the author proves her point.

Rossing also shows how Revelation overturns the selfish, individualistic, and self-protective ethos of Rapture theology. Where Rapture proponents consider only the fate of an individual believer, Revelation envisions a new community of abundance for all, one in which no one will be left behind.

And finally, Rossing argues that Revelation's message itself is a complete reversal of Rapture theology. It is "Rapture in reverse"

(Rossing, 147), bringing a message not of God snatching believers out of this world, but one of God being incarnate in our midst. Like the rest of holy Scripture, Revelation teaches that "God loves the world so much that God comes to earth to dwell with us" (Rossing, 148).

Because this book is written primarily for a lay audience, Rossing does not directly employ scholarly methodologies to make her case. In talking about Rome's worship of victory (Chapter 5), however, she does use historical (social-scientific) criticism to give readers an idea of the context in which Revelation was written. This is designed to give readers a better grasp of the message Revelation conveys about the power of Jesus' nonviolent, self-giving love—within the framework of Rome's imperial rule. Rossing does not include the perspective of minority interpreters, but she does touch briefly on the view of oppressed peoples in a discussion of "the courtroom of the lamb," pointing out that victims of injustice must know that they will be vindicated by God. She also makes a passing reference to the "feminine characterization of the evil empire" (Rossing, 132) claiming the image of Babylon (Rome) as a whore is not to be taken literally. Although it is not necessarily within the scope of this book to incorporate perspectives of individuals in marginalized groups, Rossing's analysis seems incomplete without them.

The review discusses the author's methodology and audience. It also critiques the book for not addressing the perspectives of those in marginalized groups.

The Rapture Exposed is extremely useful for gaining a clear understanding of the primary messages in Revelation, specifically *how* it says what it says. It also is very relevant for my ministry. Because it is written for a lay audience—clear, engaging, and readable—it would be highly effective in a Bible study class, a book discussion group, or even a workshop. Rossing points out that nearly 60 percent of Americans believe the events in Revelation to be true literally (Rossing, 72). For this reason, it would be very helpful for congregation members to read this book, in order to debunk popular ideas about the Apocalypse and to help them understand Revelation in a deeper way. I could foresee a workshop on a topic such as "The Already and Not-Yet Reign of

The final paragraph highlights the book's usefulness in various ministry settings. What would strengthen this review is more of the reviewer's engagement with ideas she agrees with and those she does not—a more in-depth critique of the author's key ideas in addition to the clear summary.

God" or a Bible study (similar to one Rossing describes on p. 166) focused on the question of "What might the new Jerusalem look like?"

Melanie Baffes
Garrett-Evangelical Theological Seminary, Evanston, IL

* * *

CHAPTER TWO

Exegetical Papers

A blank piece of paper is God's way of telling us how hard it is to be God.—Sidney Sheldon

What Is Exegesis?

One of the first assignments you'll be asked to do in seminary is write an exegetical paper. Biblical Studies professors often assign papers in the first few weeks of the semester, provide a brief handout with basic guidelines, and expect students to cobble together something resembling exegesis. Your work will proceed more enjoyably if you take time first to understand the basics of exegesis.

EXEGESIS

The word *exegesis* comes from the Greek *exēgeisthai*, which means "to lead out of," "to interpret," or "to explain." Exegesis is the process of interpreting the meaning of biblical passages or verses, not by means of your own creative imagination, but through a systematic approach.[i] This approach uses a particular set of *methods* (such as the historical-critical method, which you will learn more about shortly) and a specific set of *tools* (Bible commentaries, dictionaries, concordances, etc.).

In writing exegesis, your goal is to guide readers through a biblical passage in order to help them understand the text. Exegesis is important for seminary students because it's an important step in preparing for Bible study, teaching, preaching, or pastoral care. You won't be able to help others comprehend the biblical text unless you yourself have entered into the world of a particular passage and gained a deeper understanding of the text in all its complexity. Keep in mind that reading and interpreting Scripture for the purpose of exegesis is *not* the same as reading the Bible for prayer, Bible study, devotion, or spiritual formation. Please note that exegesis is *not*:

- reading the text in light of your personal faith journey;
- a reflection on what the passage means to you;
- a sermon or a homily;
- a review of the commentaries or literature;
- a verse-by-verse translation or explanation;
- a summary of what you have learned about the passage; or
- an explanation of the one true meaning of the text.

When you exegete a text, you're not setting out to prove or disprove foundational beliefs; instead, you're trying to discover what the author is saying, what means he uses to say it, and what the passage might have meant to those who first read or heard it. Exegesis is an interpretive process involving the study of several different dimensions of the text.

- *Audience.* Biblical texts were written for a specific audience in a specific place and time.
- *Language.* The Hebrew Scriptures were written in Hebrew (later translated to Aramaic); the books of the New Testament were written in *Koine* Greek, the everyday Greek language used by inhabitants of the Roman Empire.
- *Social world and culture.* The social and cultural world of the authors of the text (and the first readers) differs significantly from our cultural world.
- *History.* Different books of the Bible were written in different historical contexts that influenced their emphasis and perspective.
- *Authorship, source, and tradition.* Many of the books of the Bible were written by more than one person, reflecting traditions that evolved over a period of time.
- *Genre and form.* The Bible consists of a variety of genres and forms, including visions, oracles, speeches, psalms, poetry, liturgies, miracle stories, parables, dialogues, and epistles.
- *Text variations.* The texts we have are copies made centuries after the originals were written (there are about 5,000 different frag-

ments or manuscripts of the New Testament, for example). The texts also were translated into other languages, such as Aramaic, Latin, Syrian, and Coptic.[ii]

HERMENEUTICS

Students new to biblical studies often confuse exegesis with hermeneutics; in fact, the terms are sometimes used interchangeably. Although exegesis and hermeneutics are related, they refer to distinct aspects of the interpretive process. The term *hermeneutics* refers to the "rules one uses for searching out the meanings of writings, particularly biblical texts."[iii] The field of hermeneutics studies the theory, methodological principles, or underlying assumptions that guide interpretation of a text. In reading any biblical text, you use hermeneutic (or interpretive) principles at every stage–whether or not you're aware of doing so. Some common types of hermeneutics (or presuppositions) include:

- *Literal interpretation.* Some interpreters of the Bible view it as being divinely inspired, revealed, or "dictated" to writers and, as a result, believe that the text should be read as literally true.
- *Moral interpretation.* Interpreting the Bible through this lens involves seeing the text as a code of conduct or ethical lessons for everyday life.
- *Typological interpretation.* This interpretation presupposes that persons, objects, and events in the Hebrew Scriptures are meant to "pre-figure," typify, and predict persons, objects, and events in the New Testament.[iv]

Methods of Biblical Criticism

Also related to exegesis is biblical criticism, a broad discipline that investigates various questions related to the Bible–questions related to the history of the text (the world *behind* the text), the text itself (the world *of* the text), and the impact of the text on readers today (the world *in front of* the text).

Like exegesis, biblical criticism involves the process of interpreting the biblical text. But the term *biblical criticism* refers to a broad range of interpretive activities that are used to evaluate a text from different perspectives: "Biblical criticism is 'critical,' not in the sense that it 'criticizes' the Bible, but in the sense that it carefully and deliberately engages the text and assumes the freedom to derive from the Bible meanings that may differ from those that traditional religion has seen in it."[v] Any exegetical analysis you complete—whether in preparation for writing a paper, preaching a sermon, or teaching a Bible study—draws from the established methods of biblical criticism.

Exegesis, hermeneutics, and biblical criticism can be summarized as follows:

Exegesis	Hermeneutics	Biblical Criticism
A *systematic and individual study* of various elements of a biblical text (studying authorship of the Deutero-Pauline Epistles, for example)	The *principles, set of rules, or interpretive lenses* used to read a biblical text (reading the text from a feminist or womanist perspective, for example)	A *broad discipline* that includes a range of interpretive activities for evaluating Bible texts (the branch of biblical criticism that studies the text to identify its underlying ideologies, for example)

COMMON APPROACHES TO THE TEXT

Historical criticism—study of the historical background of the text from the viewpoint of social setting, location, and date—often has been considered the foundation of biblical criticism, although it's only one among many methods. The Bible's meaning can be found in other approaches, including source criticism, form criticism, and literary criticism. Different critical methods address different questions and aspects of a text (although there's a great deal of overlap among them), and many scholars utilize a combination of approaches, as you will do when exegeting a text. Your task is to choose the methods most appropriate and revealing for the biblical text you've selected. Oftentimes, your instructor will tell you what method to use.

The following is a broad overview of common approaches to the world *behind* the text, the world *of* the text, and the world *in front of* the text.

THE WORLD BEHIND THE TEXT

The biblical texts were written by human authors who lived in particular historical and social settings that determined their beliefs, worldviews, and experiences. Looking at the world behind the text involves exploring the text's history (**historical criticism**); its authorship and source (**source criticism**); different layers or breaks in the text (**redaction criticism**); the oral traditions that preceded the written documents (**tradition criticism**); and the social context in which it was developed (**social-science criticism**).

THE WORLD OF THE TEXT

Exploring the world of the text itself involves examining its literary genre, a particular kind or type of literary work (**literary criticism**); the smaller units that make up the text, the type of language used, word choice (**form criticism**); techniques used by the author to persuade readers and/or listeners (**rhetorical criticism**); or the narrative arc of a story (**narrative criticism**). Studying the text in this way can offer clues to the author's intent and to the potential impact on the first readers.

THE WORLD IN FRONT OF THE TEXT

Looking at the world in front of the text means studying the impact of a particular passage on a reader or a community of readers—in light of the specific context in which the text is read (**reader-response criticism**). The social location or context may include the community's history, values, attitudes, experiences, and worldview. This approach emphasizes the role of the reader and the process of interpreting the text—as opposed to the world of the author or the world of the text itself.

Two basic principles underlie in-front-of-the text methodology: (1) the understanding that meaning is not contained within the text itself but is created in the dialogue between the reader and the text; and (2) the assumption that the meaning of a text is different for each reader.[vi] In the last several decades, in fact, post-modern scholars have continued to challenge the idea that there is one ultimate truth or meaning inherent in the biblical text. Instead, they suggest, there are a variety of *potential* meanings. For post-modern critics, any reading of the biblical text is valid, and scholars do not have privileged access to the "right" interpretation. Similarly, post-structuralists have called attention to the fact that all concepts of reality are historically based (and therefore biased), and they have raised awareness of the role of power in determining what individuals think and believe. Political/ideological criticism, for example, is a hermeneutical perspective that reveals the ways in which the biblical text has been used to justify practices of domination and oppression.

Feminist, womanist, and post-colonial theorists, in particular, have revealed the historical interpretation of the Bible from a white, Euro-centric perspective—a reading that has relegated all other perspectives to the margins. Recent scholarship has attempted to "de-center" biblical interpretation, giving voice to individuals and groups previously ignored (**feminist, womanist, liberationist, and post-colonial criticism**). Although these perspectives are still considered "alternative" in some seminaries, a comprehensive exegesis will take into account the perspectives of individuals or groups for whom traditional historical-critical interpretations have been oppressive.

Overview of Biblical Criticism: The World Behind the Text			
Method	Key Questions	Approach	Example
Historical criticism (this is an umbrella term for different types of criticism listed below)	What is the context and setting of the passage? Under what historical conditions does it appear to have been written?	Researches historical, social, political, and cultural background of text from the perspective of social setting, historical foreground, geographical location, and date	Determining whether a psalm is pre-exilic, exilic, or post-exilic
Source criticism	Who wrote the text? If an author is assumed, did that person actually write it? What sources did the author use? Are there inconsistencies, shifts, or repetitions that suggest more than one author?	Examines the biblical text to determine the sources or written documents the author drew from in producing a finished text (and how the different texts relate to each other)	Tracing the *Yahwist* (J), *Elohist* (E), Deuteronomist (D), and Priestly (P) sources of the Pentateuch
Tradition criticism	What oral traditions shaped the text into its present form? What different traditions are discernible in the text? What different stages of development can be seen?	Explores the ways in which various oral traditions of a community were passed on, how they evolved over time and influenced the development of the text	Tracing the theme of exile and return in Hosea
Social-science criticism	What are the social structures and conventions of the author's world? How are they reflected in the text?	Looks at the world of the author from a historical viewpoint, focusing on values, social structures, conventions, interactions and experiences	Studying the first-century concept of "anti-society" as it relates to the Gospel of John

Overview of Biblical Criticism: The World of the Text			
Method	Key Questions	Approach	Example
Literary criticism (this is an umbrella term for different types of criticism listed below)	What is the genre of the text? Is it narrative, poetry, apocalyptic literature, an epistle, wisdom literature?	Investigates the Bible as literature, looking at genre, styles, patterns, and narrative approaches used in creation of a text	Examining differences in language and style in the Pauline Epistles
Form criticism (related to literary criticism)	How do smaller units of a text function? Why did the author choose them? Is a particular type of language used, or are certain words significant?	Analyzes the form and function of smaller units of a text to identify the underlying purpose for the use of that particular form	Studying the use of dialogue vs. monologue in the Book of Proverbs
Redaction criticism (related to source criticism; also known as editorial criticism or composition criticism)	Are there different layers or breaks in the text that point to different editorial stages? What is the theological perspective of the editor/redactor? How has the text been altered to reflect that viewpoint?	Studies the way in which smaller units from written sources or oral traditions were combined, adapted, or reinterpreted for a particular audience or to accomplish a specific theological agenda	Examining the textual variants in the texts of Psalm 18 and 2 Samuel 22
Rhetorical criticism	What are the rhetorical techniques the author used? How did the writer employ these techniques to persuade readers and/or listeners?	Considers the Bible as rhetoric and looks at an author's intent to persuade, convince, or reinforce convictions	Considering the purpose of the Sermon on the Mount in Matthew 5-7
Narrative criticism	Why did the author tell the story in this particular way? What impact does it have on those who read or hear the story?	Explores plot, conflict, character, setting, and point of view — as well as the function of the story and the narrative world of the text to understand the effect the text has on the implied reader and why it has that effect	Identifying the differences in the birth narratives of Jesus in Matthew vs. Luke

Beginning the Exegetical Paper—Analysis

ANALYSIS AND SYNTHESIS

Writing an exegetical paper has often been characterized as a process of analysis and synthesis. In the first stage, you analyze different elements of the passage—such as history, socio-cultural setting, or literary genre—taking apart the components in order to study them separately. Once you've examined the component parts using the approaches and tools available, the second stage is one of synthesis. This involves reviewing the various pieces of your research, considering the significance of each, and determining how they fit

Two. Exegetical Papers

| \multicolumn{4}{c}{Overview of Biblical Criticism: The World in Front of the Text} |
Method	Key Questions	Approach	Example
Reader-response criticism (this is an umbrella term for different types of criticism listed below)	How do a reader's beliefs, values, and worldview influence reading of the text? How does the reader interpret the text as a way to make sense of the world?	Examines the role of the reader in determining the meaning of the text and in interpreting it in order to make sense of the world	Interpreting a gospel passage by imagining, constructing, and forming ideas about the text through an intuitive reading
Feminist, womanist, and liberationist criticism	How has the text been interpreted in the past? Who has been doing the interpreting? What impact have those readings had on women and other marginalized groups? How can the text be read "from the margins?"	Studies the text in light of the political, social, and economic rights of groups marginalized by traditional readings and historical interpretations	Reading Genesis 16 from the perspective of Hagar, Sarah's maid
Political, ideological, socio-economic, post-colonial criticism	How has the text been used to justify practices of oppression, domination, and imperialism?	Analyzes the text from the perspective of political, ideological, or socio-economic power, including issues of dominance and resistance, oppression and marginalization, and politics of imperial and colonial	Understanding the motif of "the world above" in the Prologue to the Gospel of John as a colonizing idea

together into a cohesive interpretation of the text. Sometimes your investigation will reveal that previous understandings do not fit with the evidence gathered.[vii]

CLARIFYING THE ASSIGNMENT

The professor who assigns an exegetical paper may or may not provide guidelines. You may be asked to focus on an historical analysis of the text in its original setting, or you may be free to select the area on which you want to concentrate. If the instructions are vague or unclear, ask probing questions to focus your thinking about the assignment:

- How large a pericope should I select?
- Is there a particular critical method I should use?
- Can I choose methods best suited to the passage?
- Do you want to see implications for contemporary readers?
- Should there be a section on applications for ministry?

- Is there a specific organization of the material you would prefer?
- Do I need to identify my social location or hermeneutical lens?
- Is this an objective historical-critical analysis or do I need to propose an argument of my own?

Guiding Questions

You may begin your research by consulting one or two Bible commentaries just to gain a general idea of the passage. Once you begin your research in earnest, however, it's helpful to have some guiding questions in mind. If you take time to develop a few focused questions up front, your research will be much more productive than if you try to read everything you can on a given text. Keep in mind that your questions may change or expand as you complete your research. Read the passage several times slowly, reflecting on the following questions:

- What interests you most about this text?
- Are there any words or phrases that jump out at you?
- How would you describe in your own words what happens in this passage?
- What primary message do you understand from this passage?
- What's one question related to this text that would you like to explore?

Steps for Exegetical Analysis

There are different ways to approach exegesis, but they all involve similar steps and, as you gain experience, you'll develop your own process. Here are some basic guidelines to get you started, but keep in mind that you may use only some of these steps—depending on the specific assignment, the length of paper required, or the biblical passage you've chosen. We've also pointed to a few resources to begin your exploration, but don't forget to check other materials (including Internet Resources) listed in Appendix B—Research Sources—and to compile your own list of resources as you go along.

1. *Determine the boundaries of the text.* How much of the passage should you include in your study? If there were no chapter and verse divisions, how much of the surrounding text would belong to the

selected passage? Are there things that happen immediately before and after this text that may help you understand what these particular words are trying to accomplish? How does this larger unit relate to what seems to be the major themes and concerns of this text?

2. *Research the historical context.* Look at the historical setting in which the text was written. Who is the author? What were the circumstances under which the text was written? Who is the audience? What were their circumstances when they first heard this text? Was there a specific historical event or situation that caused the book (and not just the specific text) to be written? Would what was communicated to the original hearers be different from associations made by today's readers? Do any of these differences significantly alter the meaning or add to your understanding of it? (Start with Bible Commentaries and other resources listed in "Historical Context of the Bible" in Appendix B—Research Sources.)

3. *Analyze the source of the passage.* What is the original source of the material? What other ancient documents did the author use in composing the text? What is the relationship of this text to its sources? How did the author alter the source materials for his own purposes? Are there inconsistencies in the text as a result of the different sources used? (See materials listed in Appendix B—Research Sources; for NT exegesis, see *The Sources of the Synoptic Gospels*; for OT exegesis, see *Readings from the Ancient Near East: Primary Sources for Old Testament Study*.)

4. *Look at how the passage appears in other books.* Does this same story or parable appear in other books or gospels? If so, how does it compare to other versions? Are the words and ideas presented in the same way? Is the larger context of the passage in other books different from the one you are studying? Does the passage allude to, quote, or contain "echoes" of other biblical texts? If so, how do they compare? What other passages help us understand this text? Does this passage affect the meaning or value of others? (See materials listed in Appendix B—Research Sources; for NT exegesis, consult *Synopsis of the Four Gospels: Greek-English Edition* and *Commentary on the New Testament Use of the Old Testament*; for OT exegesis, see *Ancient Israelite and Early Jewish Literature*.)

5. *Reflect on key words and themes.* What specific words did the author use (as opposed to others he might have chosen with similar

meaning)? Are there words in your passage that do or do not occur frequently elsewhere in the author's writings? Are there themes or images in your text that appear elsewhere in the Bible? Or is there a theme that is unique to your chosen passage? (See Bible Concordances suggested in Appendix B—Research Sources.)

6. *Review the original text/translation.* Examine key words as they appear in the original language. What are the nuances of the various words used? (See materials listed in Appendix B—Research Sources; for NT exegesis, see *A New Reader's Lexicon of the Greek New Testament*; for OT exegesis, see *The Hebrew and Aramaic Lexicon of the Old Testament.*)

7. *Look at grammar and syntax.* After reviewing key words and themes, look into the grammatical elements of the passage: sentence structure, verb tenses, and the connections between words. Look for unusual constructions, unexpected verb tenses, or the choice to use singular or plural pronouns. Does it suggest that some phrases could be read in a new light if translated differently? Are there any ambiguities in the Hebrew or Greek that make different interpretations possible? (See materials listed in Appendix B—Research Sources; for NT exegesis, consult *The Idiom Book of New Testament Greek, Analysis of the Greek New Testament,* and *The New Linguistic and Exegetical Key to the Greek New Testament*; for OT exegesis, see *A Guide to Biblical Hebrew Syntax* and *Basics of Biblical Hebrew Grammar.*)

8. *Determine the form or genre of the passage.* What are the literary features of the text? What kind of saying is it? Is it an apocalyptic saying? Is it a prophetic utterance? Does it have poetic elements? Does it employ overstatement? Is it a parable, historical narrative, dialogue, or epistle? What function did the form serve in its original community? How would the form have influenced original listeners' understanding of the passage? (See materials listed in Appendix B—Research Sources; for NT exegesis, consult *Literary Forms in the New Testament*; for OT exegesis, see *Style and Structure in Biblical Hebrew Narrative.*)

9. *Consider the setting of the story.* At what point in the narrative does the writer place this passage? Should any significance be attached to *when* in the story the author places the text? What was the role and function of various characters (such as prophets, scribes, or Pharisees) in the culture of the narrative? How do the story's

events, characters, timeline, and settings contribute to the overall message the author is trying to convey?

10. *Explore the theological themes.* What are some key theological themes and messages expressed in this text—themes such as covenant, law, revelation, baptism, etc. Where else in the chapter (or book) do these same messages occur? Is there a relationship between these texts?

QUICK TIP: CHECKLIST FOR EXEGETICAL PAPERS

☐ Decide on the best text to use and determine the original wording, as best you can.
☐ Gain a sense of the context of the passage and its place in the developing narrative.
☐ Determine the form of the passage—whether the text is a discourse, parable, narrative, pronouncement story, miracle story, etc.
☐ Analyze grammar and syntax and investigate significant terms.
☐ Be clear as to how the passage is structured by noting the sequence of events.
☐ Note significant historical, social, cultural, and geographical background and events.
☐ Trace tradition history and sources and the concerns of the original writers.
☐ Determine how the passage functions in the overall narrative of the book.
☐ Note any important conflicts and resolutions in the passage.
☐ Sum up the main thrust of the passage. How does it function as the Word of God?
☐ Show that you've understood and synthesized the commentaries and work of others, but thought about the passage yourself and included your own original thoughts. Remember, your thoughts are valuable as well.

Completing the Exegetical Paper—Synthesis

The synthesis stage involves reviewing the elements of your analysis, identifying the significant points in each, and finding a common thread running throughout your findings. Your study may suggest insights that are counter to traditional readings of the text, or it may indicate new possibilities for expanding on those insights. You may find that the text doesn't answer the questions you originally posed, but instead points in new directions; this is a positive sign because it shows you're being open to what your research has revealed.

Reviewing Your Research

You began by identifying a few key questions to explore; as you have conducted your analysis, new questions also will have emerged. These provide a starting point for synthesizing your findings into a clear and compelling interpretation of the text. Review the notes you've gathered in your research and consider the following questions:

- How has your initial impression or understanding of the text changed?
- How does your research relate to your initial impression?
- Do you agree with traditional interpretations of this passage?
- If there is more than one interpretation, with which do you agree and why?
- How can you enlarge or expand on the interpretation that speaks to you?
- What is the one most important question you would like to address?

Identifying the Unifying Theme

In using the methods of biblical criticism for exegesis, it's not possible to develop a strictly "neutral" or objective interpretation of the biblical text. Interpreters cannot help but bring their own theological concerns and presuppositions to their reading of the text, and these concerns and presuppositions will no doubt influence the questions you raise and the interpretation you shape in response to those questions. Keep in mind, however, that you can't "force" a certain argument, but you can present your interpretation if you've found evidence in your research to support it. Say, for example, you're curious about Jesus' statement in the Gospel of John, "for salvation is from the Jews" (John 4.22b), and you suspect that this text can be read against the grain (contrary to traditional readings). You might ask yourself, who Jesus is referring to when he says "the Jews?" How does this statement compare with others Jesus makes about this group in John's Gospel? What was the prevailing attitude of the Johannine community toward those in the synagogue at the time the Gospel was written? What events occurred around the time that the Gospel was written that may have influenced what the Johannine Jesus said and did? As you answer these questions, a thread will begin to emerge, some element of the passage that stands out for you. More research may be needed at this point, but it will be clearly focused on your unifying theme.

COMPLETING THE EXEGETICAL SYNTHESIS

Depending on the type of exegesis the professor has asked you to focus on, your final paper will contain several elements. In most cases, you'll be asked to do a paper that focuses on a "behind-the-text" approach, combining historical and social-science criticism. Other professors may ask you to focus on the world of the text—literary, form, rhetorical, or narrative criticism. Increasingly, you may be asked to focus on the world in front of the text and interpret the passage from a particular perspective or social location. But *all* the methods of biblical criticism can be employed in your research—and to support your interpretation as it is emerging. How you decide to present your interpretation (provided the professor doesn't specify) is entirely up to you, but it is important that you build your argument in a clear and straightforward, but also engaging, way. Here are the various elements that may be included in a basic exegetical paper:

- Introduction
  - ➢ translation of the text passage
  - ➢ summary of the text's message
  - ➢ a clear thesis statement
- Historical analysis
  - ➢ authorship (location and timeframe)
  - ➢ background of the author's setting (cultural, religious, social, and political)
  - ➢ original audience (and how they may have heard the text)

- Literary analysis
  - larger context/location of the passage
  - content of surrounding passages
  - genre, form, and structure of the text passage
- Word study and textual analysis
  - alternate translations of words in the original language
  - interesting or unusual grammatical constructions
  - relationship between this text and other biblical passages
- Your interpretation
  - theological message or implications
  - summary of your interpretation
  - implications for a contemporary audience
  - conclusion

Keep in mind that you don't have to include *all* of your research in the paper, nor do you have to present your findings in a linear, step-by-step manner. You may find that it's more effective to weave in your interpretation as you complete different segments—such as literary/textual analysis or historical analysis. The important point to remember is that you *build* your interpretation out of the various elements, so the presentation must be clear and easy to follow. Remember, the first part of exegesis is analysis, in which you take apart the text—this second segment involves synthesis, so you must do more than just lay it all out on paper. It's at this point that you assemble your findings into a cohesive interpretation. Through practice, you'll develop your own approach to the exegetical process.

Quick Guidelines for Exegetical Papers

You'll discover that exegesis does not have absolute rules. Indeed, your best rule of thumb is to check with individual instructors to see if they have a pattern they want you to follow, and then you'll know that you're on the right track. But just in case, here are guidelines we've found can help you, in most cases, do a good job on an exegetical paper.

A. Beginning Research and Reflection

- If you're not assigned a specific pericope by the instructor, decide on which text you wish to work. The best results will come from choosing a passage you find most interesting or challenging. Consult several good translations of the Bible, as well as a few commentaries. There are a lot out there.

- Read the entire chapter of which your passage is a part. Where does it start and end? Look at the context of the passage and determine how it relates to the entire book of the Bible.
- What is the form of the passage, i.e., is it a parable? A miracle story? A pronouncement? Again, Bible commentaries are helpful here. Translation footnotes are also helpful with this.
- Locate the historical and geographical setting of the passage and who is in it. Who are the people, and why are they here? Where are they, and what is going on? What's happening in their history? If it concerns Jesus, where has he been and where is he going? What's the social location? Try to see if you can figure out the reaction of the first readers or listeners.
- Look at the content of the passage. In English class, you'd be asked to find the thesis of the story: what's the main idea the author is trying to get across? What is the form (genre) of the story, the rhetorical style? What kind of language is the author using— everyday language or formal? Does the story develop chronologically, logically, etc.?
- Concentrate on the words as well. Are there words that need explanation?
- What are the theological implications of the passage for today? This is often the most difficult part of the paper for students, especially if the exegesis is Old Testament/Hebrew Bible. Take into consideration your social location, because it impacts the way you look at the passage, and include it in your writing toward the end of the paper.

B. Writing the Paper

It's impossible to address all the issues relevant to a biblical text in one paper, especially if it's a short paper, so concentrate on one that interests you the most. Begin with analysis and then move on to your interpretation and the theological implications. In the end, you're dealing with the ethics of the issue for today's church.

- You can begin by copying in the passage itself.
- Then write a clear introductory paragraph, with a clearly stated

thesis, i.e., the point you are examining and why you feel it's important and worth looking at.

- Look at the examples of exegesis papers (especially the comments); you can use these as possible models for developing the body of your paper.
- Avoid doing a verse by verse commentary, which can get boring. Be creative.
- Before your concluding paragraph, give a paragraph with implications for today. This is important and often is left out. Don't forget it.
- Write a strong, clear conclusion. Don't just slap something on at the end. You're probably tired by this time, but remember—this is the last thing your reader sees. Leave them with a strong impression of how good you are.

* * *

Exegetical Paper: The Gospel of Matthew
Jesus Grants Honor, Equality, and Voice to the
Canaanite Woman
Introduction to the New Testament
Melanie Baffes

Introduction and Background

In Matthew 15:21–28, the author presents a fascinating and puzzling story about an exchange between Jesus and a Canaanite woman. The story is familiar enough: a Gentile woman approaches Jesus for help with her daughter, whom she believes to be demon-possessed. Jesus first ignores the woman by not responding at all, and he then refuses to help her, claiming, "I was sent only to the lost sheep of the house of Israel" (15:24). Finally, Jesus insults the woman by saying, "It is not fair to take the children's food and throw it to the dogs" (15:26). But the woman will not be dissuaded, and she respectfully challenges Jesus with an insightful response, "Yes, Lord, yet even the dogs eat the crumbs that fall from their master's table" (15:27). Jesus hears in her words the depth of the woman's commitment, praises her for

A brief summary of the passage helps readers recall important highlights of the story.

Two. Exegetical Papers

her faith, and agrees to help: "Woman, great is your faith! Let it be done for you as you wish" (15:28).

One of the pivotal stories about women in the Gospel of Matthew, this passage tells of an ironic reversal in which an individual succeeds in challenging Jesus. When the Canaanite woman questions Jesus' response to her request, she engages in a challenge-and-riposte interaction—in which she questions not only his comments, but also, implicitly, his social space and even his authority. The woman's remarks prompt Jesus to accept the challenge (rather than reject it or refuse to respond), and he ultimately praises her and grants her request.[1]

> *A paper cannot answer every question about a text, so choose one that is most significant to you. The question behind this study was "Why does Matthew portray Jesus as rude and dismissive in this story, and is there another way to understand his actions as positive and life-giving?"*

This story, the only narrative in which an individual succeeds in a challenge with Jesus, is significant in that it is centered on a *woman* and a *Gentile*, someone doubly marginalized. And because a challenge-response typically involves a confrontation over honor and dishonor between those of equal social standing,[2] it also is noteworthy that a marginalized person has the faith, the wisdom, and the courage to challenge someone from whom she needs help, someone she calls "Lord." This paper explores the interaction between Jesus and the Canaanite woman—by studying the language, themes, rhetorical devices, and literary structure of the text—in order to show that the story is central to the writer's agenda. The thesis is that the author presents Jesus as a model of transformation who moves from exclusion to inclusion and embodies the theme, "the last will be first, and the first will be last" (20:16).

> *The thesis statement, in the last sentence, tells what the paper is going to prove and how it will do so. It can be one sentence or two, but it should be clear and succinct.*

---

1. According to Bruce Malina, the challenge-and-riposte process is characterized by three stages: (a) original **action**, a positive request for help or a negative insult, threat or affront; (b) **perception**, in which the receiving individual evaluates the potential dishonor that will result; and (c) **reaction**, which can be a lack of response, rejection through contempt, or acceptance, a response that involves engagement and counter challenge. See Bruce J. Malina, *The New Testament World: Insights from Cultural Anthropology* (3rd ed.; Louisville: Westminster John Knox Press, 2001), 33–36.

2. Malina, *The New Testament World*, 35.

Historical Setting

Authorship and audience. Matthew was written around 80 to 85 CE by an Israelite male, somewhere near Palestine in a major urban area like Antioch in Syria.[3] The author himself may have been a Jew, and the emphasis on Jewish scripture and law suggests a predominantly Jewish audience. On the other hand, the author's presentation of Jesus' urging missionary work among the Gentiles (28:19) indicates that the audience for this Gospel was most likely a combination of Jews and Gentiles. The Gospel also appears to be written for a primarily male audience; (indicated by passages such as "everyone who looks at a woman with lust...." [5:28]).[4]

Socio-cultural background. The broader socio-cultural context in which this Gospel was written was slightly different from the social world depicted in the narrative. One example of this is in the role of women. During the time of Jesus' ministry, women played a prominent role, accompanying Jesus on his journeys, providing financial and other support, and being present on his final trip to Jerusalem and at his crucifixion. Even in Paul's time (50 to 60 CE), women had roles as pastors, teachers, and prophets. But, by the time Matthew's Gospel was written some 30 years later, the situation was changing; near the end of the first century, women began to face serious challenges from those opposed to their having status or holding positions of power. Yet the author of Matthew, in direct contrast to the prevailing ethos of the time, portrays women as having worth, purpose, and dignity. In similar fashion, the narrative in Matthew's Gospel gives the impression that Christ's followers are predominantly Jews when, in fact, it is likely that more Gentiles were following Jesus at the time the Gospel was written.[5]

It is in this context that the story of the Canaanite woman would have been heard, and it most likely was met with surprise and curiosity by people of the first-century Mediterranean world. Because Matthew's Gospel acknowledges the contributions of

> Although this is primarily a literary analysis of the text, a brief overview of the historical setting helps set the stage for further analysis.

---

3. H. W. Attridge, ed., *The HarperCollins Study Bible* (New York: HarperCollins Publishers, 2006), 1666.

4. Janice Capel Anderson, "Matthew: Gender and Reading," in *A Feminist Companion to Matthew*, ed. Amy-Jill Levine (Sheffield, UK: Sheffield Academic Press, Ltd., 2001), 29.

5. Bart D. Ehrman, *The New Testament: A Historical Introduction to the Early Christian Writings*, 3rd ed. (New York: Oxford University Press, 2000, 2004), 106.

women and others excluded from status and positions of authority,[6] all those hearing the stories about women, Gentiles, and other marginalized persons would have seen the discrepancy between the ideal and their reality. They would have understood the call to be radically welcoming, to include everyone in the Matthean community.[7]

Context of the Passage

Matthew 15:21–28 appears directly after two other narratives about purity laws. At the start of Chapter 15, when the Pharisees question Jesus about his disciples not keeping the purity laws, he censures them for placing their traditions above "the commandment of God" (15:1–3). Following this exchange, Jesus makes his well-known speech to the crowd about things that defile: "it is not what goes into the mouth that defiles a person, but it is what comes out of the mouth that defiles" (15:11). In both passages, the author strongly suggests that the purity laws insisted upon by the Pharisees are not important when placed next to the teachings of Jesus and the commandments of God. The stories also seem to be a tacit condemnation of the laws that separate clean from unclean and Jew from Gentile. These two incidents introduce Jesus' movement to Tyre and Sidon, two Gentile cities on the Mediterranean coast. He leaves the land of the Pharisees, which is clean, to travel to the land of the Gentiles, which is unclean, and here he meets the Canaanite woman.[8]

This paper uses primarily "the-world-of-the-text" methods of biblical analysis—form criticism, rhetorical criticism, and narrative criticism.

This section begins the literary analysis. It studies placement of the passage in the gospel, how it relates to the larger context of the book, and what that might mean for how it can be understood.

Both before and after the story of the Canaanite woman, Jesus performs a series of healings, miracles, and exorcisms and, on several occasions, he specifically mentions having compassion for oth-

---

6. Amy-Jill Levine, "Gospel of Matthew," in *The Women's Bible Commentary*, ed. Carol A. Newsom and Sharon H. Ringe (Louisville: Westminster/John Knox Press, 1992), 253.

7. Esther A. de Boer, "Review of *Jesus and Marginal Women: The Gospel of Matthew in Social-Scientific Perspective* by Stuart L. Love," *Review of Biblical Literature* (2010), accessed August 31, 2010, http://www.bookreviews.org.

8. Gail. R. O'Day, "Surprised by Faith: Jesus and the Canaanite Woman," in *A Feminist Companion to Matthew*, ed. Amy-Jill Levine (Sheffield, UK: Sheffield Academic Press, Ltd., 2001), 115.

ers: "Moved with compassion, Jesus touched their eyes" (20:34). In addition, narratives in Chapter 12—the story of plucking grain on the Sabbath and the man with a withered hand—also stress the importance of human need over observance of the Law. Most striking is the juxtaposition of the feeding of the 5,000 and the feeding of the 4,000 right before and after the story of the Canaanite woman, which makes the woman's willingness to receive crumbs of bread even more poignant and significant.[9]

The story is placed next to others in which Jesus points to the hypocrisy and irrelevance of purity laws, feels compassion and performs miracles and healings, and stresses human need over observance of the Law—setting up a sharp contrast to the way Jesus refuses to help the woman, rebukes her, and compares her to a dog. Finally, the author of Matthew gives the story special significance by its central placement in the overall chiastic structure of the Gospel:

> A Two blind men (9:27–31)
>   B Sign of Jonah (12:38–42)
>   C Feeding of 5,000 (14:13–21)
>   **D Canaanite woman (15:22–28)**
>   C' Feeding of 4,000 (15:32–38)
>   B' Sign of Jonah (16:1–4)
> A' Two blind men (20:29–34)[10]

Form of the Passage

Although some scholars consider this passage a miracle story, the miracle itself is not the most important aspect.[11] Others have classified it as a "sayings of Jesus" story or an "apophthegm" (sayings of Jesus in a brief context), but the focus is not on something Jesus says but instead on what someone else says to him.[12] Bultmann identifies the story as a "controversy dialogue," which occurs when an "action or attitude is seized on by the oppo-

This section studies the form of the passage, explores why the author may have chosen it, and what it says about how the passage can be understood.

---

9. Anderson, "Matthew: Gender and Reading," 38.

10. Ibid., 37.

11. Rudolf Bultmann, *The History of the Synoptic Tradition*, trans. J. Marsh (Oxford: Basil Blackwell, 1963), 209.

12. O'Day, "Surprised by Faith," 116; Bultmann, *History of the Synoptic Tradition*, 11; and Martin Dibelius, *From Tradition to Gospel* (New York: Charles Scribner's Sons, 1965), 261.

nent and used in an attack by accusation or question," but even this form is not entirely accurate since Jesus does not come out on top of the controversy.[13]

Feminist scholar Gail R. O'Day suggests that the story is "a narrative embodiment of a lament psalm."[14] It demonstrates the characteristics of a lament psalm, including an opening *plea*—with address, complaint, petition, motivations, and imprecations—that leads to words of *praise*—in which there is a shift to words of change and transformation. In using the form of lament psalm, the author of Matthew sets the story against the backdrop of Israel's laments to God. The woman's words of faith before Jesus, then, are a reminder of the Jews placing their concerns before God as an act of faith.[15] Because the author's goal, in part, is to present Jesus as the Messiah who comes in fulfillment of Jewish scriptures,[16] he chooses a form that will be recognizable to his Jewish readers or listeners.

Content of the Passage

Key words. Several striking features distinguish the story, including the author's choice of language. The story comes from Mark, but in that version, the woman is referred to as "Syrophoenician" rather than "Canaanite." The author has changed the word intentionally to designate the woman not only as a Gentile, but even worse, as the traditional enemy of Israel.[17] Also interesting is the fact that the word "Gentile" is used only twice in Mark (and not in derogatory ways), but it appears as many as 11 times in Matthew, sometimes in a positive light and sometimes not. The author of Matthew has deliberately added the word "Gentile," perhaps to emphasize Jesus' Jewishness and his coming in fulfillment of the Jewish scripture. Because the word "Canaanite" is used only one time in Matthew (and not in the other gospels at all), it is likely that the author chose the term intentionally to draw attention to the

> The emphasis here is on key words in the text. Have certain words been chosen intentionally to convey a particular message?

---

13. Bultmann, *History of the Synoptic Tradition*, 38–39.
14. O'Day, "Surprised by Faith," 119.
15. Ibid., 120–25.
16. Ehrman, *The New Testament*, 93.
17. O'Day, "Surprised by Faith," 115.

woman's "otherness" and to the centrality of the story to the message of this Gospel.

Rhetorical devices. One device the author uses is the *anonymity* of the woman. The fact that she has no name may function to make her plight more universal, to highlight the significance of her role, or to call attention to her placement in the overall narrative plot.[18] At the same time, the woman's *particularity* as a female and as a Canaanite also serves as a rhetorical device because it is what advances the meaning of the story. The author of Matthew generally has an androcentric perspective, but he includes women prominently, especially the four women named in Jesus' patriarchal lineage. The fact that women are mentioned in a male line of descent is remarkable enough, but they also are all Gentiles. The other women in Matthew—those present at the tomb—also play a prominent role and are sometimes considered disciples. In this Gospel, the women "played an important role in God's plan and so came to be considered the instrument of God's providence or of His Holy Spirit."[19]

A major part of this analysis looks at rhetorical techniques the author used and how he used them to persuade readers.

Another rhetorical device is the *role reversal* between Jesus and the woman. Because the Canaanite woman is doubly marginalized, her accomplishment in winning the challenge and riposte with Jesus is heightened. The reversal of roles—between Jesus as learner and the woman as teacher—is even more striking because she is Gentile, unclean, *and* a woman.

But there also is a role reversal between the woman and the Jewish leaders. Her lowly status makes a sharp contrast between her "model faith and the failings of those more privileged such as the Jewish leaders and disciples."[20] If the author of Matthew intended to show Jesus as both the fulfillment of Jewish scripture *and* the Jewish Messiah rejected and unappreciated by the Jewish leaders,[21] this story reinforces both of those themes at once. Matthew's Jesus is able to be an observant Jew by upholding the Jewish Law and remaining faithful to his mission, while at the same

---

18. Karla G. Bohmbach, "Names and Naming in the Biblical World," in *Women in Scripture: A Dictionary of Named and Unnamed Women in the Hebrew Bible, The Apocryphal/Deuterocanonical Books, and the New Testament*, ed. Carol Meyers (New York: Houghton Mifflin Company, 2000), 38.

19. Anderson, "Matthew: Gender and Reading," 31.

20. Ibid., 39.

21. Ehrman, *The New Testament*, 93, 105.

time subtly pointing out the shortcomings of the Jewish leaders who reject Jesus himself and reject the truth he brings.

Closely related to this theme is the Gospel's use of another rhetorical device common to Jesus' teachings: *antithesis*. As Ehrman points out, Jesus often "states a Jewish Law and then sets his interpretation of that Law over and against it."[22] In this case, the *woman* is the one who gets to the heart of the matter, interpreting for Jesus what is truly important, expanding his statement (and his insult), and opening it to new interpretations and possibilities.

Narrative structure. The overall plan of the story follows a "U-shaped plot," which is characterized by a state of equilibrium at the start, followed by a disruption—adversity or misunderstanding. In a story with a U-shaped plot, the lowest point is followed by a reversal, a divine deliverance or awakening of a character, or an action that turns things for the better. In a story of this type, typically the character "recognizes something of great importance that was previously hidden or unrecognized."[23] In the story of the Canaanite woman, it is Jesus who appears to recognize something that was previously unknown.

> *This section explores how the author tells the story, and why he might have chosen a particular narrative approach.*

Common interpretations. There are several different interpretations of the surprising outcome of this story and the message it conveys. One perspective is that Jesus learned from the woman "that the outsiders he encountered were not outside the activity of God, the heart of God, the care of God."[24] This reading of the text proposes that the woman "taught" Jesus that all are welcome in the kingdom of God, suggesting that Jesus himself had lost sight of this truth.

> *Before bringing together elements of your analysis to prove the thesis, it is helpful to provide a brief overview of common readings of the text as a context for presenting your own argument.*

Some scholars argue that Jesus was caught up in his mission, distracted, in grief over John's death. Others claim that "we need to readjust our understanding of Jesus to accommodate the understanding that, from time to time, he could be as rude and chauvin-

---

22. Ibid., 102.

23. James L. Resseguie, *Narrative Criticism of the New Testament: An Introduction* (Grand Rapids, MI: Baker Academic, 2005), 205.

24. John D. Haughey, S.J., "There's No 'Them' There," *Living Pulpit*, Oct/Dec (2004), 13.

istic as any of his male counterparts."[25] Each of these readings has merit, particularly in light of Matthew's depiction of Jesus as the Jewish Messiah, the new Moses, the healing descendant of David.[26]

An alternative reading. There is evidence to suggest, however, that the author of Matthew intentionally portrayed Jesus in this story as the learner (rather than teacher) so that he could demonstrate first-hand the transformation that needed to occur in the disciples and the Jewish leaders.

Several key themes support the interpretation of Jesus as a model for transformation. One is a prevailing theme in Matthew that God is always present and active in the world, and everything that happens relates to God's purposes. "Though Jesus is the main character in the Gospel, God is the primary force behind the narrative and in the world as the author of Matthew understands it."[27] From this perspective, the author presents Jesus having the humility to know that *he* does not have to be the only agent of revelation and new learning, but can allow others to "teach" what he himself already knows as God's agent. In this view, the story is a reminder that it is ultimately God at work in the world.

Another important theme involves Jesus' teaching the disciples to do what he does. "The disciples replicate Jesus' work in their lives: they heal, teach, and exercise authority."[28] Jesus' goal for his disciples is that they obey God's will as revealed through his teaching and, perhaps, through the teachings of others commissioned by him and by God. Jesus wants the disciples to go forth, making other disciples, baptizing and teaching in the same way that he does. The Canaanite woman, then, foreshadows and models "the final command for the disciples to teach and baptize the nations."[29]

> *This is where the paper brings together the various pieces of analysis into a cohesive whole. By looking closely at different elements of the story through the lens of literary criticism—and always with the guiding question in mind—it is possible to suggest an interpretation that is counter to conventional readings of this story.*

---

25. J. Martin C. Scott, "Matthew 15.21–28: A Test-Case for Jesus' Manners," *Journal for the Study of the New Testament* 63 (1996): 25.

26. Ehrman, *The New Testament*, 110.

27. Anthony J. Saldarini, "Matthew," in *Eerdmans Commentary on the Bible,* ed. James D.G. Dunn and John W. Rogerson (Grand Rapids, MI: Wm. B. Eerdmans Publishing Co., 2003) 1002.

28. Ibid., 1004.

29. Ibid., 1036.

Matthew's Jesus demonstrates this theme through another reversal. While in most stories, the disciples and followers identify with the person to whom Jesus is speaking; in this story, however, Jesus aligns himself with the position he knows the disciples will take, and he gives them an opportunity to identify with *him*. In doing so, he shows them the transformation that is possible, giving them the chance to change along with him. By positioning Jesus as the learner in this challenge and riposte, the author allows the disciples and the Jewish leaders to learn along with him. At the same time, he allows women, Gentiles, or other marginalized individuals to be empowered and affirmed by identifying with the Canaanite woman.

The primary message, however, has to do with inclusion and on Matthew's "emphasis on the marginal and disempowered."[30] Earlier in Matthew's Gospel, Jesus states that "he will proclaim justice to the Gentiles" and "in his name the Gentiles will hope" (12:18b, 12:21). The author's message is for Jews and Gentiles alike, and he uses the story of the Canaanite woman to show that God's kingdom is for everyone: men and women, Jews and Gentiles, clean and unclean. The story emphasizes that even those at the margins will find entry into the kingdom if they have faith; the true followers of Jesus are those who love others as they love themselves regardless of who they are. Women, in fact, for the author of Matthew, are often the ones who are significant enough to further God's plan.

Theological implications

Theological message. In the story of the Canaanite woman, the author has chosen a marginalized person as a model for faith, someone living at the boundaries.[31] In doing so, the author reminds listeners that God is present for all who are faithful, regardless of class, race, ethnicity, gender, age, or any other culturally or socially-imposed distinctions. According to Amy-Jill Levine, the writer of Matthew "attempts to eliminate all relationships in which one group exploits or dominates another."[32] There is no "other" in God's realm.

> *The paper should relate your alternative reading to the here-and-now, answering the question, "What possible theological implications does this have for us today?"*

---

30. Amy-Jill Levine, "Gospel of Matthew," 259.
31. O'Day, "Surprised by Faith," 125.
32. Amy-Jill Levine, "Gospel of Matthew," 252.

Social location. This reading of the text emerges from my experience as a woman living in a patriarchal culture. Although women in the U.S. today have greater access to resources than do women in almost any other country in the world—access to education, employment prospects, leadership opportunities—this access is limited to women of certain races, ethnicities, cultures, religions, and socioeconomic groups. Despite talk of equality in a first-world, democratic society, members of many groups—people of color, foreign-born residents, Muslims, those living in poverty—continue to be marginalized in subtle, yet powerful, ways. Immigrants are unwanted, Muslims are feared, and the poor are ignored. Many groups have diminished voice, influence, and impact in arenas considered most important by the hegemonic culture, a culture in which being male, Caucasian, American (and often Christian) has been normative—relegating everyone else to "other."

> *It is always a good idea to take into account your own social location as a point of departure for your interpretive reading.*

Implications for today. The story of the Canaanite woman is a reminder that God is at work outside and beyond the bounds of cultural norms that define human identity and worth. What this means is that setting ourselves apart from others —by virtue of race, gender, class, ethnicity, religion, or any other criteria—will always result in someone being marginalized or excluded. The message in Matthew is a call for us to examine the unconscious beliefs we have about *our* way being the *right* way, believing that whoever "we" are is the norm and everyone else is "other." The story of the Canaanite woman helps us recognize that we are not as different from each other as we would like to believe.

Conclusion

The author of Matthew places the story of the Canaanite woman in the structural center of the Gospel in order to convey its centrality to the primary message. Because it is in form of lament psalm, it makes Jewish listeners remember the lament of the Israelites before God and realize that the woman, a Gentile, is more like them than they think. She is the underdog, and Jews familiar with their history will recall what it was like to be in that position.

> *The conclusion succinctly restates the thesis, what the paper has proved and how it has done so, as well as a concise re-statement of what this reading suggests to us in our present-day lives.*

But her faith is stronger than theirs, so they must learn from her, as Jesus does, and recognize that faith and entry into God's kingdom is not dependent on being Jewish, being male, or being a member of any other "in-group." Women and Gentiles are not excluded from God's care, love, or plan. In fact, like the other women in Matthew, the Canaanite woman plays a prominent role in furthering God's plan.

Through this story, Matthew shows Jesus as living out his statement, "So the last will be first, and the first will be last" (20:16). Jesus, the Messiah rejected by the Jewish leaders, knows what it means to be marginalized. By making himself last to show that the outcast and rejected can be first, Matthew's Jesus gives honor, equality, and voice to the Canaanite woman and to all other marginalized persons. By making himself last, Matthew's Jesus reverses the idea of teacher and learner, in and out, Jew and Gentile, clean and unclean, first and last. By making himself last, Matthew's Jesus demonstrates first-hand the transformation possible when one has humility, openness, faith, and a willingness to see God's movement in everything and everyone.

Works Cited

Anderson, Janice Capel. "Matthew: Gender and Reading." In *A Feminist Companion to Matthew*, edited by Amy-Jill Levine, 25–51. Sheffield, UK: Sheffield Academic Press, Ltd., 2001.

Attridge, Harold W., ed. *The HarperCollins Study Bible*. Rev. ed. New York: HarperCollins Publishers, 2006.

Bohmbach, Karla G. "Names and Naming in the Biblical World." In *Women in Scripture: A Dictionary of Named and Unnamed Women in the Hebrew Bible, The Apocryphal/ Deuterocanonical Books, and the New Testament*, edited by Carol Meyers, 33–40. New York: Houghton Mifflin Company, 2000.

Bultmann, Rudolph. *The History of the Synoptic Tradition*. Translated by J. Marsh. Oxford, UK: Basil Blackwell, 1963.

de Boer, Esther A. "Review of *Jesus and Marginal Women: The Gospel of Matthew in Social-Scientific Perspective* by Stuart L. Love." *Review of Biblical Literature*. Accessed August 31, 2010. http://www.bookreviews.org.

Dibelius, Martin. *From Tradition to Gospel*. New York: Charles Scribner's Sons, 1965.

Ehrman, Bart D. *The New Testament: A Historical Introduction to the Early Christian Writings*. 3rd ed. New York: Oxford University Press, Inc. 2000/2004.

Haughey, John C. S.J. "There's No 'Them' There." *Living Pulpit*. Oct/Dec (2004): 13–14.

Levine, Amy-Jill. "Gospel of Matthew." In *The Women's Bible Commentary*, edited by Carol A. Newsom and Sharon H. Ringe, 465–77. Louisville: Westminster/John Knox Press, 1992.

Malina, Bruce, J. *The New Testament World: Insights from Cultural Anthropology*. 3rd ed. Louisville: Westminster John Knox Press, 2001.

O'Day, Gail R. "Surprised by Faith: Jesus and the Canaanite Woman." In *A Feminist Companion to Matthew*, edited by Amy-Jill Levine, 114–25. Sheffield, UK: Sheffield Academic Press, Ltd, 2001.

Resseguie, James L. *Narrative Criticism of the New Testament: An Introduction.* Grand Rapids, MI: Baker Academic, 2005.

Saldarini, Anthony J. "Matthew." In *Eerdmans Commentary on the Bible,* edited by James D.G. Dunn and John W. Rogerson, 1000–1063. Grand Rapids, MI: Wm. B. Eerdmans Publishing Co., 2003.

Scott, J. Martin C. "Matthew 15.21–28: A Test-Case for Jesus' Manners." *Journal for the Study of the New Testament* 63 (1996): 21–44.

* * *

Exegetical Paper: The Gospel of John
Martha as an Exemplar of Jesus' Sheep
The Gospel of John
Sarah Lee

Introduction and Background

In John 11:17–27, the evangelist gives us Martha's conversation with Jesus and her following confession in the story of raising Lazarus from the dead. The story of the passage is well-known: When Jesus arrived at Bethany, the village of Martha, Mary and Lazarus, he found that Lazarus had already been in the tomb four days. Martha, who heard that Jesus was coming, went to meet him. Martha first complained to Jesus, saying "Lord, if you had been here, my brother would not have died" (John 11:21). Soon, however, she showed her belief about Jesus, saying, "But even now I know that God will give you whatever you asked of him" (11:22). Jesus responded to Martha, promising that her brother would rise again (11:22–23). Martha first misunderstood Jesus' remark (11:24). To Martha, Jesus explained again what it meant, saying that "I am the resurrection and the life. Those who believe in me, even though they die, will live, and everyone who lives and believes in me will never die," and asked her if she believed this (11:25–26). After listening to Jesus, Martha said to Jesus, "Yes, Lord, I believe that you are the Messiah, the Son of God, the one coming into the world" (11:27).

One of the remarkable stories about women in the Gospel of John,

> *A clear presentation of the passage that is the focus of this exegesis is immediately presented.*

> *The entire first paragraph presents the Gospel story—a good way to begin the paper.*

> *This beginning phrase points out what is unusual about this story: it is about a woman.*

this passage shows Martha as an exemplar of the sheep that belong to Jesus. With the help of Charles H. Talbert's literary analysis, my argument is based on the close relationship between John 10 and 11. In connection with the previous chapter, John 10, which is about Jesus as the good shepherd, Martha, in this passage, symbolizes how the sheep act, listen to Jesus, believe in Jesus, and confess their belief about Jesus.

From the passage, there are two reasons Martha stands out as an exemplar of Jesus' sheep in the Gospel. First, her conversation with Jesus and her confession are in contrast to the dispute between Jesus and the Jews, who were depicted as the sheep who did not belong to Jesus in John 10. Second, a sign that she finally gained in the following passage—her brother Lazarus was raised from the dead—was Jesus' promise to his sheep: Jesus gives his sheep eternal life and his sheep never perish (John 10:28).

| *The author makes her points by using "first" and "second" and then explaining them clearly.* |

| *Martha often is seen as exemplar of faith, belief, and discipleship; the author is tying these themes directly to the sheep motif.* |

Context of the Passage

John 11:17–27 is a part of John 11, the story of raising Lazarus from the dead. Before the story of Lazarus begins, the previous chapter, John 10, is about authentic shepherding.[1] It includes not only Jesus' parables and words about authentic shepherding, but also the following misunderstanding and trial from the Jews who do not believe in him. When Jesus first talked about the parable of the gate, the shepherd of the sheep, and the sheep following the shepherd, the Jews did not understand what he was saying to them (John 10:6). So again Jesus said to them, "I am the gate for the sheep (10:7)" and "I am the good shepherd" (10:11, 14). As the good shepherd, he owned the sheep and the sheep would listen to his voice (10:16). The Jews were divided because of Jesus' words (10:19). They had doubts about whether they had to listen to his words or not.

| *It is important to place context here; this paper has a clear explanation of the passage's context and what it means.* |

---

1. Michael D. Coogan, ed., *The New Oxford Annotated Bible with the Apocrypha: New Revised Standard Version* (New York: Oxford University Press, 2010), 1899.

The story moved to the Festival of the Dedication in Jerusalem (10:22). The Jews gathered around Jesus and asked if he was the Messiah. Jesus answered, "I have told you, and you do not believe." (10:25). Here, Jesus brought up the theme of "the sheep" again, saying "you do not believe, because you do not belong to my sheep" (10:26). Jesus' explanation of his sheep appears in the following verses: "My sheep hear my voice. I know them, and they follow me. I give them eternal life, and they will never perish" (10:27–28). Then, Jesus added that the Father and he were one (10:30). When the Jews heard what Jesus said, they took up stones to stone him for blasphemy (10:31, 33). After the Jews' misunderstandings and trials surrounding Jesus as the good shepherd and his sheep who believe in him, John 11 begins, and Martha's conversation with Jesus and her confession appear.

After the passage, what follows is Mary's conversation with Jesus, which is quite different from Martha's. As Martha did, Mary first complained to Jesus (10:32).

> *The author contrasts Martha and the unbelieving Jews; she will then relate it to her central claim.*

Instead of continuing the conversation, however, Mary wept. Jesus also began to weep, went to the tomb, and raised Lazarus from the dead. Many of the Jews, who had seen what Jesus did, believed in him (10:45). But some of them went to the Pharisees and told them what he had done. So the chief priests and the Pharisees called a meeting of the council, and began a plot to kill Jesus (10:53). Because of their unbelief, they were still not the sheep who belonged to Jesus and listened to him.

Form of the Passage

As I mentioned earlier, my argument for the passage is based on the close relationship between John 10 and 11. For this reason, I would like to look at the form of the passage in light of the relationship between John 10 and 11 as a whole.

> *This is a good use of a strong source to explain the form of the passage. Use your sources to support your argument.*

According to Talbert, "John 10:1–11:54 is a large thought unit set temporally at or near the Feast of Dedication (10:22)."[2] Throughout John 10 and 11, the Fourth

---

2. Charles H. Talbert, *Reading John: A Literary and Theological Commentary on the Fourth Gospel and the Johannine Epistles* (New York: Crossroad, 1994), 169.

Gospel portrays Jesus as the fulfillment of the hopes of Dedication, which is quite related to "shepherd" and the shepherd's "sheep."[3] He explains that there are multiple ways to tie the two chapters together. First, the two chapters consist of the usual discourse (John 10) and sign (John 11). Second, cross-references appear in both chapters. For example, "The Jews took up stones again to stone him (10:31)" echoes "Rabbi, the Jews were just now trying to stone you, and are you going there again?" (11:8). Third, certain themes such as a good shepherd and his sheep hearing his voice run through both chapters. In this light, it is reasonable to think of John 10 and 11 together.

| *The author has made her point well here.* |

Talbert continues to argue that "If John 10 functions as the thought unit's discourse/dialogue, John 11:1–53 functions as the accompanying sign."[4] He also explains that "John 11:1–53 is an expanded miracle story with the three customary components: (1) the problem (vv. 1–17), expanded by dialogue and action; (2) the miracle (vv. 17–44), expanded in two cycles that loosely correspond to one another (vv. 17–24; vv. 28–44); and (3) the reactions to the miracle (vv. 45–53), expanded by a plot for Jesus' death."[5] The passage, John 11:17–27, is a part of the miracle story. And the passage is a "Martha cycle," one of the two cycles in the miracle, since Talbert names the passage a "Martha cycle" and the following passage (11:28–44) a "Mary cycle."[6]

However, Talbert does not approach the Martha cycle as one of the multiple ways to tie John 10 and 11 together. For him, the Martha cycle is just a part of the miracle that is about raising Lazarus from the dead. It neither stands out solely nor has an importance in the two chapters as a large thought unit. For me, the passage plays an important role to tie the two chapters together. Unlike the Mary cycle, the Martha cycle has dialogue and Jesus' response in the form of a promise: "Your brother will rise

The author employs the various methods of biblical criticism—in this case, literary analysis—to build and demonstrate her claim.

The author points to the significance of Martha's profession of faith— because it comes after Chapter 10 and contrasts her with the Jews, who are unbelievers.

3. Ibid., 170–174.
4. Talbert, *Reading John*, 176.
5. Ibid., 176.
6. Ibid., 177.

again (11:23)."⁷ Compared to the Mary cycle, why is the Martha cycle distinctive in that way? I think that this can be understood in connection with John 10, because the Martha cycle shows an exemplar of Jesus' sheep, contrasting Martha and the Jews (who do not belong to Jesus) in John 10. The two chapters are also tied together because of the passage.

Content of the Passage

Common Interpretations. There are many different interpretations of Martha's confession in John 11. Regardless of methodology, with the exception of feminist methodology, most interpretations tend to focus on Martha's inadequate belief in the passage. One of the traditional commentaries says that "Throughout the incident involving Martha we see that she believes in Jesus but inadequately," because "'[s]he regards Jesus as an intermediary who is heard by God (22), but she does not understand that he is life itself (25)."⁸ Another interpretation, which is from socio-science analysis, says that the passage shows how Martha, who was not initially a full insider (24), became a full insider when she recognizes that life is in Jesus (27).⁹ In those interpretations, Martha is not depicted as an active character and Martha's confession does not carry much weight for the whole Gospel. I propose that Martha plays an important role in the Gospel of John through her conversation with Jesus and the following confession particularly in the connection with the previous chapter.

| *Feminist Interpretations.* Unlike the traditional interpretations above, feminist biblical scholars approach the passage in a more active way. Martha is interpreted as an active character, and her conversation with Jesus and her confession

> *Here, the author lays out the conventional readings of the text as she prepares to give her own interpretation.*

> *This is an excellent re-statement of the author's argument.*

> *Here, she compares Martha with male characters (disciples) in the Gospel, proving her point about Martha's importance in the narrative.*

---

7. Ibid., 178.

8. Raymond E. Brown, *The Gospel According to John*, Anchor Bible, vol. 30 (Garden City, NY: Doubleday, 1966–70), 433.

9. Bruce J. Malina and Richard L. Rohrbaugh, *Social-Science Commentary on the Gospel of John* (Minneapolis: Fortress, 1998), 199.

play an important role in the entire Gospel. Collen Conway put a great emphasis on the confession of Martha and its role in the Fourth Gospel, contrasting it ("You are the Christ," John 11) with Peter's ("You are the Holy One of God," John 6). According to Conway, "That Martha voices this confession in the Gospel of John hints at a deliberate displacement of Simon Peter."[10] Martha's confession is what the Johannine community believed because "[w]ith this confession, she embodies the stated aim of the entire narrative, 'These things have been written in order that you might come to (or continue to) believe that Jesus is the Christ, the Son of God' (20.31)."[11] However, Peter's statement does not satisfy the Johannine faith because "the title that Peter uses for Jesus is not clearly messianic."[12] I agree that Martha's confession shows the Johannine credo here. But for me, Martha embodies the confession of the Johannine community as an exemplar of Jesus' sheep, which is the Johannine community itself.

The Jews vs. Martha. In John 10 and 11, there is a parallel between the Jews and Martha. When Jesus describes himself as a good shepherd and explains how the sheep that belong to him act, the Jews and Martha act differently. This contrast between the Jews and Martha indicates that the Jews are the sheep who do not belong to Jesus but that Martha is the sheep who does belong to Jesus.

> The author highlights Martha's role in the Gospel's progressive revelation *of who Jesus is, along with the increasing* rejection *by those who do not understand or see him.*

I will look at Jesus and the Jews in John 10 first. Jesus said that as the good shepherd, he laid down his life for the sheep (10:11, 15, 17) and knew his own (10:14). The sheep who belonged to him also knew him (10:14). The Jews first did not understand him. Jesus said it to them again, but the Jews had doubts about his words. They did not believe Jesus, which meant that they did not belong to Jesus' sheep. In the next story in John 10, the Jews first asked if Jesus was the Messiah. Jesus explained again that Jesus knew his sheep (10:27) and gave his sheep eternal life (10:28). His sheep heard his voice and followed him (10:27). When Jesus concluded, saying that the Father and he were one, finally the Jews tried to stone him for blasphemy (10:33). They did not believe stories about Jesus in terms of two things:

---

10. Colleen Conway, "Gender Matters in John," in *A Feminist Companion to John*, vol. II, ed. Amy-Jill Levine and Marianne Blickenstaff (London: Sheffield Academic Press, 2003), 87.

11. Ibid., 87.

12. Ibid., 89.

Jesus was the Messiah and the Son of God. It meant that they did not belong to Jesus' sheep.

> *This is a good connection/return to the core subject of the paper.*

How the Jews acted in John 10 contrasts with how Martha acted in John 11:17–27. When Martha heard that Jesus was coming, she did not stay at home as her sister Mary did (the posture for the female mourner).[13] Instead, she went and met him (10:20), which meant that she followed Jesus as his sheep. Then, Martha complained to Jesus, saying "Lord, if you had been here, my brother would not have died" (11:21). Her complaint, however, does not express Martha's unbelief; rather, it shows her faith about Jesus. According to Gail O'Day, "Complaint belonged to the language of faith in Judaism (e.g., Psalms 4; 6; 13; 22)" and "the edge of complaint in v. 21 gives greater impact to Martha's statement of confidence in Jesus in v. 22; 'Even now,' in the face of Lazarus's death, Martha's confidence is undiminished."[14] In this respect, once she followed him, she showed her faith in Jesus.

To Martha, who followed him as his sheep followed him, Jesus said "Your brother will rise again" (11:23) in the form of a promise which echoed what he said in John 10: "I give them eternal life" (10:28). First, Martha did not understand Jesus' words (11:24) as the Jews did not in John 10. As Jesus did to the Jews, then, Jesus said again to Martha what it meant. What Jesus said to Martha again, "I am the resurrection and the life. Those who believe in me, even though they die, will live, and everyone who lives and believes in me will never die" (10:25–26) is also related to Jesus' words about his sheep in John: "I give them eternal life, and they will never perish" (10:28). After Jesus said this, he asked if she believed it. Unlike the Jews who tried to stone Jesus because they did not believe Jesus was the Messiah and the Son of God, Martha said "Yes, Lord," and her confession about the two things followed: "I believe that you are the Messiah, the Son of God" (11:27). Even though Martha did not understand Jesus at first, she listened to Jesus' words and believed them: Jesus was the Messiah and the Son of God. As she confessed her faith in Jesus, she gained a sign of eternal life as her brother Lazarus was raised from the dead. Raising Lazarus from the dead was the fulfillment of the promise to Jesus' sheep (Jesus gave his sheep eternal life and they never perished) in John 10. In this, Martha was an exemplar of the sheep which belonged to Jesus.

---

13. Malina and Rohrbaugh, *Social-Science Commentary on the Gospel of John*, 199.

14. Gail R. O'Day, *John, New Interpreters Bible*, vol. 9 (Nashville: Abingdon, 1995), 688.

Historical Setting

Authorship and Audience. The Gospel of John was written about 90 CE by a disciple of John from a "'Johannine school,' which ancient tradition perhaps correctly locates at Ephesus in western Asia Minor at a time when persecution by Roman authorities was becoming more frequent, and conflicts between Gentile Christians and Jewish Christians as well as between Christians in general and Jews were becoming more intense."[15] In terms of the audience, Craig Koester assumed that there might be three groups of readers who were scattered abroad among the Johannine Christians: Jewish, Samaritan, and Gentile Greek Christians. If this is correct, the Gospel might include various perspectives from various readers and might also convey truth which is multidimensional.[16] Therefore, in a time of various conflicts among the community which also had diverse readers, it may have been important for the Johannine community to point out who were the sheep that belonged to Jesus. In that time, the evangelist picked up Martha as an exemplar of the sheep who belonged to Jesus and a spokeswoman for the messianic faith of the Johannine community.[17]

> *This is an important element of all exegetical papers! Note that you can use annotated Bibles or commentaries to find information on the historical setting of a passage.*

> *The author relates the authorship and audience to her argument.*

Socio-Cultural Background. Bruce J. Malina and Richard L. Rohrbaugh approach the Gospel of John based on the thesis that the Johannine community was an antisociety and the language of the Fourth Gospel was antilanguage.[18] For Malina and Rohrbaugh, therefore, the sheep that belonged to Jesus and Martha's confession are all related to the theme of antisociety and antilanguage. In terms

> *This is another important element of exegesis: Who were the people involved here? To what group did they belong?*

---

15. Coogan, *The New Oxford Annotated Bible*, 1879.

16. Craig R. Koester, "The Spectrum of Johannine Readers," in *"What Is John?" Volume 1: Readers and Readings of the Fourth Gospel* (SBL Symposium Series), ed. Fernando Segovia (Atlanta: Scholars Press, 1997), 9–11.

17. Adeline Fehribach, *The Women in the Life of the Bridegroom: A Feminist Historical-Literary Analysis of the Female Characters in the Fourth Gospel* (Collegeville, MN: The Liturgical Press, 1998), 84.

18. Malina and Rohrbaugh, *Social-Science Commentary on the Gospel of John*, 59.

of Martha's confession, in particular, they argue that "Martha acknowledges her belief, indicating she is a member of the core group."[19] If these were the Johannine community who heard about the sheep (insiders) and the Jews (outsiders) in John 10, they may have well recognized Martha was as an exemplar of the sheep, a core insider of the community. In that way, Martha was a model for the community to emulate.

> Here, she clearly concludes her analysis with a restatement of the thesis she has proved.

Theological Implications

Social Location. My interpretation emerges from the Korean church in which I was brought up, witnessing a lot of limits as a woman because of its male-dominancy. At the same time, I saw many times that Korean male pastors liked using the Gospel of John because of its strong high Christology. However, no one focused on Martha's conversation with Jesus and her confession. When they mentioned Martha in John 11, they focused more on her misunderstanding about Jesus' words and diminished her role in the chapter. From my perspective, the Gospel of John put emphasis more on female characters and their roles than any other Gospel. But the Korean church, which likes the Fourth Gospel the most, does not recognize it but diminishes the role of women in the church a great irony! My interest and interpretation of the passage starts from this irony I have felt in my faith community.

> This is another important place to spend time writing clearly. Often, students get to this point in an exegetical paper and do not reveal their social location—failing to let the reader know who they are. This is important for fully understanding the author's reading of the text.

Theological Message. In John 10, when Jesus explained authentic shepherding and his sheep, there was no one among the Jews to understand his words and become his sheep as he described. However, in John 11, the evangelist has picked Martha, a woman, as an exemplar of the sheep who belong to Jesus. Moreover, she stands out as a spokeswoman for the credo of the entire community. Among the members of community, the model of Jesus' sheep, who listened to his words and believed in him, and finally received a sign of eternal life, was a woman. The Gospel of John reminds us

---

19. Ibid., 199.

that there are no limitations for anyone to become the sheep of Jesus if she/he follows Jesus, listens to him, and believes him as the Messiah and the Son of God. Finally, she/he will receive the eternal life from Jesus, who is the resurrection and life.

Implications for Today. In this passage, Martha reminds us that women can actively appear as a core member of the faith community and play an important role of showing the credo of the community. This provides many implications for today's church, which has various groups and different members like the Johannine community, but still limits women in terms of leadership and ordination, accepting gender discrimination in the ministry work. If the conservative Korean church, in particular, likes reading the Gospel of John, they should also accept what the Gospel brings up in terms of the role of the female character, Martha, in the passage.

> Here is another important element to include. Often, this can form the basis for a future sermon. How does the Gospel speak to us today?

Conclusion

Reading John 10 and 11 together, we come to know that these two chapters show us who are the sheep who belong to Jesus and who are not. The Jews in John 10 were not Jesus' sheep because they did not follow Jesus, listen to Jesus, and believe his words. They tried to kill him, rejecting the belief that Jesus was the Messiah and the Son of God. However, Martha in John 11 shows how Jesus' sheep acts as an exemplar. She followed Jesus, listened to him, and believed his words. She confessed that Jesus was the Messiah and the Son of God. Finally, she received a sign for the sheep that belonged to Jesus (the promise of eternal life) through resuscitation of his brother, Lazarus.

The Johannine community had different groups of members and was faced with various conflicts. To guard against those difficulties, the Johannine community may have picked up Martha as an exemplar of Jesus' sheep (the Johannine community itself) and as a spokeswoman for what the community believed. In this way, Martha in the passage plays an important role in the entire Gospel and offers implications for today's church, which tends to limit women's roles and leadership in the

> This is a very strong exegetical paper, with careful attention to the interplay of themes between John 10 and 11. It's a feminist reading that the author proposes after looking at more traditional, historical-critical readings.

ministry. For this reason, we cannot diminish the passage but pay attention to and actively read Martha's conversation with Jesus and her confession in John 11.

Works Cited

Brown, Raymond E. *The Gospel According to John*, Anchor Bible, Vol. 30. Garden City, NY: Doubleday, 1966–70.

Conway, Colleen. "Gender Matters in John." In *A Feminist Companion to John*, Vol. II, edited by Amy-Jill Levine and Marianne Blickenstaff. London: Sheffield Academic Press, 2003.

Coogan, Michael D., ed. *The New Oxford Annotated Bible with the Apocrypha: New Revised Standard Version*. New York: Oxford University Press, 2010.

Fehribach, Adeline. *The Women in the Life of the Bridegroom: A Feminist Historical-Literary Analysis of the Female Characters in the Fourth Gospel*. Collegeville, MN: The Liturgical Press, 1998.

Koester, Craig R. "The Spectrum of Johannine Readers." *"What Is John?"* Volume 1: *Readers and Readings of the Fourth Gospel* (SBL Symposium Series), edited by Fernando Segovia. Atlanta: Scholars Press, 1997.

Malina, Bruce J. and Richard L. Rohrbaugh. *Social-Science Commentary on the Gospel of John*. Minneapolis: Fortress, 1998.

O'Day, Gail R. *John. New Interpreters Bible*, Vol. 9. Nashville: Abingdon, 1995.

Talbert, Charles H. *Reading John: A Literary and Theological Commentary on the Fourth Gospel and the Johannine Epistles*. New York: Crossroad, 1994.

* * *

CHAPTER THREE

Theological Essays or Summaries

> *A theological sentence does its proper work just to the extent it makes the familiar strange. Much of modern theology, however, has been the attempt to show that the familiar is just that—familiar.*—Stanley Hauerwas, "How to Write a Theological Sentence"

General Guidelines

In this chapter, we'll address various types of essays that you might be asked to write in seminary. First, however, here is a general list of points to keep in mind when presented with an assignment that asks you to examine an original source document, take it apart, and develop an argument around its most important points. In other words, what is the author trying to say? If the author is an ancient church father, like Origen for example, what point might he be making in one of his original writings? What thesis can you develop based on this writing? Here are the steps to attacking an assignment of this type:

1. Read the original source document carefully. What is the author's thesis? In other words, what is the point of the document?

2. If there are several main points in the document, determine which one is the most important. Which one interests you the most?

3. Note the points that you feel are the most important and write them down.

4. Look for secondary sources that relate to the points or point that you found to be the most important in the document. Read at least three.

5. Use the encyclopedias of biblical history, volumes that give a biography of the author of the passage (e.g., Origen), and get to know the author before you attempt to write.

6. Spell out your thesis idea in the first paragraph, while noting others that you may or may not agree with. Make your thesis clear.

7. Make sure the first paragraph includes the supporting points for your thesis and states them clearly.

8. Develop one point per paragraph in the body of your paper, if the paper is a short one. You may use several pages if the paper is a long one. Use support from the primary document.

9. Make sure the conclusion solidly re-states your thesis, your support point, and your conclusion in a way that will reinforce your idea to the reader. Don't just throw on a conclusion as an afterthought. The conclusion should make your point again and show how you have proven it.

10. Always proofread carefully. Do not expect spell-check to find your spelling errors. Remember that the computer does not "read" your text—if you meant "or" and you typed "of," spell-check will not catch that mistake.

QUICK TIP: WHAT IS A THESIS AND
HOW DO I WRITE ONE?

Remember that every paper you write MUST have a thesis. You know this, you've learned it all through your schooling, but it never hurts to repeat it. All a thesis is is the main idea about the subject you intend to prove in your writing, and you'll prove it either through your research or through your thought process if this is a reflection paper (more on that in another chapter). You'll choose a thesis that is not too broad to cover in a short paper, and support the thesis with specific evidence, i.e., you will PROVE it, not just give your opinion about the subject. A good thesis should be: (1) *debatable*, something that someone might disagree with; (2) *reasonable*, a claim you've thought about and arrived at through critical evaluation; (3) *specific and focused*; (4) *significant*, something that makes a meaningful contribution; and (5) *interpretive*, offering an evaluation of the evidence rather than just a description.[i]

See if you can write your thesis in a single sentence (this is often the most difficult step in the entire writing process). This step will help you determine if you really have a workable idea for the paper. It also will guide you in your writing, because you can focus yourself by referring back to the thesis as you write. Do NOT let yourself stray too far afield. Ask yourself, "Does this sentence support my thesis? Is it really necessary to put this material in my paper?" If you cannot answer "yes" to these questions, then take out the extraneous material.

These general rules being noted, let's begin looking at how to write a theological paper.

How to Write a Theological Paper

At this point, we'll begin our look at various types of theological essays, summaries, or brief chapter reviews you may be asked to write in seminary. In some cases, you may be given part of an original source document and asked to give a detailed exposition of the passage as if you were writing for a dictionary of theology. Let's begin with this type of short, 750-word essay and look at how you would develop it. This is the type of paper that you might be assigned in a History of Christianity course.

Extract from Luther's Smalcald Articles (1537)
Article XIII: How One is Justified before God, and of Good Works
What I have hitherto and constantly taught concerning this I know not how to change in the least, namely, that *by faith*, as St. Peter says, we acquire a new and clean heart, and God will and does *account us entirely righteous and holy for the sake of Christ, our Mediator*. And although sin in the flesh has not yet been altogether removed or becomes dead, yet He will not punish or remember it. And such faith, renewal, and forgiveness of sins is *followed by good works*. And what there is still sinful or imperfect also in them shall not be accounted as sin or defect, even [and that, too] for Christ's sake; but the entire man, both as to his person and his works, is to be called and to be *righteous and holy from pure grace* and mercy, shed upon us [unfolded] and *spread over us in Christ*. Therefore we cannot boast of many merits and works, if they are viewed apart from grace and mercy, but as it is written, 1 Cor.1, 31: He that glorieth, let him glory in the Lord, namely, that he has *a gracious God*. For thus all is well. We say, besides, that *if good works do not follow, faith is false* and not true.

F. Bente and W. H. T. Dau, trans., Triglot Concordia: The Symbolical Books of the Ev. Lutheran Church (St. Louis: Concordia Publishing House, 1921), 453–529.

The directions you receive for an assignment of this kind may be as follows:

Provide a brief but detailed exposition of the above passage in 750 words. Imagine you are writing an entry for a dictionary of theology. Try to be as concise, but clear, as possible while using information from your reading and class notes. You might also think of this as an exercise in preparation for clarifying church concepts to congregation members in an easy-to-understand manner. Certain key expressions have been underlined, and your exposition should focus on these. You may choose either of the following:

1. *Do a short exposition of each key expression in order.*
2. *Write a continuous narrative, weaving in the expressions as you write.*

The following paper, with explanatory notes, is an example that may help you on your way.

* * *

Theological Essay: Historical Document
How One Is Justified Before God
History of Christianity
Diane Capitani

When Luther insists that one is justified before God by faith, he gives voice to the central element of his theology: how the individual is able to enter into fellowship with God. The sinner must believe (have faith) in God's promise in the Covenant He makes with each individual sinner. Once the sinner believes, he or she is fully assured of salvation because of a complete and personal trust in the sin-forgiving grace of God. This is not a product of reason, but rather a feeling, an impression that God makes on the heart of the sinner. God is worthy of the sinner's trust and the sinner can trust absolutely in what God promises. It is through this faith that one enters into a relationship with God, who does not need to be appeased with

This is a clear and concise opening sentence that gets to the heart of Luther's theology.

The author is able to capture, in just a few sentences, the essence of Luther's complex ideas.

Three. Theological Essays or Summaries 63

good works and does not need to harshly judge the faithful sinner. Faith is a gift of God; one is passive as God works within.

In possessing this faith, the sinner is accounted entirely righteous. For Luther, righteousness is shaped by the idea of a relationship based on trust between God and the sinner. Each fulfills their obligation toward the other. For the sinner, to be "right with God" is to trust and believe, to have faith. For God, to be "right," He must fulfill his promise of salvation for the sinner. This is the Covenant. Alistair McGrath notes that "righteousness is a fulfillment of the demands and obligations of a relationship between two persons."[1] A just God will keep his promise of salvation if the sinner keeps his promise of trust and faith.

> Here, the author might have teased out the meaning of "accounted" more—exploring how it refers to Christ's righteousness being "imputed" to the sinner—an alien righteousness. God credits humans with the righteousness of Christ on the basis of faith, which is itself a union with Christ. This is good narrative flow here, as Luther's point is well made.

Luther is fighting against the idea of salvation through good works, i.e. earning one's place in Heaven. Faith awakens love of one's fellow man: if one believes, one will do good works from one's own impulse. This is what makes the works morally right, what makes the works valuable: because they are performed out of love, not as an effort to appease an angry God. One who has faith and

> This is exactly the point of good works. The author of this piece makes complex ideas clear and understandable.

is "right" in their relationship with God no longer need worry about justice from God: good works flow from the heart. Luther, in his work, *The Freedom of a Christian,* sees this as a totally freeing act for the Christian who should "lay aside all reliance on works, and strengthen his faith alone more and more, and by it grow in the knowledge, not of works, but of Christ Jesus, who has suffered and risen again for him..."[2]

It is in and through Christ that pure grace and mercy makes us righteous and holy. Through faith, the soul is united to Christ: this is Luther's "third incomparable grace of faith."[3] "Christ and the

---

1. Philip Meadows, Class Lecture Notes, History of Christianity II, Garrett-Evangelical Theological Seminary, Evanston, IL, February 18, 1999.

2. Philip Meadows, Class Handout: Excerpt from Martin Luther, *The Freedom of a Christian,* History of Christianity II, Garrett-Evangelical Theological Seminary, Evanston, IL, February 18, 1999.

3. Ibid.

soul are made one flesh" ... "as the wife to the husband."[4] All that is belongs to the other: "Let faith step in, and then sin, death and hell will belong to Christ, and grace, life and salvation to the soul."[5] Christ takes upon himself our sin and gives us grace in return.

> *This is a good use of quotes in this paragraph to explain Luther's work.*

In sum, what Luther tells us is that the sinner must first have faith in God's righteousness, trust in God's promise of salvation and grace, to enter into union with Christ. Christ then transforms the sinner by uniting with him in faith. Through this unity with Christ, the sinner receives God's grace, while Christ, like a good husband, takes upon himself the sinner's degradations and sins. Faith dwells "in the inward man,"[6] in his heart. With faith in God's promise, the sinner receives the gift of righteousness, which alone justifies: "It is evident that by no outward work or labour can the inward man be at all justified, made free, and saved; and that no works whatever have any relation to him ... therefore the first care of every Christian ought to be, to lay aside all reliance to him ... therefore the first care of every Christian ought to be, to lay aside all reliance on works, and strengthen his faith alone more and more, and by it grow in the knowledge, not of works, but of Christ Jesus, who has suffered and risen again for him..."[7] Works and penance do not earn salvation for the sinner; belief, faith, and trust in God's grace, received in uniting with Christ, lead the sinner to do good works freely, of his own desire, pleasing God and himself at the same time. Thus, the sinner is justified by faith.

> *This piece shows skillful use of primary-source material, which is always of major importance.*

Works Cited

Meadows, Philip. Class Handout: Excerpt from Martin Luther, *The Freedom of a Christian*, History of Christianity II, Garrett-Evangelical Theological Seminary, Evanston, IL, February 18, 1999.

Meadows, Philip. Class Lecture Notes, History of Christianity II, Garrett-Evangelical Theological Seminary, Evanston, IL, February 18, 1999.

* * *

4. Ibid.
5. Ibid.
6. Ibid.
7. Ibid.

Writing the Chapter Review

In addition to analysis of primary historical documents, you most probably will be asked to write short chapter reviews of current books that you read for classes you're currently taking. This is both a review of a chapter and an analysis of it, so you'll include:

- the author's thesis in the chapter
- the theory the author is developing in the chapter
- a brief summary of the chapter
- the strengths and weaknesses in the chapter
- your opinion as to whether the author succeeds in proving what he or she intended to prove.

Remember, in the short chapter review paper, you may only have a page and one-half to do this, so you must be clear, succinct, and concise as you write. In your opening summary/thesis statement, tell what the chapter is about, and then develop that idea in the rest of the opening paragraph, as you will see in the sample papers provided. The second paragraph will begin with the author's thesis of the chapter that you feel is the most important, followed by a strong example that you then develop in the rest of the paragraph. By the third paragraph, you might begin to present an opposing point of view to the author, if you have one, as you'll notice in the examples. Your use of secondary material is appropriate here, always makes your argument stronger, and proves that you're able to think across disciplines. By the time you reach your final paragraphs, you're able to critique the author's specific treatment of his or her theory or thesis: was the author able to prove the thesis? Did the author do what he or she said they intended to do or to prove what the chapter set out to prove? What is your critique of the chapter? Was it clear? Did the narrative flow?

With these thoughts in mind, let's consider the following annotated paper.

* * *

Chapter Review: Current Book

The Social World of Jesus and the Gospels
by Bruce J. Malina
(Chapter: "Christ and Time: Swiss or Mediterranean")
New Testament Studies: Matthew-Acts
Diane Capitani

Malina's Chapter 7, "Christ and Time: Swiss or Mediterranean" develops the theory that the "investigation of time in the New Testament writings" (Malina, 18) is important to an understanding of the way in which first-century Mediterraneans would have received Jesus' account of the coming of the Son of God and Man. His theory posits the idea of a present-oriented people who would have looked at the pronouncements of Jesus in a totally different way than 20th century–Americans who are future-oriented. To prove his theory, Malina develops a rather complicated system of time analysis that asserts the importance of studying human conduct within a theory of temporality.

| *The first sentence says immediately what the author's theory is in the chapter. It is also the thesis statement for the short essay.* |
| *The second sentence offers a more complete statement of the theory developed in the chapter.* |
| *End the first paragraph stating how the author intends to proves his theory. Your essay will show how the author proves it or does not.* |

Malina insists that 20th-century Americans look at Jesus and his pronouncements as indications of future happenings. One example from his text is a passage where Jesus states "Truly, I say to you, this generation will not pass away before all these things take place" (Mark 13:30; Matt. 24: 34; Luke 21[qm] 32–18). Malina insists that U.S. future orientation determines the way in which we read that passage, i.e. as a future prediction of an event that could take place at any future time. A first-century Mediterranean, coming from a peasant society, where "the present as first-order temporal" (Malina, 182) is the preference, saw the pronouncement as an indicator of a present event, since long-range planning or ideas was not part of their world view. Malina argues

| *Each paragraph should have a thesis statement; this is the thesis statement of the second paragraph. It is also Malina's main thesis in the chapter. A good beginning for the short essay.* |
| *Always give a strong example of the author's proof of support for the thesis—and develop it, as this paragraph does.* |

Three. Theological Essays or Summaries 67

that contemporary U.S. residents have difficulty with this concept because, for example, they see this as a future indicator, even if the future is only five minutes away. Further, he insists that U.S. time is unusual anywhere on the planet, except in highly-industrialized, developed, and "enlightened" cultures.

| *This is the final support point for the thesis in this paragraph.*

One might agree with Malina's theory to this point. Certainly, peasant societies operate on a day-to-day basis, as do most primitive cultures. Getting through each day is the center of life; what one may do ten years from now is of no import. E. P. Thompson, in his famous work, *The Making of the English Working Class,* indicates the same thing: that temporality changed when rural, agrarian societies became industrialized and the time clock was invented. Like Thompson, Malina argues that a resident of a peasant culture who ate because he was hungry, not because the clock told him it was noon, and who worked as and when it was necessary to do so, changed only when forced to adopt schedules and timetables in order to survive in a world taken over by a ruling elite that forced him to.

| *Since this is a very short essay, you can now begin to agree or disagree with the author's thesis. Here, the author of the essay offers a point of agreement with Malina.*

| *Bringing in an outside source is always good. It shows that you can read across disciplines. This is a very well-known book that applies here.*

What this means for an understanding of Jesus, then, is that any promise of future reward for leaving everything behind to follow him has to be looked at differently. Malina insists that "there is no expressed concern for the future in the Synoptic story-line. And it would appear that the same holds for the entire New Testament since any time description consisting of this age ... has no room for a future of the sort we speak of " (Malina, 184). He goes even further: "I would contend that the presumed future-oriented categories of the Bible are in fact not future-oriented at all, but present oriented" (Malina, 185).

| *This paragraph continues Malina's argument.*

From this point on, Malina attempts to encourage a reading of the New Testament with a "primary temporal orientation" (Malina, 187). What is key is his interpretation of the word "present": Malina sees the present as "a single context of meaning that often is of long dura-

| *This points out Malina's key argument. The last paragraph sums up all Malina's arguments and then points out why the reviewer does not feel that Malina's argument works.*

tion (189), where a "generation" could refer to the present, not, as we see it, as something in the future. He offers no specific proof for this theory, except in developing his theory of modern abstract time vs. traditional experienced time. This experienced time is rooted in the organic nature of things and one may agree with him that the culture of Jesus was much closer to the organic, imaginative world than late 20th-century America. I found his argument difficult to follow, perhaps because he systemizes a variety of time experiences: modern linear separable time vs. cyclical time, etc. At some point, the argument seems repetitive, i.e., re-introducing the idea of linear, scheduled time on p. 198 and his constant referencing of cyclical time. Ultimately, when Malina claims to superimpose his system of reading the New Testament over those of other historian/theologians, he ends by making assumptions about first-century Mediterraneans that he can never really prove, only assume from historical research he attempts to discredit.

| *Here is the summation, strongly argued.*

Work Cited

Malina, Bruce J. "Christ and Time: Swiss or Mediterranean?" In *The Social World of Jesus and the Gospels,* 179–214. New York: Routledge, 1996.

* * *

Another type of chapter review assignment may require a summary and evaluation of a chapter in a well-known textbook, like Raymond Brown's *Introduction to the New Testament,* used in many seminaries and theological schools around the country. The following annotated example paper presents a short (one-and-a-half-page) paper that gives a concise summary of Chapter 7 of Brown's text, explains his theory and the way in which he develops it, then critiques his theory and method by presenting an alternative theory and plan of attack to examining the Book of John.

* * *

Chapter Review: Course Textbook

Introduction to the New Testament by **Raymond Brown**
(Chapter: "The Gospel of John")
Introduction to the New Testament
Diane Capitani

The Gospel of John, and the writings attributed to "John" in general, continue to be some of the most controversial of all New Testament writings. It is easy, even when evaluating the Fourth Gospel at an introductory level, to raise many questions in interpretation. The most striking contrast between my reaction to the composition of the Gospel and Brown's analysis of it, is in the definition of the structure of the text. While one could consider many facets of this observation, the focus here is broader, and my thesis is to disagree with Brown's outline of the book as a traditional two-part "Signs/Glory" narrative format of the life and teachings of Jesus Christ, and submit that the book is actually a single summary text of the revelative teachings of Christ and a complete retelling of the entire Bible story.

| *A clear first sentence tells us what the essay is about.* |
| *We know immediately that the writer is going to disagree with Brown.* |
| *This is a strong, clear statement of the thesis, a very good opening paragraph for this short essay.* |

Brown's analysis chooses to bifurcate the book into two sections, based on the order of the text: The Book of Signs (1:19–12:50) and The Book of Glory (13:1–20:31), with a prologue and epilogue on either end. Furthermore, in his discussion, "Is John a genuine Gospel?," Brown explains this structure as the result of a three-stage development: (1) The recording of various memories and stories of Christ, (2) the influence of the surrounding Johannine community, and (3) the literary work of an "evangelist" who shaped the first two influences, along with his own "creative ability" into the written form (Brown, 363). The end result was a narrative history in the more traditional gospel form, but strikingly different from the Synoptic Gospels. The focus of the book

| *Clear description begins the second paragraph, which is devoted to Brown. It shows how he will develop his point and tells us what it is.* |
| *This entire paragraph is an excellent summary of Brown's chapter.* |
| *End the paragraph with a strong finish, again making clear what Brown's focus is and that he has achieved it in the book.* |

is the birth, life, death, and resurrection of Christ, through which the reader will understand a higher level of the teaching of the "Good News."

One can, perhaps, agree that there is a certain flow to the book that could be read in that way, but I was overwhelmed in my reading by the observation that the Gospel of John is one continuous text, a true retelling of the entire Bible story, Genesis to Revelation, through the words of Christ. It is almost as if John has taken all of the teachings that Jesus may have done, and ended them with the words, "He who has ears, let him hear," then collected them together as a single manuscript. John, with his self-impression as "the disciple whom Jesus loved" would certainly have felt close enough and qualified enough to arrange such a collection, as, through the Gospel, we find John around Jesus at his most intimate moments.

> *This third paragraph begins the author's disagreement with Brown and details what it is. This is an interesting argument.*

There are examples that bolster the idea of the creation/salvation story: a series of miracles and other related anecdotes scattered within the text in order to illustrate, explain, validate, and bolster the story. This large current is so strong, I argue that the book must be seen that way.

> *This paragraph simply gives more support for the reviewer's argument against Brown's point of view.*

Obviously, I am not the first to make the observation. Brown does describe the work of German theologian Rudolph Bultmann in the early 1900s. Bultmann did extensive work proving a theory on the existence of a revelatory source as the foundation for the Gospel. He took the book apart, line by line and reconstructed it as a three-source theory, a "Signs Source" or miracles, "a Revelatory Discourse Source," and a third "Passion and Resurrection Account" similar to Synoptic accounts (Brown, 363). The revelatory source that came from this has been referred to as the "Redenquelle" (RQ).

> *In making any claim in an essay, always attempt to find out if anyone else has ever made the same argument before you. If so, pull it into your paper, particularly if it is a well-know theologian like Bultmann.*

While Bultmann's critics have had to concede that his work has been important and significant for study in the exegesis of the Gospel of John, nevertheless it has been dismissed in the years since his writing for a number of reasons, among them the fact that it requires significant orderly re-distribution of the text to fit correctly into the prose he envisioned. However, in a 1946 book review of Bultmann's theory of the RQ source, B.S. Eastman acknowledged its significance as a contribution to Johannine criticism, commenting that a short review did not lend itself to giving Bultmann's theory proper exposition.

> *If a theologian has been discredited, it is still acceptable to include his or her argument and explain the reasons others have argued against it. Then explain why it is that you feel the argument is valuable, as this paper does.*

Coming full circle, reviewing Bultmann's regeneration of the RQ, one's original impression of the Jesus statements—"In the beginning was the Word" through "That I might bear witness to the truth"—can be seen as a recreation of the Bible in Jesus' light. However, it also becomes obvious how the work was re-ordered for contextual flow, thus generating considerable cloud over Bultmann's methodology. Yet, one cannot wonder if another perspective might yield additional insight.

> *This concluding paragraph takes us back to the beginning, reinforcing the author's thesis in a strong fashion and showing the possibilities for further study. The entire paper shows that the student has done careful reading and has creative insights.*

Perhaps the writer of the Gospel was close enough to the actual revelatory source that no third document preexisted the writing of the Gospel, so no reorganization was needed. The miracle stories and other historical and anecdotal inserts into the text seem to be consistent with the intention of the original writer who states: "these texts are written that you may believe." I argue strongly that my original impression that Brown's more traditional "Signs/Glory" understanding may be overlooking a powerful and theologically significant interpretation of the Book of John.

Work Cited

Brown, Raymond Edward. *Introduction to the New Testament.* New York: Bantan Doubleday Dell Publishing Group, Inc., 1997.

* * *

QUICK TIP: LEARNING TO PARAPHRASE WELL

With almost every paper you write, you'll be integrating someone else's published (or unpublished) material into your own writing. In order to use these source materials effectively and responsibly, without plagiarizing, it's important that you learn to paraphrase well.

When you paraphrase, you restate *in your own words* the author's claim. Not only does paraphrasing help you avoid including too many quotes in your paper (a sure tip-off to your professors that you're "padding" the paper), but also it forces you to understand and articulate the full meaning of the source material—which is, after all, the point of reading it in the first place. Here are some general guidelines for paraphrasing source material:

1. Review a passage once to get a general idea of the meaning. Read it again carefully to make sure you understand fully what the author is trying to say.

2. Narrow your focus to identify the elements relevant to your own writing.

3. Without looking at the source, jot down a few notes about what the passage says.

4. Consider how you would translate these ideas into your own words if you were saying them out loud to someone else.

5. Summarize the key points in a sequence that best supports your paper topic.

6. If you borrow any phrases or specialized words from the passage, cite the source.

Remember, when including *any* material from another author in your paper, you must acknowledge the source—and this applies whether you are referring broadly to the author's theories *or* citing specific points of an argument, listing steps in a process, following the arrangement of an author's line of thinking, or using some of the author's original language.[ii]

Tips for Reading Critically

When reading source materials in preparation for writing any type of paper, use these strategies to improve your understanding and retention.

1. *Do a preliminary review.* Begin by reviewing the back cover, the preface or foreword, the introduction, appendices, and the author biography. These sections give you a good preview of the book's content. Remember that the introduction is where the author outlines

the plan for the book, the purpose for writing, his or her unique perspective, and the primary claim the book will make.

2. *Read with a question in mind.* If the professor has assigned an essay, reflection, or response paper, he or she may provide specific questions to guide your reading. If you're reading in preparation for other types of writing, it's helpful to identify a few questions you hope the reading will answer—even if you haven't yet settled on your final paper topic or thesis. Your questions may be general, as in "What is this author's theology?" or you may focus on a specific aspect of the reading as, "How does this author understand grace?"[iii]

3. *Make annotations.* As you read, make notes about your responses to the material or questions it raises. This is what annotation means. These annotations provide clues for areas you want to explore in more depth; they also can suggest topics for class discussions or spark ideas for paper topics.[iv]

4. *Record your initial impressions.* After each reading session, take a few minutes to write your initial impressions of the material while it is fresh in your mind. This is different from ordinary note-taking because it allows you to record your understanding of the material, your response to it, and any remaining questions.[v]

5. *Identify relevant or interesting points.* If the assignment is a reflection or response paper, you may be asked to select one or two points that resonate with you. But even if you are reading for a longer research or exegesis paper, reading critically involves narrowing your focus; as you read, it is important to identify what interests you most, what best answers the question(s) you have in mind, or what you find most compelling.

6. *Write a brief summary of the reading.* After finishing a reading, record your response to the piece in its entirety. Consider how the reading relates to the course topic and themes you've been discussing in class. Sometimes taking detailed notes can cause students to lose sight of the big picture, but this strategy gives you the chance to synthesize the key points of what you've read with the overall topic.

* * *

Theological Essay: Christian History
Unity and Diversity (Final Exam)
Roots of Diversity
Krista J. McNeil

From the white-washed walls of the American rural Protestant chapels to the ornate Baroque cathedrals of Europe to the golden domed churches of the Coptics, the rising Sunday sunlight reveals Christian devotees gathered in worship. Their hymns and chanting, rising like incense, or nay with incense, reveal a united theology, nuanced through anthropology, culture, and symbolism. The balance of unity and diversity within the Church is two-fold: unity resides within the central creed that each devotee confesses; diversity *should* exist in how the central creed is symbolized and practiced.

> *A beautiful opening paragraph immediately grabs readers and makes the central theme of the essay—unity and diversity—relevant to a contemporary context.*

Unity, thus, is defined as consensus in core theological/Christological beliefs as revealed to us in Scripture, explicated by the apostles, apologists, church fathers, embodied in the words of the Nicene Creed, and explained in the Chalcedonian Definition. Unity is neither simply peace nor agreement, but transformative love. Unity is realized salvation on Earth and future salvation in the new kingdom, as the body of Christ. Establishing this in doctrine and practice filled the first six centuries of the Church's history. Unity in doctrine, and diversity in culture through history, will be considered below, followed by how this affects my own ministry.

> *This is a clear and concise definition of the term* unity.

> *The author gives a brief preview, so readers know what to expect.*

As early as the writings of Paul, there is clearly diversity in Christian beliefs and culture. Paul's determination that we are one in Christ was not his own conception, but that of Christ himself. In the Gospel of John, Christ describes this unity as those who love him and keep his commandments, who love one another (John 15), and again in his prayer to the Father for

> *Be careful when writing about something Jesus did or said; the author here refers to the Jesus as depicted in the Gospel of John, not the historical Jesus. Remember, they're not the same!*

the disciples that they would remain one in unity, as the Son and the Father are one (John 17). Christ's concerns about the unity of his people manifested in practices, writings, and worship.

Part of the disunity stemmed from the heritage of the converts. This was the case with those who converted from paganism,[1] with syncretistic beliefs intertwined with philosophical dualism between corporality and in-corporality, such as the docetics.[2] Believing that the divine was opposite of the flesh, the incarnation became impossible for the proto–Gnostics. God simply appeared as flesh in Christ. On the way to his martyrdom, Ignatius of Antioch questioned why we would live our lives for God if God had not truly become human and truly suffered, "But if it be, as some godless men, i.e., unbelievers assert, that he suffered in phantom only—it is they that are phantoms—why am I in bonds? Why, moreover, do I pray that I may fight with the wild beasts? Then I die for naught. Then I lie against the Lord."[3]

This is an excellent use of a quote to show the persistence of various groups' beliefs.

Disunity also stemmed from those who converted from Judaism. The Judaizers of Antioch believed that Jesus was a teacher within Judaism, and the Ebionites believed that if Christ suffered, he could not be God. They also asked if Christ were God, then how could Christians be monotheists. They believed Christ was the son of God only so much as any other human is God's son or daughter (they were adoptionists, which will be considered later on).

Ignatius, being "set on unity,"[4] urged the avoidance of divisions. He regarded docetists as apostates, but not heretics, as they had not fully broken off from the Church, which was still being established. Ignatius believed in the importance of bishops and adherence to the structure established by Christ through the presbytery of the apostles. Through structure, unity was manageable and pleasing to God.[5] The sacraments were central to unity, so

---

1. For more detailed information on the traditional religion of these converts, particularly on the syncretism of their gods, see James S. Jeffers, *The Greco-Roman World of the New Testament Era: Exploring the Background of Early Christianity* (Downers Grove, IL: InterVarsity Press, 1999), 94–96.

2. James Papandrea, Class Lecture Notes, History of Christianity I, Garrett-Evangelical Theological Seminary, Evanston, IL, February 16, 2010.

3. J. Stevenson, ed., *A New Eusebius: Documents Illustrating the History of the Church to AD 337* (London: SPCK, 1999), 15.

4. Papandrea, Class Lecture Notes, February 16, 2010.

5. Stevenson, *A New Eusebius*, 15.

Ignatius taught that they must occur under the direction and approval of a bishop from within the hierarchy.

Contrary to this hierarchy, Marcian established a new church through a new set of Scriptures. He believed there were two gods: one ruled the material world, and the other god was love. The former is the God of the Old Testament. The latter is the one revealed in the New Testament. Marcian therefore rejected the Old Testament[6]: "Marcian took scissors to the Scriptures at the very time that the Scripture was being made."[7] The establishment of a unique canon, in combination with his belief in two gods, moved Marcian from heretic to apostate. Scripture is central to unity, for we are defined by it and Christ defined within it.

> *The author succinctly traces several historical movements to show the disunity that characterized the early church.*

Another movement to break off completely from the mainstream church was the Gnostics. Gnosticism was rooted in dualism and syncretism. In one sense, there was no such thing as "Gnosticism" proper, as there was no unity amongst the Gnostic sects. However, the various groups (Sethian, Valentinian, Manichaeism) held in common "Hellenistic syncretism, or the mingling of Greek and Oriental traditions and ideas subsequent to the conquests of Alexander the Great."[8] The various schools did have "gnosis" as a common element—a secret knowledge only revealed to elite persons. The cosmogony of the Gnostics was varied and diverse; it borrowed from many traditions, including Judaism and Iranian Zoroastrian dualism. Gnosticism placed culture and philosophical cosmogony over and above the centrality of Christ. Christ became one of many bearers of secret knowledge.

Another threat to unity was the struggle between prophesy and hierarchical order. By the 90s CE, distinction was being made within the offices of the Church: the presbyteros (presbyters, elders, priests), and the episcopes (bishops). It is speculated that the seat of the bishop may have started as the chairperson of the clergy and transitioned into a singular point of

> *Simple transitions make each paragraph flow smoothly from one to the next.*

---

6. Justo L. Gonzalez, *A History of Christian Thought*, vol. 1 of *From the Beginnings to the Council of Chalcedon* (Nashville, TN: Abingdon Press, 1970), 137–39.

7. Papandrea, Class Lecture Notes, February 16, 2010.

8. Kurt Rudolph, *Gnosis: The Nature and History of Gnosticism* (San Francisco, CA: HarperSanFrancisco, 1987), 55.

Three. Theological Essays or Summaries 77

authority.⁹ One of the challenges to this was Montanus and the New Prophesy, also called "Cataphyrgianism."

Though not schismatic, this group was critical of the newly forming Church, and they questioned where authority resided. For the Church, authority came from the Rule of Faith, the Apostolic Tradition, and from Scripture. For Montanus and his daughters, Maximilla and Priscilla, authority came through revelation. In the early 170s CE, Montanus surfaced claiming to be a prophet. He was accused of claiming to be the Holy Spirit itself. He asserted charismatic authority to re-interpret the Scriptures. The mainstream Church, however, had decided that prophecy of this sort ended with the apostolic age, and the gift of prophecy had been replaced with preaching. The Church was a church of the bishops; authority resided with the bishops among equals, as authority resided with the Father in the Godhead among equals. For the Montanists, authority resided with the prophets, who were above the laity.¹⁰

Unity and diversity were also in tension concerning liturgical practices, such as with the Novationists. In 202, Emperor Septimius Severus issued an edict making Christianity illegal. He required all inhabitants to sacrifice to the traditional Roman gods in the honor of the emperor to prove their adherence to Roman civic religion. Many Christians sacrificed, but many did not. Some were martyred. One of the first to die was Fabian, the bishop of Rome. Novatian, a priest, became the acting bishop. Once the persecution ended, questions arose as to how to deal with the lapsed Christians—some had made the sacrifice, others paid a non–Christian to make the sacrifice for them, others just burned incense. The key players in the situation were the rigorists (Novation, Hippolytus, Tertullian), who argued that the lapsed should not simply be let into the Church again; the Laxist (Cornelius and Cyprian), who argued that the lapsed should be dealt with on a case-by-case basis and with adequate grace; and the Confessors. The latter were Christians who had suffered torture during the persecution. They began to assume charismatic authority among the laity, who believed the Confessors could grant readmission to the Church.¹¹

Meanwhile, the Church met to vote on the new bishop of Rome. A small group consecrated Novatian bishop, while Cornelius

---

9. Papandrea, Class Lecture Notes, February 23, 2010.

10. Ibid.

11. Stevenson, *A New Eusebius*, 216–246; Papandrea, Class Lecture Notes, March 2, 2010.

was properly elected into the seat. This became the first schism of the Church. Both the rigorists and the laxist were seeking unity. Novatian sought unity by excluding the lapsed from the body of the Church. The laxist sought unity by allowing them back in through penance. In 251/2, a series of synods held in Carthage and Rome excommunicated Novatian and his followers. Converts to Novatian's church were re-baptized on the basis of it not being clear if the person had first been baptized by someone who had lapsed during the persecution. Likewise, Cyprian began re-baptizing converts to the mainstream Church from the Novatianists.[12] More synods were held in 254. Baptism was ruled valid no matter who performs it as long as it is done in the name of the Trinity.[13] The schism affected more than reconciliation and penance; it also affected the sacrament that defined Church membership.[14]

> *In detailing the historical movements, the author gives just enough information to allow readers to follow the thread—the ongoing struggle for unity in the church.*

In 325 CE,[15] Christianity, being the faith of the emperor, allowed unity to take on a new dimension, that of politics as seen in the Council of Nicea. Arius was a presbyter in Alexandria who proclaimed that "the Son of God has come into existence out of the non-existent and that there was when he was not, that as possessing free will he was capable of virtue or of vice, and that he was created and made."[16] Arianism was a form of Adoptionism, the belief that God adopted Jesus as his Son. The main difference was that Arianism attached deification to adoption, "God [...] ensured the Son's closeness to himself by giving him all the glory he is able to receive and

---

12. Papandrea, Class Lecture Notes, March 2, 2010.

13. I would also like to draw attention to the debate over baptism between Augustine and the Donatists. Augustine concluded that grace flowed from God directly to the person receiving the sacrament and not through the person performing the sacrament. The redemptive grace could therefore not become "damaged" by the sins/actions of the clergy performing the sacrament. Papandrea, Class Lecture Notes, March 25, 2010.

14. Papandrea, Class Lecture Notes, March 2, 2010.

15. This paper is silent about Pelagius and Augustine, not for lack of knowledge or understanding, but for space constraints. Suffice it to say that the very nuanced debates between them at the end of the fourth century demonstrate that even if two persons affirm the Nicene Creed, diversity can exist within the Christian understanding of human will, God's grace, and sin. This very detailed diversity at the time led to Pelagius being condemned and Augustine's position being affirmed, though not completely adopted by the Church, which settled for a "middle of the road" position on grace, sin, and the human will. Papandrea, Class Lecture Notes, March 23, 2010 and March 25, 2010.

16. Stevenson, *A New Eusebius*, 322.

Three. Theological Essays or Summaries 79

by bestowing upon him some sort of participation in the divine intellect."[17] Adoptionism had the ascent of Jesus, but not the ultimate divinity. Furthermore, as a pre-existent creature, the Arian Jesus did not have the same divinity—substance—as God the Father. Arius and Adoptionists were preserving the immutability of God.[18]

The Creed of the Council of Nicea, under the influence of Constantine, was written to make sure that Arianism was completely excluded—to ensure that the divinity of Christ was professed, the unity of the Son and the Father made central, and that this was pivotal for salvation. The crucial phrasing: "begotten from the Father [...] from the substance of the Father, God from God ... begotten not made, of one substance with the Father [...] who because of us humans and because of our salvation came down and became incarnate [...]." Constantine later imbued the Council with divine favor: "For that which has commended itself to the judgment of three hundred bishops cannot be other than the judgment of God; seeing that the Holy Spirit dwelling in the minds of persons of such character and divinity has effectually enlightened them respecting the Divine will."[19]

> The author does well in summarizing key schisms that moved the church toward disunity, and the church's attempts to find a way to bring it back into unity.

A little more than a century later, disunity was once again threatening the Church. This time it came at the craftsmanship of Nestorius and Eutyches. Nestorius, patriarch of Constantinople, said Mary gave birth to Christ, not God. She was *Christotokos*, not *Theotokos*. Cyril, the bishop of Alexandria, believed Nestorius had divided the "oneness" of Christ by saying this—Nestorius was stressing the distinction of the human nature from the divine nature within the person of Christ. Cyril responded by speaking of the person of Christ as being one nature *of two natures* or "one composite nature after the incarnation."[20]

> This paragraph begins with another good transition statement.

This ensured that the divine and the human are united in one person equally. Rome and Constantinople meanwhile, advocated

---

17. Rowan Williams, *Arius: Heresy and Tradition* (Grand Rapids, MI: Eerdmans Publishing Company, 2001), 106.

18. Papandrea, Class Lecture Notes, March 16, 2010 and March 18, 2010.

19. Stevenson, *A New Eusebius*, 350.

20. Papandrea, Class Lecture Notes, April 22, 2010.

for "in two natures" to protect against the heresy of Eutychianism. Eutyches, archimandrite of Constantinople, argued against Nestorius' two-natures with one-nature Christology. However, he combined the natures to the extent of erasing the humanity with the divinity. The Church was facing division over this. The emperor Marcian, like Constantine, called for another Council, the Council of Chalcedon.

The Chalcedonian Definition aimed to maintain unity, to end both Nestorianism and Eutychianism and to pacify both the Alexandrians and the Romans. The prologue of the Definition explains its purpose, "no one should vary from his neighbor in the doctrines of religion, but that the preaching of the truth should be uniformly set forth to all."[21] It was not a new creed, but a means by which to measure theological and Christological statements to ensure that they adhered to the Creed of Nicea and to the mainstream Church's interpretation of Scripture. It was necessary to ensure that the humanity of Christ was not diminished. To do so would dissolve the link between humans and God, thereby destroying salvation.[22]

The fallout after Chalcedon was quite complex, as it led to a permanent split in the Church. Those who were opposed to Chalcedon rejected it because it favored the writings of Leo, bishop of Rome. Many attempts were made at reconciliation. I believe they ultimately failed because they all were made with the assumption that the anti–Chalcedonians should simply "accept" the linguistic formulation of "in two natures." Language is rarely *just* language; it is culture, heritage, ethnicity, and nationalism. What the anti–Chalcedonians, specifically the proto–Coptics, believed was completely in line with what had been established at Chalcedon. They were rejected by the favoritism of Roman theological linguistics and Latin over Alexandrian theological linguistics and Greek. It is as if those who were attempting to "convert" the proto–Coptics failed to recognize that distinctive culture does not equal heresy.

| Here, the author offers her own opinion of these events.

My Own Ministry and Conclusion

As an academe and lay person, the influence of my beliefs on unity and diversity in theology are different from those of the

---

21. J. Stevenson, *Creeds, Councils, and Controversies: Documents Illustrating the History of the Church AD 337–461* (London: SPCK, 1989), 350.

22. Papandrea, Class Lecture Notes, April 22, 2010.

ordained clergy. I will not be making decisions about baptizing, marrying, or determining who is and who is not ready for confirmation. I am in ministry as an advocate to those who are becoming clergy at seminary. My sensitivity to culture helps me to be sympathetic to the students as they struggle to understand Christology and to reconcile what they learn in seminary with the theology that they were raised in. I am drawn into students' discussions as they prepare for the Board of Ordained Ministry, as they write careful answers to difficult and vital questions. I try to hold their statements up to the Nicene Creed and the Chalcedonian Definition, to the formulations in Paul's writings, and Christ's own few self-revelations in Scripture. As an editor for our international students, their writing must fall in line with these formulations, but their culture need not. I try to help them understand the nuances of English and Greek prepositions that are so important in Christology. It is a fine line to walk, though, as many of them come from Confucian backgrounds which bring the principles of yin and yang into their understanding of God and Christ—it is so easy to fall into syncretism and the dichotomy between corporality and incorporality. I revisit the struggles of the Church over and over again as I seek ways to explain Christology to them, and to make sense of their unique perspectives in Christology as non–Westerners.

| *The professor will specify whether the paper should address the topic in light of your ministry.* |

| *The author reveals her own commitment to* unity *in terms of the theological formulations and to* disunity *in terms of diversity—and how she lives this out in her ministry.* |

We must have unity in our confession, in order to even be defined "Christian," but we should also have uniqueness in our cultures, as each person/culture experiences the Godhead through many varied and rich facets. The history of the early church shows us that for unity to exist, the church first had to determine its doctrine, and upon what the doctrine was built (Scripture). This can be seen in the push and pull between Docetism, proto–Gnosticism, and the Judaizers. Once doctrine was formed, it was necessary to apply hierarchy to it to determine what it meant to be Christian, such as with Montanus. It is also seen through the Novatianist schism, where liturgical practice and the sacraments were realized as central to defining who was and was not part of the Church and what it

| *This is a clear and well-written conclusion that captures the ongoing tension between unity and disunity in the church—both then and now.* |

means to be Christian. Finally, unity is defined systematically in the Councils of Nicea and Chalcedon. Here, Christology determines how we ought to live (ethics), and what we believe about eschatology (both realized and future). Both the Nicene Creed and the Chalcedonian Definition allow space for cultural variations and diversity, while maintaining unity in profession of faith and by being grounded in Scripture. We must also be graceful towards one another's diversity, emanating the grace of God and the *imago Dei*.

Works Cited

Gonzalez, Justo L. *A History of Christian Thought*. Vol. 1 of *From the Beginnings to the Council of Chalcedon*. Nashville: Abingdon Press, 1970.

Jeffers, James S. *The Greco-Roman World of the New Testament Era: Exploring the Background of Early Christianity*. Downers Grove, IL: InterVarsity Press, 1999.

Papandrea, James. Class Lecture Notes, History of Christianity I, Garrett-Evangelical Theological Seminary, Evanston, IL, February 16, 2010; February 23, 2010; March 2, 2010; March 16, 2010; March 18, 2010; March 23, 2010; March 25, 2010; and April 22, 2010.

Rudolph, Kurt. *Gnosis: The Nature and History of Gnosticism*. Translated by Robert McLachlan Wilson. San Francisco: HarperSanFrancisco, 1987.

Stevenson, J., ed. *A New Eusebius: Documents Illustrating the History of the Church to AD 337*. London: SPCK, 1999.

_____. *Creeds, Councils and Controversies: Documents Illustrating the History of the Church AD 337–461*. London: SPCK, 1989.

Williams, Rowan. *Arius: Heresy and Tradition*. Grand Rapids, MI: Eerdmans Publishing Company, 2001.

* * *

CHAPTER FOUR

Reflection Papers

All of my writing is God-given.—Ray Bradbury

Steps for Writing a Reflection Paper

We approach this chapter with some trepidation, in part because there is no specific process that we can hand you that will work for all theological reflection papers. The student must always be sure to understand the assignment, i.e., does the instructor want a *personal* reflection written from the first-person point of view, in a conversational tone, reflecting on a personal experience that the student has had—or is this an *academic* assignment, requiring a more academic and formal vocabulary, employing a third-person point of view? We will break this down as we go along.

A good practice for writing reflection papers is to keep a journal as you enter seminary. Some of you may have begun to do this already, and in some courses, especially in pastoral counseling, professors often ask students to keep a journal for the duration of the course. Usually, these are informal journals, reflections on readings in the course or discussions that take place and should reflect your thoughts on the coursework. You should feel free to express yourself honestly in these journals without judgment. Journals are a form of free writing, so you should not attempt to force yourself to write in them as you would a formal essay. But they are a good basis for work in writing personal reflection papers, so keeping the journal will help you later on. Some students have commented that they've found them helpful in later sermon writing as well, by allowing them to reflect on past experiences they had recorded in their journals.

What is "theological reflection?" It's a term that is prominent now in theological seminaries and divinity schools and can be defined as a process in which you, as an individual, or you, as part of a group, reflect on an experience, a faith-based one of your own, or one you've read about. It's a way to reach a new understanding about human experience, your own or that of others, and a way to observe and connect with the way people live and participate in their faith experiences. This is part of faith formation, and reflecting theologically is one way for you to develop your own faith. For those of you in seminary who will enter the ministry, theological reflection is an important tool in aiding you to grow your ministry, as you grow in faith.

Theological reflection requires more than simply "thinking about things." Spiritual discernment is part of the process as well. As you reflect, try to put yourself in a frame of mind to be receptive in being guided by the Holy Spirit. Be open to this, if you can. We acknowledge that this is not always easy, particularly in today's busy world. If you can remove yourself to a quiet place, at a quiet time, early in the morning, perhaps, it will help you on this journey. As noted above, there are different types of theological reflection, and you may receive instructions that are specific to a class requirement, i.e., to reflect upon a book the class is reading or a piece of music the entire class is listening to, etc. But most theological reflection can be broken down into a few main steps:

1. *Personal or shared experience.* Your reflective writing can be based on a life experience that has had an impact on you and has led you to God, or has influenced you spiritually, either in the past or currently. The writing also can be based on a shared experience that a group has had together; for example, a mission trip to the Mexican-American border where you may have worked with those trying to enter the United States and, as a result, were suffering in imprisonment in desperate conditions. You might be reflecting on "the least of these." Writing theological reflection papers of this type often flows more easily because these memories or thoughts are those that are difficult to get out of your mind. They might cause you to think more deeply about what you really believe and what the role of the Christian really is. If this is to be a group project, you may share your

thoughts with the group as you write. This type of project might test your faith, but that is not necessarily a bad thing. This is how you grow, and that is the purpose of theological reflection. The experience isn't requiring you to do research; personal reflection papers are not research papers, but thoughtful, perception papers. Those based on events or personal experiences are not based on church doctrine or practices, for the most part.

2. *Learning how to reflect.* You would think that it wouldn't be necessary to "learn" how to reflect, and formal lessons are certainly not what we're advocating here, but you do, in writing theological reflection, view an experience or event through a different "lens" than if the paper were being written in an English literature class. For example, your faith tradition informs your reflection, even if you don't realize it. How you have participated in that tradition also has had an impact on forming your theology. The values your faith tradition gave you form part of that response, and some of those values were imparted by your culture. Your response to any event or experience, theologically or otherwise, comes through because of these lenses. Allowing time for prayer, for the Holy Spirit to be with you before you begin any free writing, may help you clear your head, and be sure your vision is not clouded by false judgments that may distort your vision of the Divine. Some of us need to be in a peaceful place in order to reflect. It's a good idea to adopt an attitude of contemplation, to place ourselves *inside* ourselves, as it were, in order to find the Divine and be ready for the encounter. Others may be able to simply listen, no matter where they may be and encounter the Divine on a crowded street or see the Divine in the face of a homeless person. It will be up to you to discover your own path to personal reflection.

3. *Learning how to respond.* You are now ready to write your theological reflection. If this is part of an assignment for a specific class, you may have been given something specific to which you have to write a response. You will still need to center yourself around the assignment or question you've been given and follow the steps noted above. However, if you're able to select your own experience to write about, then the task is done more easily, because you can approach it by covering something that may touch you more deeply. In either case, provide as many details to describe the situation as clearly as possible. Try to recreate the situation or revisit the experience so that

readers feel they are present with you. Imagine that you are *in* the experience once again. As much as you can, imagine that you are there. If you felt filled by the Holy Spirit, pause as long as it takes to see if you can summon the presence once again—not easy, we know, but pray and hope.

4. *Writing the reflection paper.* When you return to write the final draft of your paper, you're refining what you just did. The pedagogy of writing tells us to "write three times." Ideally, this is always what one should do, although often time runs out and we don't do it. However, that first writing experience should have fallen under the heading of "free writing"—the process of simply allowing your thought to flow onto the paper as your memories came forth, as the Spirit filled you. This draft is rough, perhaps containing misspelled words and grammar errors. That's just fine. Now you will create an outline and fill it in.

Here are your steps:
  A. Prayer
  B. Reflection and inspiration
  C. Free writing—putting your thoughts into words
  D. Rough outline
  E. Uncorrected rough draft
  F. First draft
  G. Final draft

While this may look like many steps, there really aren't that many. For example, the rough draft may consist of just a few words in each paragraph to give yourself the main ideas of where your final draft will go. In the same way, the outline is there to help you by providing a pathway on which you can walk to get the paper going. Then, remember that a first draft just allows you to put in additional ideas and thoughts that your free writing may have left out. Each stage allows you to keep adding ideas and thoughts; you'll be surprised that more experiences in your reflection will occur to you the longer you are writing. Don't worry about grammar snags until your final draft; there will be time enough to correct spelling errors and other faults. Don't take time to correct words or sentences that you might remove later. Indeed, that's something to think about in all your writing.

Style Guidelines

The types of writing you do in seminary will vary based on the course requirements, the subject area, and the type of assignment. In every case, however, ==your audience will be a seminary professor who expects a certain standard of quality in your work.== By following these simple style guidelines, you can greatly improve the quality of your writing:

1. *Use straightforward language.* Many students mistakenly believe that writing for the academic community means using academic jargon, multi-syllabic words, overly complex sentences, or pretentious language. But good writing is clear, direct, and unaffected; your goal is to be understood, not to sound erudite. ==Write as naturally as you can.==

2. *Avoid clichés, slang, and a too-casual tone.* At the same time, writing in the seminary is a specific type of formal writing, so it is important to avoid clichés, slang expressions, or an overly-casual style. You also should avoid using contractions in formal writing (we have used them in this book to make it more reader-friendly) and, for the most part, you will not use the first-person pronoun, "I" (although there are times when this may be appropriate; see "Academic Voice vs. Personal Voice" in this chapter), because this suggests a subjective viewpoint when the goal of academic writing is to be objective. = sticks to facts, have no personal feelings

3. *Eliminate redundancy.* Students often use repetition—piling up adverbs and adjectives or using too many qualifiers such as "basically," "really," or "very"— to shore up their arguments (or to extend the page count of their papers). Wordiness stems from not having enough to say or not knowing how to say it. It is important to decide what you want to say before you say it. Eliminate the filler, and you will have a stronger paper.

4. *Choose active voice.* Most of you know by now that the use of passive voice—a sentence that puts the actor after the action, as in "Six hymns were sung by the children's choir"—generally weakens your writing and makes your meaning harder to discern. Active verbs give your writing energy and keep the reader engaged. In certain cases, passive voice can be used strategically, in cases where the object of the verb is important, as in "The Pentecost liturgy was enhanced by liturgical dance."

5. *Use parallel structure.* Using parallel forms can make your writing more clear and powerful. Instead of writing, "God is omnipotent, has no beginning and no end, and we cannot understand God," it is stronger to use a parallel structure such as, "God is omnipotent, eternal, and incomprehensible."

6. *Be specific.* Vague language and ideas tell readers that the writer does not have enough concrete information to make a compelling point. A very general sentence such as "The Gospel of John was written by different people over time" does not tell the reader nearly as much as "The Gospel of John evolved from an early document based on a personal experience of Jesus, to a literary creation developed from other sources in the tradition, to the final New Testament Gospel included in the canon today." Specific, descriptive words and content make your ideas clear, forceful, and interesting.

7. *Choose verbs over nouns.* Your writing will be much stronger if you avoid verbs made into nouns by the addition of a -tion ending, such as "An assessment of the problem needs to be completed by the group." Instead, it's stronger to write, "The group needs to assess the problem."[i]

8. *Watch for empty or inflated expressions.* When you are tempted to use a longer phrase such as "in reference to" or "with regard to," choose a simpler option such as "about" to convey the same meaning. Eliminate empty phrases to start a sentence, such as "it was found that" or "it is important to note that."[ii] Do not begin your sentence with "In my opinion." You are writing the paper, so the reader assumes it is your opinion. It is better to say, "my argument is ..." or "my thesis is..."

9. *Avoid confusing constructions.* Journalists often write confusing sentences that are time-consuming for readers to decipher: "the education committee voted not to overturn the ban on limiting the use of computers in the classroom." Don't frustrate your readers by forcing them to deconstruct your sentences. Stay away from double-negative phrases such as "not unlikely" or "not impossible" when you can say directly whether something is likely or possible.

10. *Do not use different words for the same concept.* When your paper requires you to use a certain key word over and over again, do not replace it with a different synonym each time. This can be confusing for readers. The repetition of key words throughout your paper

can provide transitions and help readers follow the thread of your argument.[iii]

Academic Voice vs. Personal Voice

One of the greatest writing challenges for beginning seminary students is finding a writing style, tone, and voice that are appropriate for an academic audience.

A. Academic Voice

- The purpose of academic writing is to take a position on something, build a persuasive argument, and provide evidence to support it. You will be including the voices of other authors in your paper, but this should be done in moderation, which means that your voice must carry the weight of the argument and supporting evidence.
- The purpose of academic writing is to be objective, accurate, and impersonal. Use of the pronoun "I" generally is not appropriate since it introduces personal observation. It makes no sense to write, "I think Ephesians is a genuine Pauline epistle," when it is understood by the reader that the paper is the product of your thinking. State your position directly—"Although Ephesians uses language that differs significantly from the undisputed Pauline epistles, the similarity of themes suggests a common author"—then build a strong argument by supporting your claim with concrete evidence.
- In addition to the style issues discussed in Style Guidelines in Chapter Four, strong academic writing is free of *vague language* ("in many ways," "they," or "things"); *hyperbole* ("awesome," "super," or "fabulous"); and *combined verbs* ("starting out," "finishing up," or "checking in"). Use precise, descriptive language and check the definition of a word if you are unsure of its meaning.
- Watch out for tentative language that weakens your position and undermines the confidence of your voice—words such as "may," "could," "kind of," "seems," or "might." Choose language to strengthen your claims, such as "must," "definitely," or "certainly."
- When introducing an author's idea, avoid bland phrases such as "according to" or "in so-and-so's view." Instead, state your assessment of the work by using evaluative language: "Witherington's interpretation fails to take into account the voices of marginalized readers."

Take a stand, but be sure to present others' arguments fairly; while it is entirely appropriate to critique an author's claims, your evaluation must have a balanced and respectful tone.

B. Personal Voice

- Some seminary assignments are specifically intended to draw out a student's personal insights: response papers, case studies, spiritual autobiographies, or other types of personal reflections in which a first-person perspective is desirable.
- When writing in a personal voice, it is acceptable to use language that is more natural and less formal than academic writing (although still following many of the same style conventions). The goal is to be honest, to express personal insights or emotions, and to articulate your commitment to certain values. At the same time, it is important to balance your personal perspective with a sense of objectivity.
- Until relatively recently, the first-person perspective was rarely used in academic writing, and many scholars still avoid it in an effort to maintain "objectivity." But, increasingly, scholars acknowledge that all writing, no matter how objective it seems, is the product of an individual writing from a particular point of view. Feminist scholars argue that scholarly writing is designed to maintain the *appearance* of objectivity—and to dismiss opinions that do not conform to the accepted style—when in fact, what appears to be objective, scholarly writing actually is a type of discourse common to patriarchy.
- The decision to use an academic voice vs. a personal voice in your writing depends on the type of assignment, whether your personal experience and insights are relevant to your overall purpose, and to what extent they influence your understanding and approach to the questions you are exploring.[iv]

Reflection Paper: Reading Reflection

Letter from a Birmingham Jail
Theology of Martin Luther King, Jr.
Thomas Yang

My reflection of Martin Luther King, Jr.'s *Letter from Birmingham Jail* is influenced by an Asian-American constructive theological method. From this perspective, I interpret King's letter using assumptions asserted in Andrew Sung Park's reinterpretation of the Christian Doctrine of Sin, which incorporates the Asian concept of *han* (한). Park's Doctrine of Sin articulates a way of salvation that considers the perspective of *both* the sinner/oppressor—the victim/oppressed—whereas traditional doctrines of salvation and sin focus solely on the actions of the sinner/oppressor and neglect a theological analysis of the victim/oppressed.[1] *Han* is a Korean term to describe the depths of human suffering, an experience which is essentially and unfortunately untranslatable. *Han* expresses itself in active and passive forms as aggression and acquiescence, respectively.[2] In short, my methodology notices the perspective of the victims/oppressed in King's letter by identifying *han* in their experiences, and as such, I find this methodology useful in extracting new meaning from King's writings.

> This is a very strong opening paragraph that lays out the integrative approach the author is taking—exploring the relationship between MLK's theology, the doctrine of sin, and the concept of han.

> Even in a very brief paper, the author makes a clear statement about methodology and purpose.

King is "cognizant of the interrelatedness of all communities and states."[3] Even though I know that many of King's statements likely arose from his study of Personalism, understanding the interconnectedness of *han* and sin also buttresses King's statement. When I read sentences like, "We are caught in an inescapable network of mutuality," I am especially reminded of the precarious rela-

---

1. Andrew Sung Park, *The Wounded Heart of God: The Asian Concept of Han and the Christian Doctrine of Sin* (Nashville: Abingdon Press, 1993), 69–70.

2. Ibid., 15.

3. Martin Luther King, Jr., *Letter from a Birmingham Jail*, 1963, accessed March 26, 2013, http://www.africa.upenn.edu/Articles_Gen/Letter_Birmingham.html.

tionship between the oppressor and the oppressed. When the oppressor sins against the oppressed, their victims experience passive *han* and acquiesce to their subjugation. However, such a relationship does not remain static. Rather, the oppressed may quickly transform their experience of passive *han* into active *han*,[4] retaliate against their oppressors, and become oppressors in their own way. King describes the *han* of the leaders of the Alabama Christian Movement for Human Rights when he writes, "As the weeks and months went by, we realized that we were the *victims* of a broken promise... We had no alternative except to prepare for direct action" (italics added). The nature of *han* reveals how these cyclical dynamics truly embody a "network of mutuality."

> *This is an insightful and original reading of han in a new context.*

Although King appears to use rhetoric to equate segregation to a "disease," the Christian Doctrine of Sin does not necessarily define sin in biological terms. Sin attempts to accurately relate the human condition and experience to misery and suffering, which does not necessarily imply sin in terms of biological parameters.[5] On the other hand, the concept of *han* includes a biological component. *Han* can be successfully transmitted biologically from one generation to the next. In the case of the Black experience of King's day, the DNA encoding skin pigments to express dark skin tones became a biological cause for the *han*/suffering of Blacks in a segregated climate. From an Asian-American constructive theological perspective, King's message could be reinterpreted as a call for Blacks to recognize their *han* masked in forms of complacency and in their implicit participation of their own demise by injustices created from invisible systemic structures.

> *The author is skillful in exploring the interrelationship of these ideas at a deep level.*

In many experiences of *han*, the victims feel powerless to change or resist the systemic structures in place that perpetuate oppressors to continue in their oppression. Such feelings of powerlessness become the passive experience of *han*, which can create a collective consciousness of acquiescence. I believe King saw this collective consciousness dangerously setting in within the minds of his colleagues and fellow Blacks as a "degenerating sense of 'nobodiness.'" I feel King's disappointment in his ministerial colleagues

---

4. Active *han* that violently works to counter the injustice is called *dan* (단).

5. Park, *The Wounded Heart of God*, 79–81.

that "fellow clergymen would see [his] nonviolent efforts as those of an extremist." From the perspective of *han*, I see more deeply King's desire to stir the complacent attitudes of many within his time.

> *Here is another original and perceptive observation.*

The more I interpret King's letter from the perspective of *han*, the more I see King's awareness of his social location. One of King's many insights is that "few members of the oppressor race can understand the deep groans and passionate yearnings of the oppressed race," which was true not only when he was alive, but also true today. Therefore, my understanding of *han* becomes a way for me to theologically interpret my social location. There will always be injustice, suffering, and oppression in the world, but through the perspective of *han*, I more clearly see the intertwining relationship between the oppressor and the oppressed. I believe that forgiveness, from a Christian perspective, must include perspectives from both the sinner and sinned against, which *han* and Martin Luther King, Jr. acknowledge. Thus, I will continue to integrate *han* into my theological methodology in further academic studies and in my exegesis.

> *Here, the author reveals how his own thinking has changed as a result of this reflection.*

> *This is an excellent example of reflecting deeply on theological concepts and considering how they inform the way we live. Exploring these ideas in the context of historical events and present-day realities moves them beyond academic concepts; they have become part of the author's experience and understanding.*

Works Cited

King, Jr. Martin Luther. *Letter from a Birmingham Jail*, 1963. Accessed March 26, 2013. http://www.africa.upenn.edu/Articles_Gen/Letter_Birmingham.html.

Park, Andrew Sung. *The Wounded Heart of God: The Asian Concept of Han and the Christian Doctrine of Sin*. Nashville: Abingdon Press, 1993.

* * *

Reflection Paper: Pilgrimage

Thin Places
Celtic Christianity
Melanie Baffes

And in that moment, the luminous One appeared and she lifted the veil which lay over his mind.[1]

> *A Scripture text from a non-canonical gospel previews the overall theme of the paper.*

It's a cool and sunny June day when I arrive on Iona, yet I feel a wave of disappointment. The setting is unimaginably beautiful: the tiny island, a rocky coastline, sapphire-colored water, white-sand beaches, a clear and cloudless sky. But it doesn't feel very holy to me; tourists with cameras are everywhere and there are way too many people for my liking. I've learned that Iona's visitors come in many forms and for many reasons, which is why it's so crowded: People come to tour the island, to shop, to see the beaches, to visit the abbey. Some come to make a pilgrimage, but a surprising number of visitors appear not to know it's a sacred site at all. Many of us have come because we're curious about the Celtic beliefs and rituals that call us. We're eager to circle the standing crosses, to stand at the edge of the world where land meets sea and sky, to experience first-hand the power and mystery of this ancient tradition.

> *Since this is a reflection on a personal pilgrimage, use of the first-person (I/we), an informal tone, and sensory imagery all are appropriate.*

Iona is known for being the place where Christianity first came to Scotland in 563 CE, when Columba and his followers arrived from Ireland. One of the meeting points for Celtic spirituality and Roman Christianity, Iona has a restored Benedictine Abbey and nunnery ruins dating from the twelfth century, and these are destinations for travelers from all over the world. Over the past 15 centuries, Iona has been a place of learning, Christian mission, and pilgrimage.

For most pilgrims, it's the threads of Celtic spirituality that draw us to places like Iona. The idea of pilgrimage itself was an important part of the Celtic tradition; it was a journey to seek God, to leave one's familiar home to find new life. Iona was an ideal site for pil-

---

1. "The Secret Book of John," in *Lost Scriptures: Books that Did Not Make It into the New Testament*, ed. Bart D. Ehrman (New York: Oxford University Press, Inc., 2003), 305.

grimage, not only for its history as the birthplace of Celtic Christianity in Scotland, but also for its natural beauty. For the Celts, the immanence of God, the presence of God in everything, was evident in the beauty and wildness of the created world. But the presence of God also was found in the soul of every human being. To the Celtic imagination, not only were humans created in God's image, they were imbued with God's wisdom, passion and creativity. Pilgrimage then was more than an outward voyage to a holy site; it was an inward journey to the sacred center within.

| *Here the author introduces some background on the Celtic theology she will reflect on in this piece.* |

As I walk about the Abbey, the village and the nunnery, I begin to feel the magic of this island, so different from the places most of us inhabit. The land seems flat, at least right here, and the sky wide and welcoming. I'm reminded that as a child, I wondered why everyone focused so on the surface of the Earth. Even then, I knew there were worlds beyond our understanding, and we seemed to live in just two dimensions, oblivious to the vast depths and soaring heights of sea and sky. And now this, another unimagined life, people living and working on a 1,800-acre island jutting boldly into the Atlantic on the western coast of Scotland. No skyscrapers, highways, 18-wheelers, bridges, trains—a place rumored to have more sheep than people. I wander about the small village of Baile Mór: a few shops, a single hotel, one restaurant, several dozen modest and colorful homes. It's as if I've entered another time.

Is this what Iona was like when the Celts inhabited the island so many years ago? I think about what happened when Christianity came to their world. By integrating their own pagan beliefs with the new Christian way of thinking, they were able to forge a faith that was true to their origins and to the new Roman tradition as well. If you were a Celtic Christian, you believed women and men were born not with original sin, but with original grace. To the Celts, the light of God was found not only in Christ, but also in each human soul; Christ came to remind us that we are made in God's image, that we carry the light and presence of God within us. I wonder if coming here now is a way to remember and awaken the collective memory of God's light and presence within each of us.

Awakening is, in fact, the theme for our group's time here on Iona. Our trip leader reminds us that, at the heart of any pilgrimage, there is always a central question. For me, the question is: *How can I awaken to a deeper life? How can*

| *This is where the author makes a connection between the Celtic tradition and the experience she is living right in this moment.* |

I live my life as passionately, fully, authentically as possible? I've come here to find what makes me feel most alive, although I can't say why I think I might find it on a small island in the Hebrides.

The pilgrim's path leads through the ruined nunnery, so our group gathers here for an opening prayer. While it is home to beautiful gardens, the abandoned nunnery has no roof, and it seems fitting that we worship in the open air of this glorious day. It's noisy and tourists are milling about and gawking, but we quiet ourselves to begin our day of pilgrimage. At the only crossroads on the island, we begin in earnest, thinking about the crossroads in our lives. Another brief prayer and we make our way toward Columba's Bay, the ultimate destination. This is the place Columba landed when he came from Ireland, and our agreement is to walk there in silence. At last there is quiet: all we can hear now is the rustle of the wind, the occasional bleating of sheep, our boots on the path, and the sound of our own breathing.

We walk though beautiful fields with sheep and cows, and the landscape becomes hilly and rocky. This is where the crofters live, still farming and working the land, and I imagine their impatience with the tourists and hikers traipsing earnestly across their pastures. What must they think of our striving for something that comes naturally to them? The connection to the earth, to the spirit of God in the natural world; it's what we seek, but we are strangers in a strange land.

Fresh in my mind this morning is *The Secret Book of John*, one of the gospels found in the Nag Hammadi desert that did not become part of the New Testament canon. In this secret gospel, Christ appears to John in a dream and tells him that humans have forgotten who they are, forgotten that they are made in the image of God: "And he made them drink water of forgetfulness ... in order that they might not know from where they came."[2] John hears Christ say that he is the memory of what humans have forgotten. Later, in the *Acts of John*, dancing the Round Dance of the Cross with the apostles, Christ sings a hymn, "I am a lamp to you who see me, I am a mirror to you who perceive, I am a door to you who knock on me, I am a way to you, wayfarer."[3] Thinking of this as I make my way across the rocky terrain, I'm

The author finds an interesting link between a non-canonical Scriptural text and Celtic theology.

---

2. "The Secret Book of John," 305.

3. "The Acts of John," in *Lost Scriptures: Books that Did Not Make It into the New Testament*, ed. Bart D. Ehrman (New York: Oxford University Press, Inc., 2003), 95:105.

curious about how the Celts came to believe something so similar, their conviction that Christ came to remind us of our origins in God. I'm drawn to the idea of Christ the awakener, Christ the mirror, Christ the memory, and I feel the truth of it deep inside me.

I'm reminded then that what makes Iona special, both to the ancient Celts and to modern-day pilgrims, is its reputation as a "thin place," a spot where people feel a powerful connection to God's presence, where the veils between the worlds part just enough to allow us a glimpse of something beyond. Are these veils what blind us to a deeper reality? Are they what keep us from seeing our origins in God, from remembering who we are?

> *"Thin place" is the thematic thread that links the Scripture texts to the Celtic tradition* and *to the sacred site the author is visiting on this pilgrimage.*

Suddenly I remember being in a church several years ago watching a man sitting nearby. Something made him move in strange ways; it appeared as if he were constantly wiping away cobwebs from his face, his head, his arms and legs. The movements were graceful, and in the brief moments between them, he was composed and thoughtful-looking. Watching him, you could begin to believe there really were veils of some kind he was dusting aside—you could almost see them—because his movements were so full of grace and intent, and each time he made a move, it seemed new, not just a habitual action. I tried to imagine a lifetime of this, and how exhausting it might be for him to keep chasing away the veils that only he could see.

Just a few walkers remain when we reach the top of the cliff overlooking Columba's Bay. My fellow pilgrims walk on without me, and I sit in silence to take in the beauty. The sky is overcast now and there's a sense of being enveloped by the dense clouds. I make a conscious effort to breathe the air and feel the cool ground beneath me. I study the shape of the clouds and the slope of the land, and I listen to the wind, feel it lift the hair off my neck. I hear the waves in the distance. Without warning, the world stops and there's not a sound. Everything changes before my eyes. The cliff, the stones on the beach, the sandy incline, the sea and the sky are alive, humming with a deep and potent presence. The world feels small and boundless at the same time, and I feel the hidden heart that beats beneath every living thing. Picking up a stone, I notice it shines with the colors of the sea, the texture

> *This is the turning-point, where an important change occurs. Head, heart, and experience all come together in this reflection.*

of the earth, the warmth of the sun, the shape of the world. There's only presence now at what feels like the heart of the world, and I'm soaring, only in stillness, without movement. I sit for a long time, allowing the humming energy and presence to surround and fill me.

That night, I dream. In the dream, I see Christ standing in a circle, dancing the round dance of the cross with others I don't recognize. I enter the circle and try to touch his shoulder to see if he's real. Then the group begins to dance and I am standing right beside the One I do know. He leans his forehead close to touch mine, and when I open one eye to see if it really is him, I don't see his face. Instead I see my own face looking back at me.

> In the dance I find you,
> and touch your shoulder lightly,
> trailing slowly, watchful, mute,
> as you gather us in threads of brightness.
>
> Drawn by your rhythm, your words,
> I move round you in the circle
> 'til we meet and pause,
> in a moment, an eternity of presence.
>
> You lean to touch your face to mine,
> your shadow and your light so near,
> but stepping back, I see my own image there,
> an invisible glass between us
> returns lost pieces of a shining self.
>
> I keep still, searching to know
> beyond the names others use to claim you,
> but I hear only the song you sing to me
> in the shimmering silence.
>
> You are the memory of the me who was lost,
> the one scattered to the years and days,
> given back now in the fierce light
> of your tender, loving gaze.

This is a good example of a reflection that explores theology and Scripture in light of a personal spiritual—and transformative—experience.

Works Cited

"The Acts of John." In *Lost Scriptures: Books that Did Not Make It into the New Testament*, edited by Bart D. Ehrman, 93–108. New York: Oxford University Press, Inc., 2003.

"The Secret Book of John." In *Lost Scriptures: Books that Did Not Make It into the New Testament*, edited by Bart D. Ehrman, 297–306. New York: Oxford University Press, 2003.

*   *   *

Reflection Paper: Mission Trip

Reflections on the Border
Alicia M. Van Riggs

What I bring home from El Paso is a reflection, and then a reconstruction, of my own construction of "home." Home is an address and a familiarity with cracks in the sidewalk, the nearest bus lines, and the best price for a gallon of milk. But home is more. It is a presence built by names: street names, neighbor's names, names of pets buried in the backyard, and being called by name as evening falls, called in for dinner, called in for bedtime, called home. How does God create a home for humans?

| *The author reflects on a mission trip to a border community, and she shares with readers her personal and spiritual response to that experience.* |

I also bring back from El Paso the firm belief that, as a child of God, my concept of home has been enlarged to make room for the presence of God on the U.S. border, the austere beauty of the desert bringing into even clearer relief the suffering of the people who inhabit the desert on both sides of the fence.

By the end of the first week of our immersion trip to the border, I was feeling disoriented, mentally and emotionally overwhelmed. On our "free day," I set out early for museums and to walk around downtown. I ended the day by walking along Rim Road, the road that follows the top of the old Rio Grande floodplain, up along Franklin Mountain, the southernmost tip of the Rocky Mountains. I walked higher and higher, passing larger and larger homes, and then kept walking past the end of the sidewalk and past the end of the

| *She recreates the experience in such a way that the reader can envision the scene and experience it along with her.* |

widened shoulder. I walked up and up until I was satisfied that the vista was complete and I could feel grounded again.

To my left were mountains receding into Texas. To my right were mountains receding into New Mexico and Mexico. I looked down into the valley at my feet, surrounded by such regal mountains, jagged peaks proudly ringing this basin. It is a basin of gods, but it is also a belly of a goddess whose lost children have furtively crossed boundaries, and some of whom lie half-buried in shallow graves in the sand.

The idea of a goddess searching for her lost children comes from Luis Leon's book, *La Llorona's Children*.[1] La Llorona, an image from Aztec religion, moves within shifting landscapes, weeping by day and by night, searching for her lost children, searching to bring them home. La Llorona's children are created by our borders: "they are the walking invisible dead known as the 'illegal' population; they haunt society with their invisibility." This fluidity of identity, based on porous boundaries and identities, recalls the bush that burned but was not consumed.

The author evokes a biblical text, making a clear connection between the passage and what she has experienced first-hand.	As I continued to look down into the valley, acrid smoke rose from the valley floor and pierced the sunset. The pillars of smoke reminded me of the guiding smoke from the Exodus story:

And the Lord went before them by day in a pillar of cloud to lead them along the way, and by night in a pillar of fire to give them light, that they might travel by day and by night; the pillar of cloud by day and the pillar of fire by night did not depart from before the people. (Exod 13:21–22, RSV)

I wonder if others, other strangers lost in the desert, saw the column of smoke and joined the Israelites. Was the smoke for the lost, for the unnamed and nameless, as well as for the chosen ones? Does the concept of home extend to others who are not at first included?

Upon reflection, I now think differently about the smoke over Juarez, the maquila-smokestack emissions. The smoke is there to be seen—it is an affront, it cries to be visible. I will follow the pillar of smoke too, Juarez says. An outsider standing at the river's edge, demanding to be seen, hoping against hope that someone, anyone, will believe in them and lead them home.

The author concludes the reflection by returning to the theme of home introduced in the first paragraph—but she now has an enhanced understanding of what it means.	This is another way in which I was transformed by my trip to El Paso: I am filled with the need to bring visibility to the invisible, and my call as a preacher is to invite others to do so, too, no matter where their home is.

I conclude my reflection by reminding myself that God so loved the world that God came to make a home among us, to be

---

1. Luis D. León, *La Llorona's Children: Religion, Life, and Death in the U.S.-Mexican Borderlands* (Berkeley: University of California Press, 2004).

a fully alive human being inviting us to share in the power of God's transforming love. This home that God invites us into is one where razor wire is repurposed into artwork, where concrete river culverts

This reflection is powerful because it takes a theological position on a political issue, but by sharing her experience, the author speaks to the humanity in each and every reader.

are torn up and used as building materials, where the vista from Rim Road shows all that is possible, as well as all that is hurting.

Work Cited

León, Luis D. *La Llorona's Children: Religion, Life, and Death in the U.S.-Mexican Borderlands*. Berkeley: University of California Press, 2004.

* * *

CHAPTER FIVE

Research Papers

Good writing is like a windowpane.—George Orwell

Types of Research Papers

Most of you will have had experience writing research papers as an undergraduate student, so you know that it is the culmination of your research, thinking, and interpretation of a particular topic. The purpose of a research paper is to allow you to deepen your knowledge in a certain area and to demonstrate to the professor how you've integrated the course material into your own thinking. A research paper is *not* a summary of other scholars' opinions on a given topic (unless that's the specific assignment); instead, it represents the unique point of view you develop *after* you've engaged with your sources. There are two basic types of research papers common in seminary.

Argumentative

The argumentative paper is the most common form of research paper and the type you'll most often be asked to write in seminary. The purpose of an argumentative paper is to persuade the reader of the truth of your argument—or *thesis*. Your thesis is stated clearly up front, and the remainder of the paper presents evidence to support your claim. This type of paper can:

- Present a unique and/or controversial perspective to challenge traditional interpretations.
- Compare and contrast two opinions, using evidence to prove the value of one over the other.

- Argue that author's perspective has weaknesses or problems, suggesting alternatives.

A thesis statement for an argumentative research paper makes a definite claim; an example of a thesis for an argumentative paper might be expressed something like this: "By excluding from common liturgical canon biblical texts that are emotionally, intellectually, or socially challenging, the Church impairs the ability of Scripture to offer healing and reconciliation to all."[i]

ANALYTICAL/EXPLORATORY

Similar to the argumentative paper, the analytical research paper offers a new perspective on a given topic. Its goal, however, is not to prove the truth of one particular point of view over others, but rather to explore new ways of understanding the topic. In this type of paper, you critically analyze primary and secondary research sources, arriving at a fresh interpretation of the topic that adds to accepted ways of understanding it. Since this type of paper is exploratory, the central question may remain unsolved or ambiguous, but you'll present solid evidence even to support this conclusion. A thesis for an exploratory research paper might be expressed in a statement like this: "This paper explores elements of the liturgy to identify those dimensions of the worship experience that facilitate faith development and spiritual growth in young adults."

Choosing a Paper Topic

In most cases, the course syllabus will outline the type of paper you're asked to write; if not, don't be afraid to ask for clarification. Once you understand the assignment and the specific type of paper required, you will have to choose a topic. The professor may provide a list of suggested topics from which to choose, or there may even be specific parameters for the paper, such as: "Explore the theology, theory, and practical implications of marriage and family counseling" or "Study the development of pneumatological doctrine and assess its importance for theology today." Even if you're assigned a topic, however, you still face the challenge of narrowing the focus and zeroing in on an interesting or unique perspective.

Before deciding on what to write about, you'll have to do some preliminary reading and research in order to identify areas you want to explore. Start with general sources to get an overview and to become familiar with the prevailing opinions on the topic. If you've been completing the course readings and taking notes as you go along, there's a good chance that certain ideas will already have begun to interest you. Keep track of them and, when the time comes to begin research on your paper, you'll have a good starting point. Brainstorm questions related to the key concepts until you settle on one or two that most interest you and that can guide your research.

Identifying Questions to Explore

Strong research papers begin with interesting questions; a good question gives direction to your research and can lead you to your thesis. Here are some general strategies for formulating questions[ii]:

1. *Ask "how" and "why" instead of "what" questions.* Asking "what" questions limits your topic, while "how" and "why" questions are open-ended, leaving room for exploration.
   Example: How does the author of the Gospel of John portray male characters vs. female characters in the narrative?

2. *Explore paradoxes or contradictions.* Consider opposing perspectives that appear to contradict each other or two "truths" that seem to be in conflict.
   Example: If humanity is created in the image of God, what does that suggest about human freedom and responsibility?

3. *Highlight certain dimensions of your source material.* Take a deeper look at one specific aspect of a source and its broader implications.
   Example: How has Augustine's androcentric view of humanity contributed to patriarchy in the Church today?

Researching the Topic

As you read source materials related to your research question, you'll begin to see recurring themes that will lead you in a certain direction. Following these threads can help you find an interesting perspective and possibly lead to a thesis. During the research stage, be sure to:

- Take careful notes on all your reading.
- Highlight recurring themes or concepts.
- Organize your notes according to themes or concepts.
- As you read, keep a running list of additional sources to check.
- If you are using a good source book, check its bibliography for additional resources.
- Record all citations as you go, so you do not have to go back later to find them.

(For more about *where* to look, see "The Basics of Research" on the next page.)

Once you've completed your research, you're ready to develop a preliminary thesis:

- Review your research notes with your research question in mind.
- Consider whether the question is still valid or if it leads to another, related, question.
- Look for potential answers you have found to this question or a prevailing theme that appears consistently in your findings.
- Formulate a thesis statement that answers your question or articulates the theme.
- Identify all the evidence you have to support your thesis.

Here's an example of narrowing a topic to a question and finally to a thesis/argument:

- *Topic*. The Holy Spirit as Gift and Reception
- *Research question*. The Eastern Church came to think of the Holy Spirit as "the breathing out of the breath of God" while the Western Church thought of it as "the breathing forth of an inner love." In what ways is this concept embodied in the Church today?
- *Thesis/argument*. The theme of gift and reception expresses the inter-relationship of the three persons of the Trinity, but it also describes the inter-relationship of the Holy Spirit and the Church; related to "the breath of God" are *communal* gifts that empower the Church and related to the "inner love" are *individual* gifts that indwell believers.

You cannot read everything available on a given topic, but you'll know you've read enough when you are confident that you have a strong thesis statement and enough evidence to support it.

The Basics of Research

Research at the master's level involves using two different types of inquiry: (1) *first-hand research*, which includes information you have gathered yourself from interviews, surveys, case studies, observations, or personal experience; and (2) *second-hand research*, which is an investigation of other authors' work that you access through various books, journals, and online sources. Here are some very basic guidelines for conducting research in seminary:

A. First-hand Research

- First-hand research is less common at the master's level than at Ph.D. level, but you may occasionally be asked to do your own evidence-gathering for certain course assignments.
- In most cases, the professor will say exactly what you are expected to do—for example, interview clergy members, survey congregation members, or observe specific aspects of a worship service.

B. Second-hand Research

- Second-hand research involves investigating the works of other scholars. Generally, it is a good idea to move from general to more specific treatments of your chosen topic.
- Begin with Bible commentaries, theological dictionaries, concordances, and other standard reference tools to become familiar with your topic generally and to begin to build a bibliography customized to your writing.
- Check periodical literature to find chief articles addressing your paper topic. Start with the most recent, and pay attention to agreements or disagreements among scholars and the questions being asked. A good place to start is the ATLA Religion Database, which indexes book reviews, articles, essays, and dissertations.
- Identify other source materials most relevant to your topic. Check *primary* sources—first-hand historical documents such as the

Bible, writings of the Church Fathers, or documents from ecumenical councils—and *secondary* sources—all the books and articles that interpret or analyze the primary sources.

- Evaluate sources to make sure they are credible. Is the author respected in the field? Is the publisher well-known? Are all of the author's sources cited accurately? How recent is the source? Is the author presenting one perspective or attempting to give an objective and neutral view? Be careful with Internet sources, especially if you cannot tell who the author is or if the site is not associated with a university or other respectable organization.[iii]

Outlining the Research Paper

If you've narrowed your topic and completed the research with a guiding question in mind, you should have a strong thesis statement as you begin writing. The next step is to outline your paper, so you'll know how best to present your findings in support of your argument. Many students sit down and begin writing without any direction or end goal in mind, using the writing process itself to uncover their claim. This may work, but it will take a lot longer than if you follow the process of researching, outlining, and drafting. Remember, most bad writing isn't about students not knowing *how* to write—it's about students not knowing *what to write*. Clear thinking and clear writing go hand in hand: you can't write convincingly about a topic if you haven't thought about it before you begin to write. An outline will give you a clear road map for how to proceed; arrange the information in a way that presents the story in the way you want it to be told. Your outline might include these elements:

1. Introduction
   - Introduction of the topic
   - Statement of the problem or question
   - Background needed to understand your argument
   - Thesis statement
2. Body
   - Presentation and analysis of evidence
3. Conclusion
   - Restatement of thesis

- Summary of what you have demonstrated
- Broader implications

Writing the Research Paper

Some students prefer to create a graphic, map, or flow chart—instead of a written outline—to show how the different pieces of evidence will be presented. Whether you use an outline or a map, it helps to have a clear idea of the flow of your argument before you begin writing. With your thesis and outline (or map) in hand, now you're ready to begin writing.

1. *Introduction.* Here, you introduce the overall topic and briefly present the question driving your research. Consider the background or context the reader needs in order to understand your argument. Present a summary of dominant scholarly opinions on the topic, historical interpretations, or current understandings of it. Define important terms or concepts that are necessary as a backdrop for the presentation of your material. Present your thesis in a clear statement (one or two sentences), and what you hope to accomplish with the paper. Remember, you can go back and refine your introduction *after* you have finished the paper.

2. *Body.* Back up your argument with specific examples and citing primary and secondary sources to prove your point. Consider the best way to present the evidence: chronologically, thematically, or whatever organizational scheme best supports your thesis statement. Remember that the goal is not just to present a summary of the sources you have read, but to engage with them critically and interpret them to further your argument. For example, you might point out an inherent contradiction in a source's claim, highlight a subtext that the author may not have intended, or compare two different sources. It's also important that you explicitly state how each source supports your argument, rather than leaving it to the reader to infer. In the body, you also may present evidence that seems to counter your claim, then use supporting evidence to prove your argument as the stronger one.[iv]

3. *Conclusion.* Summarize your main argument, but do so in a more powerful and authoritative way than you did in the introduction. State

clearly how you've demonstrated your claim in the paper, and highlight what's different in your argument from others. Acknowledge your contribution and the broader implications for the field of theology, the church, biblical research, etc. Finish with a strong, dynamic final sentence.

Developing Your Argument

Developing a strong argument is the most important element of your writing—and the success of a research paper depends on how well you do it. Here are some general strategies to consider:

A. Move from General to Specific

In presenting evidence, it is most effective to move from general to specific information[v]:

- *Introduce.* Lay the foundation for the paper with a general introduction, background knowledge to set the context, or information needed to explain your thesis.
- *Focus.* State the direction the paper will take and briefly explain your organizational plan.
- *Get specific.* If your argument will be developed in several stages or include separate points, provide specifics for the first of these. Take the reader to a deeper level of understanding by discussing how this particular point backs up your broader thesis.
- *Present details.* Support your claim with data, and explain how they support your argument.
- *Conclude.* Restate your claim, summarize the main points of your argument and how you have proven them, and wrap up the paper with a strong concluding statement.

B. Analyze and Interpret

- *Interpret source materials.* You can include source materials in your paper by using direct quotations or by paraphrasing what an author has said, but you also need to state how this material supports your argument, to interpret for the reader what it adds to your claim.

- *Analyze source materials.* In addition to summarizing an author's thinking, you also need to *analyze* it by: (a) adding something to it; (b) highlighting contradictions; (c) pointing out hidden assumptions; (d) finding an interesting connection; or (e) suggesting implications.

C. Provide Structural Clues for the Reader

- *Begin with topic sentences.* A topic sentence in each paragraph alerts the reader to what the paragraph will discuss.
- *Use transitions.* By using transition sentences between major sections of your paper, you help readers progress from one idea to the next and follow your argument.
- *Clarify who is speaking.* Make sure your reader is clear when you are stating a source's position and when you are interpreting and developing your own claim.

Quick Tip: Verbs for Acknowledging Sources

You can make your writing more interesting by varying the verbs you use to introduce a quotation or another author's ideas. Here are a variety of words to use:

acknowledges	considers	investigates	replies
admits	concurs	inquires	refers to
adds	concludes	identifies	reviews
ascertains	cites	lists	reports
asks	defines	makes the case	says
analyzes	delineates	measures	shows
assesses	describes	notes	states
argues	determines	observes	stipulates
agrees (disagrees)	demonstrates	points out	stresses
addresses	discovers	posits	suggests
answers	evaluates	postulates	summarizes
believes	explores	presents	surveys
categorizes	examines	proposes	synthesizes
claims	expounds on	proves	traces
comments	emphasizes	questions	views
compares (contrasts)	envisions	rationalizes	warns
critiques	finds	reasons	writes
	furnishes	remarks	

Revising, Editing and Proofreading Your Paper

This final stage of writing the research paper (any paper, in fact) is essential, yet so many students fail to do it. It is a good idea to give yourself time to set the paper aside for a day or even a few hours, so you can reflect on it and review it with a clear mind. For many students, it is easier to spot mistakes by reviewing a paper draft rather than looking at it on a computer screen. And read it out loud. You will *hear* the errors that you pass over reading silently. If possible, have someone whose judgment you trust read the final product; they will see the errors that you have missed.

REVISING/EDITING

You need to revise/edit your paper before you can do the final proofreading. At this point, you'll review for flow, clarity, and organization. There are several areas to consider at this stage:

- *Concept.* Is your thesis too broad or too limited in scope? Is it articulated clearly? Does it answer the question you set out to answer (or the topic your paper set out to explore)?
- *Argument.* Have you developed your argument fully (rather than relying on quoted sources to do it for you)? Does your paper actually *make* the argument you're claiming to make?
- *Evidence.* Have you supported your claim with substantive evidence? Are supporting ideas adequately developed? Is there anything that doesn't fit or is irrelevant to your argument? Have you critically engaged with sources rather than just summarizing them?
- *Organization.* Do the ideas follow logically throughout the paper? Will the reader be able to follow your argument easily? Are there areas that are unclear or confusing?
- *Flow.* Do paragraphs lead from one to the next? Does each have a topic sentence? Does each accomplish what it says it will? Are there smooth transitions between them?
- *Language and style.* Have you used language appropriate for an academic paper? Are your sentences clear? Are there a variety of sentence constructions so the reading does not become monotonous? Have you used gender-neutral language?
- *Introduction and conclusion.* Are the introduction and conclu-

sion clear and compelling (and sufficiently differentiated)? Does the introduction provide a road map for the reader? Does the conclusion summarize what the paper has demonstrated?

Proofreading

When you proofread your paper, you'll look for errors in grammar, punctuation, and spelling. It is a good idea to read your paper aloud; this will help you catch missing words, redundancies, grammatical errors, or awkward constructions. Consider these questions in proofreading:

- Are the verbs in active, rather than passive, voice?
- Are subjects and verbs in agreement?
- Have you eliminated redundancies, vague language, or empty expressions? (Check your paper against the guidelines in Style Guidelines in Chapter Four.)
- Have you mixed up any commonly-confused words, such as "to" and "too," "your" and "you're," "or" and "of?" Remember that spell-check will not catch these errors.
- Have you used verb tenses intentionally? If you're using present tense in writing about biblical texts, for example, have you done so consistently?
- Are all of your citations complete and correctly formatted?

Quick Tip: Checklist for Effective Research Papers

☐ Keep the research paper assignment in mind as you complete the course readings.
☐ Make notes about concepts or questions that interest you as you go along.
☐ Begin by reading general sources to become familiar with the topic and with the perspectives of various scholars.
☐ Formulate an interesting question to guide further research.
☐ Read more specialized sources geared to your question.
☐ Take notes on your research.
☐ Outline your paper: introduction, background, thesis, evidence, and conclusion.
☐ Use the outline to write the first draft the paper.

Five. Research Papers

- [ ] Fine-tune your thesis statement.
- [ ] Add an introduction and a conclusion.
- [ ] Revise the paper, checking for flow, clarity, organization, and consistency of presentation.
- [ ] Prepare the bibliography; check all citations for accuracy.
- [ ] Edit and proofread for spelling, grammar, and punctuation.

* * *

Research Paper: *Argumentative (#1)*
Christology & Whiteness: Confronting and Resisting "Color-blind" Theological Concepts
Christology and Theological Anthropology
Nathan B. Hollifield

Two years ago my partner and I attended a presentation and discussion hosted by our church in Seattle entitled "Deliver Us from Evil: Wall Street, Imperial Economics, & the Destruction of Community." The presentation addressed questions of responsibility and salvation in the face of encroaching imperialism. Several participants were pleased that local economies and gardens would allow them to remove themselves from the evils of global financial markets. My Mexican-American partner and an African-American woman were the only two people of color in the room. Both of them spoke about their concern for communities of color and other countries where community gardens seemed far-from-realistic options in the short-term. Their concern was met with swift and abusive condemnation from the progressive white attendees. My partner and the other woman, an ordained United Methodist elder, became the enemy; they were shouted and scoffed at, accused of being uneducated, unimaginative, hopeless, and fearful. This was a transformational moment for me as a white man. I was forced to acknowledge and engage the serious problem of white privilege and supremacy within my beloved progressive, mainline United Methodist church. The purpose of this paper is to suggest a way forward for white Christians in such a context by engaging systemic whiteness theologically. My

A personal story relates directly to the topic and makes for an engaging beginning paragraph.

The introductory story ends with a clear and strong thesis statement that will drive the rest of the paper.

central argument here echoes the sentiment of the brave women who spoke that night: that white Christians have the responsibility to confront and resist "color-blind" theological concepts of Jesus. I will highlight the issue of whiteness as it affects the church's teachings about the life and ministry of Jesus, or in theological terms: Christology. In order to do this, the first section of this paper will examine the contours of "color-blind" theology within the church today. Then a brief historical analysis of the connection between race and Christology will clarify how Christian theological reflection and practice developed within the confines of systemic whiteness and often results in "color-blind" Christological conceptions. My conclusion will combine insights from womanist and liberation theologians of color to provide a framework for inviting white Christians to confront and resist "color-blind" notions of Jesus and his ministry.

> *It's very helpful to let readers know up front what to expect and how to follow the argument through the paper.*

My first task is to define *systemic whiteness* before engaging it theologically. Systemic whiteness is the social outcome of the combination of white privilege and white supremacy. If white privilege suggests invisible advantages then white supremacy signifies invisible power. In her seminal essay, "White Privilege: Unpacking the Invisible Knapsack," white activist Peggy McIntosh describes white privilege as "an invisible package of unearned assets which I can count on cashing in each day, but about which I was 'meant' to remain oblivious."[1] In other words, white privilege is a set of privileges that benefit white people but "disappear[s] before the eyes of those who live its brand."[2] References to white supremacy conjure notions of extremist groups; however, its definition refers simply to white cultural domination.[3] Philosopher Charles W. Mills makes

> *It's important to define unfamiliar terms for readers. The author has chosen quotes to help define his terms, and they are strong enough that he can quickly provide the information readers need.*

---

1. Peggy McIntosh, "White Privilege: Unpacking the Invisible Knapsack," *Independent School* 49 (Winter 1990): 31–36.

2. James W. Perkinson, "Upstart Messiahs, Renegade Samarians, and Temple Exorcisms: What Can Jesus' Peasant Resistance Movement in First-century Palestine Teach Us about Confronting 'Color-blind' Whiteness Today?" in *Christology and Whiteness: What Would Jesus Do?*, ed. George Yancy (New York: Routledge, 2012), 137.

3. Elaine A. Robinson, *Race and Theology*, Horizons in Theology Series (Nashville: Abingdon Press, 2012), 23.

this point in *What White Looks Like*, noting, "White supremacy implies the existence of a system that not only privileges whites but is run by whites, for white benefit."[4]

Systemic whiteness, therefore, is a socio-political term describing the operative system of social and economic injustice that privileges people with "white" skin to the detriment of multi-hued people.[5] Though the "regime of whiteness,"[6] as Filipino theologian Eleazar Fernandez refers to systemic whiteness, is named for its preference of skin color (a very personal trait) it is, like all regimes, a construct that functions authoritatively to control the personal at the institutional level. Systemic whiteness is racism. Unfortunately, racism today is most often construed as individual moral failure or, put theologically, personal sin. When this happens, as white theologian Elaine A. Robinson points out, alibis abound and few racists exist today.[7] My intention is not to accuse white Christians of overtly racist acts. What I am suggesting is that white Christians need to acknowledge the reality of whiteness as a systemic social construct that is just as dangerous as overt racism and recognize how their identities and faith practices perpetuate this oppressive system.

| *Here is another very clear statement of the author's claim.*

Attempts to deny and/or overlook systemic whiteness promote an ethos of "color-blindness" to which many white Christians cling. The work of prominent white evangelical pastor and author John Piper, in his book *Bloodlines: Race, Cross, and the Christian*, is characteristic of how racial blindness undermines attempts to address racial and ethnic divisions. Piper attempts to address both the personal (overt racism) and structural (systemic whiteness) aspects of racism in the United States.[8] His Christology, however, attends only to Jesus' salvific work at the level of personal sin. His proposals for engaging race, therefore, are grounded in a "color-

---

4. Charles W. Mills, "Racial Exploitation and the Wages of Whiteness," in *What White Looks Like: African-American Philosophers on the Whiteness Question*, ed. George Yancy (New York: Routledge, 2004), 31.

5. Karen Teel, "What Jesus Wouldn't Do: a White Theologian Engages Whiteness," in *Christology and Whiteness: What Would Jesus Do?* ed. George Yancy (New York: Routledge, 2012), 20.

6. Eleazar S. Fernandez, *Reimagining the Human: Theological Anthropology in Response to Systemic Evil* (St. Louis: Chalice Press, 2004), 142.

7. Robinson, *Race and Theology*, 16.

8. John Piper, *Bloodlines: Race, Cross, and the Christian* (Wheaton, IL: Crossway, 2011), 31–42.

blind" Christocentric view where "color and ethnicity will count for nothing in the court of heaven. One thing will count: the perfection of Jesus Christ."⁹ The problem with this assertion is that Piper, like many white Christians, fails to acknowledge the ways Jesus' particular ethnic life shaped the context and content of his ministry. Thus, Piper assimilates historic and current ethnic, racial, and national distinctions into his normative framework of whiteness. This is, as Fernandez points out, an untenable theological position for white Christians because it denies the unchangeable reality that God's creation is full of color.¹⁰ Theological racial blindness perpetuates the regime of whiteness by reinforcing the conditions of subordination and domination inherent to systemic whiteness,¹¹ and it promotes the illusion that Jesus' work of salvation fits squarely into normalized white categories of Christian faith and practice. White Christians, therefore, must name and resist "color-blind" theological formulations if they are to realize the goal of racial harmony. To do so, they need a clear understanding of the origins of systemic whiteness in Christian history.

> *The author states clearly why he disagrees with Piper's Christology, discussing the problems it creates.*

> *This sentence is an excellent summary of the problem the author sees in Piper's theology.*

The legacy of "whitened" Christological constructs began to take shape with the early Church Fathers who, according to African-American liberation theologian James Cone, fixated upon Greek formations of divinity to the detriment of the particular history of Jesus of Nazareth as a first-century Jew living in the Roman-occupied Palestinian state.¹² Cone states:

> *This paragraph begins the second section the author outlined at the start—a brief history of the connection between race and Christology.*

> Consequently, little is said about the significance of his ministry to the poor as a definition of his person. The Nicene Fathers showed little interest in the Christological significance of Jesus' deeds for the humiliated, because most of the discussion took place in the social context of the Church's position as the favored religion of the Roman State. It

---

9. Ibid.

10. Fernandez, *Reimagining the Human*, 149.

11. Ibid., 135.

12. James H. Cone, *God of the Oppressed* (San Francisco: Harper & Row, 1975), 116.

therefore became easy to define Jesus as the divinizer (the modern counterpart is "spiritualizer") of humanity. When this happens Christology is removed from history, and salvation becomes only peripherally related to this world."[13]

Once ripped from its historical context, the narratives of Jesus are easily assimilated into the cultural power dynamics of imperial conquest.[14] Christian theology easily goes awry when integrated into culturally accepted top-down hierarchies. The result is the gradual "whitening" of Christian faith by Euro-Christian interpreters who blindly impose their cultural norms and expectations on Jesus and his early followers.

African-American Christian ethicist Traci C. West reminds white Christians that, "For much of the first and second millennia CE, Catholic and Protestant theology was sewn from the fabric of European cultural biases, including phenotypic, anti-black racism."[15] The inheritance of this history is powerfully seen in white Christian missionary outreach to African slaves in the United States who were taught that authentic Christian conversion included "stripping away (the evil) of their African communal and cultural ties" and accepting their subservient role in the slave political economy.[16] The implication is that salvation is only available to those who assimilate white cultural norms. White Christians, both evangelical and mainline, perpetuate this exact dynamic today when they disguise their theological and political commitments behind the mask of "colorblind" discourse. The result is evangelical and mainline constructive theological proposals that fail to take seriously the ethnic life of Jesus and the lives of Christians of different races and ethnicities. They have averted their gaze and become totally blind; they see neither the whole history of Jesus nor the connection between contemporary systemic whiteness and historical Christianization as the product of imperial subjugation of people of color.

| *The author connects the historical dynamic to what is happening in mainline churches today.* |

---

13. Ibid., 116.

14. Joerg Rieger and Kwok Pui-lan, *Occupy Religion: Theology of the Multitude* (Lanham, MD: Rowman & Littlefield Publishers, 2012), 85.

15. Traci C. West, "When a White Man-god is the Truth and the Way for Black Christians," in *Christology and Whiteness: What Would Jesus Do?* ed. George Yancy (New York: Routledge, 2012), 114.

16. Ibid., 119–21.

Whether white theologians see it or not, the development of systemic whiteness is in fact closely tied to the history of imperial colonization and Christianization. It has its roots in white Euro-Christian colonial takeover of multi-hued cultures throughout the world. The scales have fallen from the eyes of white theologian James W. Perkinson, who insists in *Christology and Whiteness* that systemic whiteness emerged gradually in modern history as the byproduct of white colonizers' need to define their own identities in opposition to their negative views of multi-hued indigenous people.[17] He argues that modern understandings of systemic whiteness cannot be separated from this violent history that continues today as a militarized enterprise seemingly sanctified in the blood of indigenous cultures and baptized in their tears.[18] It is indefensible for white Christians to address the evils of imperial economics disconnected from our position of power throughout the history of Euro-Christian colonization. For today's white Christians to suddenly see ourselves as victims without acknowledging that we have seen very little of the suffering we have caused reeks of the assumption that the consequences of imperialism are burdensome only if white people experience its negative effects first-hand.

This is a deeper engagement with the consequences of systemic whiteness.

"Color-blindness" hinders white Christians' ability to see suffering, but what is more, it causes us to be blind to the irreplaceable contributions that people of color bring to bear on efforts to resist imperial encroachment as a result of centuries of resistance to colonization. White Christians paradoxically fail to recognize that their privileged lifestyles allow them to continue living comfortably in spite of their refusal to listen to diverse opinions. Their blindness toward the contributions of people of color (and their own harmful behaviors) is a direct result of systemic whiteness that is sustained today by the continued suffering and silencing of communities of color. As Perkinson has stated: "what this veil ... continues to hide today—by proclaiming [that racism is] a merely regrettable mistake of the past that has since been overcome—is simply the ruthless perpetuation of this history of gore and exploitation."[19] I am convinced that white Christians, no matter how well intentioned, will continue to suffer spiritually and psychologically until they lift this

---

17. Perkinson, "Upstart Messiahs," 137.

18. Ibid., 138.

19. Ibid., 140.

veil and theologically engage the topic of systemic whiteness so they may move beyond the narrow confines of "color-blind" theological reflection.

Thus I am proposing that white Christians turn to theologians of color to help them confront and resist commonly held "color-blind" understandings of the passion, death, and resurrection of Jesus. In her book, *Power in the Blood?*, African-American womanist theologian JoAnne Marie Terrell helps white Christians expand the meaning of the cross through the African-American religious experience and her context as a black woman who has experienced oppression. She maintains convincingly that African-American understandings of the crucifixion echo those of Jesus' earliest followers who saw his suffering and death as a "once for all" atonement signifying "both a divine rejection of sacred violence and a call to a life of service within the community of believers."[20] This transforms sacrifice into a sacrament that has saving significance for every Christian; however, it has special significance for the oppressed, including African-Americans and black women in particular.[21] The interpretive key, according to Terrell, is setting Jesus' sacrifice in historical context as a tragic event resulting from his confrontation with evil.[22] Interpreted thus, Jesus' death is understood to have profound implications for structural systems of oppression. This is difficult, I believe, for white Christians to fully comprehend, because systemic whiteness shields us from the worst forms of systemic oppression. White Christians must, therefore, take an extra interpretive step. While there is a renewed interest among white Christian scholars to place the narratives of Jesus in historical context,[23] I believe white Christian interpreters must go further to guard themselves against assuming, given the convergence of Christian theol-

> *This paragraph begins the author's third stated task— to suggest ways that white Christians might engage insights from theologians of color as a starting point for resisting color-blind theologies.*

---

20. Joanne Marie Terrell, *Power in the Blood? The Cross in the African American Experience* (Maryknoll, NY: Wipf & Stock Publishers, 2005), 33.

21. Ibid., 139.

22. Ibid., 142.

23. See Richard A. Horsley, *Jesus and Empire: The Kingdom of God and the New World Disorder* (Minneapolis: Fortress Press, 2003); John Dominic Crossan and Marcus J. Borg, *The Last Week: What the Gospels Really Teach About Jesus's Final Days in Jerusalem* (San Francisco: Harper One, 2007); and Ched Myers, *Binding the Strong Man: A Political Reading of Mark's Story of Jesus*, (Maryknoll, NY: Orbis Books, 2008).

ogy and systemic whiteness, that the historical Jesus is "one of us." The implication for white Christians is twofold: (1) Jesus cannot be understood apart from his social context as a humiliated, executed dissident against political and religious imperial forces[24]; and (2) Jesus was not "one of us" (white people).

James Cone powerfully offers white Christians a Christological path to go about this important work in his groundbreaking book, *The Cross and the Lynching Tree*. Cone, following black artists, makes the obvious comparison between the execution of Jesus on the cross and the agony of thousands of Southern black lynching victims in the United States during the late nineteenth and early-twentieth centuries.[25] Lynching was more often than not a white Christian enterprise justified as the "divine right of the Caucasian race to dispose of the offending blackamoor without benefit of a jury."[26] Cone, and this is especially important for liberal mainline readers, does not concentrate solely on blatant racists. His most critical engagement is with white theologian Reinhold Niebuhr, one of the most respected thinkers of the twentieth century. Niebuhr "was a theologian of the cross who knew all about Jesus' solidarity with the poor and the consequences he suffered for that from the Roman Empire."[27] But, he failed to make the connection between the cross and the lynching tree, because he neglected to engage in dialogue with those who suffered from the terror of the lynching tree.[28]

> *The author is able to offer a very balanced, powerful, and well supported critique without becoming polemic or judgmental.*

This is the same mistake white Christians make today when they fail to listen and respond to the victims of systemic whiteness. As a result, white Christians miss the opportunity to faithfully join the victims and discover the truth of God's love on the cross of the tortured Jesus alongside suffering black bodies hanging on the con-

> *Excellent connection between Cone's critique of Niebuhr and the author's critique of white Christians today.*

---

24. See Mark Lewis Taylor, *The Executed God: The Way of the Cross in Lockdown America* (Minneapolis: Augsburg Fortress Publishers, 2001).

25. James H. Cone, *The Cross and the Lynching Tree* (Maryknoll, NY: Orbis Books, 2012).

26. Quotation by former South Carolina governor and U.S. Senator Cole Blease as cited in Cone, *The Cross and the Lynching Tree*, 7.

27. Cone, *The Cross and the Lynching Tree*, 63.

28. Ibid., 64.

temporary "lynching tree" of systemic whiteness. Only when this happens will white Christians begin to experience the redemptive faith that is "inescapable to black people."[29] The impetus is on white Christians to join people of color and confess "white supremacy as America's great sin."[30] Without this, white Christian attempts at counter-imperialist projects or racial reconciliation will end up as empty recapitulations of systemic whiteness.

What I have argued throughout this paper is that white Christians' deliverance from systemic whiteness requires joining in solidarity with the victims of whiteness in order to truly "see redemption in the cross [and] discover life in death and hope in tragedy."[31] Terrell and Cone, and many other theologians of color spanning many ethnicities, have underscored ways in which the separation of Jesus from his social context distorts a proper understanding of who Jesus is and leads us to act out many of the most egregious contemporary betrayals of Jesus' name—including the lynching tree, mass incarceration, and military invasions. They have demonstrated that such separations are more than flashes of "color-blind" unfaithfulness; they are profound misreadings of Jesus' salvific meaning, miscomprehensions that lure believers into patterns of systemic whiteness masked as practices of social justice and evangelism.

The task for white Christians in order to avoid these mistakes is to join in solidarity with movements among the marginalized rather than perpetuating systemic whiteness from within their gentrified communities. The challenge for white Christians is clear, as white theologian and activist Mark Taylor Lewis plainly states, "White activists and thinkers should *not* expect to be the key protagonists for

| *This is a clear and powerful conclusion, summarizing the primary argument and leaving the reader with a call to action.* |

liberating the spirit's emergence in political movements. Just as 'the revolution will not be televised'—as the refrain has it—so the revolutionary transformations of liberating spirit will not be 'white-led.'"[32] While confronting and resisting whiteness will not be easy, it need not be a lonely project. In final analysis, white Christians in search of a meaningful Christology must immerse themselves in

---

29. Ibid., 159.

30. Ibid., 159.

31. Ibid., 157–58.

32. Mark Lewis Taylor, "The Role of Critical Race," accessed May 11, 2013, http://www.marklewistaylor.net, http://marklewistaylor.net/theory/#no5.

non-white traditions and movements, joining generations of Jesus' followers in their longing for freedom from the confines of systemic whiteness.

Works Cited

Cone, James H. *The Cross and the Lynching Tree*. Maryknoll, NY: Orbis Books, 2012.
_____. *God of the Oppressed*. San Francisco: Harper & Row, 1975.
Crossan, John Dominic and Marcus J. Borg. *The Last Week: What the Gospels Really Teach About Jesus's Final Days in Jerusalem*. San Francisco: Harper One, 2007.
Fernandez, Eleazar S. *Reimagining the Human: Theological Anthropology in Response to Systemic Evil*. St. Louis: Chalice Press, 2004.
Horsley, Richard A. *Jesus and Empire: The Kingdom of God and the New World Disorder*. Minneapolis: Fortress Press, 2003.
McIntosh, Peggy. "White Privilege: Unpacking the Invisible Knapsack." *Independent School* 49 (Winter 1990): 31–36.
Mills, Charles W. "Racial Exploitation and the Wages of Whiteness." In *What White Looks Like: African-American Philosophers on the* Whiteness *Question*, edited by George Yancy, 25–54. New York: Routledge, 2004.
Myers, Ched. *Binding the Strong Man: A Political Reading of Mark's Story of Jesus*, Maryknoll, NY: Orbis Books, 2008.
Perkinson, James W. "Upstart Messiahs, Renegade Samarians, and Temple Exorcisms: What Can Jesus' Peasant Resistance Movement in First-century Palestine Teach Us about Confronting "Color-blind" Whiteness Today?" In *Christology and Whiteness: What Would Jesus Do?* edited by George Yancy, 136–55. New York: Routledge, 2012.
Piper, John. *Bloodlines: Race, Cross, and the Christian*. Wheaton, IL: Crossway, 2011.
Rieger, Joerg and Kwok Pui-lan. *Occupy Religion: Theology of the Multitude*. Lanham, MD: Rowman & Littlefield Publishers, 2012.
Robinson, Elaine A. *Race and Theology*. Horizons in Theology Series. Nashville: Abingdon Press, 2012.
Taylor, Mark Lewis. *The Executed God: The Way of the Cross in Lockdown America*. Minneapolis: Augsburg Fortress Publishers, 2001.
_____. "The Role of Critical Race." Accessed May 11, 2013. http://marklewistaylor.net/theory/#no5.
Teel, Karen. "What Jesus Wouldn't Do: a White Theologian Engages Whiteness." In *Christology and Whiteness: What Would Jesus Do?* edited by George Yancy, 19–35. New York: Routledge, 2012.
Terrell, Joanne Marie. *Power in the Blood? the Cross in the African American Experience*. Maryknoll, NY: Wipf & Stock Publishers, 2005.
West, Traci C. West, "When a White Man-god is the Truth and the Way for Black Christians." In *Christology and Whiteness: What Would Jesus Do?* edited by George Yancy, 114–27. New York: Routledge, 2012.

* * *

Five. Research Papers

Research Paper: *Argumentative (#2)*

Jesus and Systemic Racism: Understanding Biblical Systemic Racism in a Mexican American Context
Christology and Theological Anthropology
Fernando Rivera

Introduction

How can we be human in the midst of constant assault of systemic evils at both the local and global level? We seem not bereft of good intentions; why is it, then, that we continue to create systems that dehumanize us... Why do we continue to justify our sinister acts and engage in organized forgetting?[1] | *Provocative opening quote lays the foundation for the paper's topic.*

For years, systemic racism has been a prominent social issue. As the opening quote suggests, society puts systems in place to help one social group but, as a result, dehumanizes another. It is important to note that there is a difference between systemic racism (the focus of this essay) and racism: "Generally understood, the term 'racism' designates prejudice, bias, discrimination, violence, and terror directed at persons or groups *solely* on the basis of what are perceived to be inferior traits, characteristics, manners, customs, or other cultural markers such as language, dress, or skin color."[2] Racism is a direct and conscious attack on a person(s) due to "them" being different as compared to "us." Systemic racism, on the other hand, is based on a *system* that is racist rather than an individual *person* who is racist. In a system that is racist, people are "unwilling to grant that they are overprivileged, even though they may grant that [others] are disadvan-

| *This is an excellent quote to incorporate because it gives such a clear definition of racism.*

| *The opening paragraph lays the groundwork by explaining basic concepts that will be explored in the rest of the paper.*

---

1. Eleazar Fernandez, *Reimagining the Human: Theological Anthropology in Response to Systemic Evil* (St. Louis: Chalice Press, 2004), 1.

2. Victor Anderson, et al, "Racism and Christianity," in *The Cambridge Dictionary of Christianity* (New York: Cambridge University Press, 2010), 1041.

taged."³ In other words, systemic racism blinds people from seeing that there is something wrong with a certain system or structure; they are not willing to acknowledge that we are all part of the problem.

This paper discusses systemic racism through the lens of my own experience. I am a Mexican-American theologian from El Paso, Texas. I grew up in a city that prided itself for being not only the largest international crossing on the U.S./Mexico border, but also the home of one of the largest Army bases in the country. I was immersed in an environment in which multiple cultures were intertwined, with very little visible segregation. After 18 years of living in this setting, I moved to Oklahoma City for college and my social experience changed dramatically. This was very much a segregated location; the Anglos had their community, the Mexicans had theirs, and so on. The city was divided into racial groups that rarely interacted with one another. When it was time for me to move to Chicago to attend seminary, many questions came to mind: *Will I be safe as an Hispanic student there? Can I walk alone at night by myself? Will I fit in?* At the same time, my Anglo friends never, or rarely, had to ask themselves these questions; the idea of not fitting in because of race was never a concern for them. This is an example of the impact of systemic racism on me personally; as a minority, it was necessary to question certain aspects of living in a new community because of my racial background. My race played a significant role in my decision to move even further north; I knew from experience that I could face oppression.

> *The paper demonstrates an effective use of personal experience. Although this is not a reflection paper, here, his experience is one of the author's primary examples; it speaks directly to the heart of the topic.*

By the same token, I also was one who oppressed others through systemic racism. In accepting a scholarship to attend my university and then seminary, I used systemic racism to my advantage. I attended both schools on a scholarship available only to Hispanic students; there may have been more qualified students who were Anglo, Asian, or African-American who had greater need for the scholarship or who could have taken better advantage of it. Instead, it was given to me because I was Hispanic and I met the criteria for it. By accepting the scholarship, I participated in a system that excluded those outside of my racial group. My race made

---

3. Peggy McIntosh, "White Privilege: Unpacking the Invisible Knapsack," *Independent School* 49 (Winter 1990), 31.

me part of the chosen group of people who qualified for the scholarship.

Being part of the chosen or in-group, unfortunately, leads us "to undergird racist practices."⁴ We forget that just as we longed not to be oppressed, we subject others to oppression. As a Hispanic student benefiting from this system, I am unconsciously standing against other ethnic, cultural, and racial groups. It is important to note that others *are* being oppressed through my actions. When we forget that or refuse to acknowledge it, we continue to do damage by reinforcing an oppressive system.

> This is where the author relates his own personal experience to the main topic of the paper.

I share these two examples to prove that systemic racism is not necessarily a personal act of evil, but rather a social struggle. We "struggle" against racism not only as an act of defiance, but also because we understand that racism is a social construct. It is not something innate in human beings: "Though it seems to be always-already-there, it is a product of history."⁵ People do not take part in systemic racism by consciously tearing down another racial group; sometimes systems and programs are put into place in such a way that one group is in a position of privilege—members of this group often unaware of this privilege—and another is oppressed.

This form of systemic racism can be seen through the ministry of Jesus, a Jew, in a Roman world. Jesus became an icon for the Jewish community, which was both oppressed by the Roman Empire and, at the same time, unconsciously oppressed others. In much the same way, there is a community of Mexican-American citizens in the United States, like myself, who find the same message in the Virgin of Guadalupe. This community, much like the first-century Jewish community, both benefitted and was oppressed by systemic racism. In this paper, I explore the role Jesus and the Jewish community played in systemic racism and the ways in which the struggle of that Jewish community relates to the struggle of Mexican-American citizens today who are affected by, and benefitting from, systemic racism.

> The author states the topic he is exploring and how he will go about it. Although the paper has elements of an exploratory research paper, it's actually more of an argumentative paper as we will see later.

---

4. Fernandez, *Reimagining the Human*, 143.

5. Ibid., 138.

The Jewish Mission of Jesus in a Gentile World

UNDERSTANDING THE CONTEXT OF JESUS' MINISTRY

Before looking at Jesus' role in systemic racism, it is important to remember that Jesus was in fact Jewish—"Numerous churches today acknowledge their intimate connection to Judaism [through Jesus]: connections born from Scripture, history, theology, and, as Paul puts it, Christ 'according to the flesh' (Rom. 9:5)."[6] Unfortunately, many times this is left unsaid. Congregants can be taught from classrooms, pulpits, and even from the pews without having to acknowledge that Jesus was Jewish: "The claim that 'Jesus was a Jew' may be historically true, but it is not central to the teaching of the church."[7] But Jesus' Jewishness was an important dimension of who he was.

After discussing his own experience in light of systemic racism, the author now turns to a discussion of the first-century Jewish community.

There is no way to fully understand Jesus' ministry and interaction with other characters without understanding his context. It would be like reading statements from Cesar Chavez and expecting to understand them without understanding the civil-rights movement.[8] Context is key to understanding any interaction between characters, especially when dealing with systemic racism. And in order to understand Jesus' actions, it is essential that we understand his context: "When Jesus is located [within] the world of Judaism, the ethical implications of his teachings take on renewed and heightened meaning."[9] You cannot have one without the other.

BEING OUTSIDERS IN A RACIST SYSTEM

Heads and subheads are used effectively to guide the reader through the author's examples.

For generations of people who came before Jesus, being Jewish meant persecution, slaughter, enslavement, and devastation: "By the time of Jesus, the Galilean, Samaritan, and Judean people had

---

6. Amy-Jill Levine, *The Misunderstood Jew* (San Francisco: HarperCollins Publishers, 2006), 18.

7. Ibid., 18.

8. Richard A. Horsley, *Jesus and Empire: The Kingdom of God and the New World Disorder* (Minneapolis: Fortress Press, 2003), 56–57.

9. Levine, *The Misunderstood Jew*, 21.

lived under the rule of one empire after another for 600 years, except for one brief interlude of less than a century."[10] It was in the midst of this that the Roman Empire tried to take over the area near Nazareth. The devastation "left collective social trauma as well as physical destruction in their wake."[11] After the Roman Empire had taken control, they established a system to collect revenues more effectively from the Galileans in order to support the new rule. This economic pressure led Jewish families to fall heavily into debt and become vulnerable to their creditors; many lost their lands and property. It is into this system of oppression that Jesus was born: the Romans, through established systems, oppressing the Jews.

The Jewish community was oppressed by virtue of who they were and their history. Interestingly, the Roman Empire was known for "establishing order and an elaborate network of roads"[12]—and it is given credit for the Hellenization that not only made Christianity possible but also paved the way to spread the Gospel faster. So, the conditions established by the Roman Empire created the very conditions by which Jesus was able to travel so easily throughout the region. And this Hellenization was made possible by the oppression of groups such as the Jewish community into which Jesus was born. Here was a system meant to help one group that affected, excluded, and oppressed another.

Hellenization is a clear example of the Jewish community being affected by systemic racism. They were the "outsiders," and they were impacted negatively by the system that benefitted the "insiders." The reality is that, when one group is oppressed by a racial system, especially to the extent that the Jewish community was, that group begins to desire to be part of the "insider" group. This was the good news that Jesus brought to the Jewish community: they were now insiders. When this longing happens, however, the group experiences a loss of identity,[13] and this loss is a result of systemic racism. Sometimes however, one group is so focused on becoming the insider group that they begin to exclude and oppress others.

BEING INSIDERS IN A RACIST SYSTEM

When understood through the lens of these struggles, the story of the Syro-Phoenician woman in Mark begins to make more sense.

10. Horsley, *Jesus and Empire*, 16.

11. Ibid., 60.

12. Ibid., 17.

13. Fernandez, *Reimagining the Human*, 146.

In this pericope, recounted in Mark 7:24–30,[14] we get a glimpse of Jesus taking advantage of systemic racism. As the story begins, Jesus is headed to get some rest when a woman approaches him about healing her daughter.

Now, the author discusses an example from Scripture, showing how it demonstrates systemic racism.

After having laid out the narrative in 7:24–25, the reader is expecting a healing to take place. A woman has asked Jesus to heal her daughter. She has heard of the healings that he has already done: "In many ways, the Syro-Phoenician woman is like many other persons in the Gospel who receive healing or ask for healing on behalf of another: she is in a house, has heard about Jesus, has a daughter in need, and she falls before Jesus begging for healing for her daughter."[15] The author of Mark however, makes it clear that something is different about this woman; he points out that the woman is not only a Gentile, but more specifically "'Greek, Syro-Phoenician by birth' (7:26b)."[16] Jesus has denied this woman healing for her daughter solely on the basis of her not being Jewish. In this Gospel, the Markan Jesus claims that the good news he brings is for the insider group only, the Jewish community. In this pericope, however, the roles of systemic racism have been reversed. Now the system benefits the Jewish community and oppresses and excludes all others.

This type of systemic racism is what I would consider privilege. Privilege is the idea that one group enjoys certain benefits while another group does not. Most importantly, privilege is enjoyed mostly because one group does not realize that they benefit automatically from an advantage denied to others: "Privilege becomes truly a privilege when we do not notice it or, in a much sharper way, when we do not have to assert or claim it."[17]

The author defines an important term—after he has given an example—so it has more meaning now for the reader.

The problem with privilege and systemic racism is that certain people are excluded; benefits and advantages are for the select few. In this pericope, Jesus makes it very clear that Jews are the privileged ones, and everyone else is not. It is not until Jesus realizes

---

14. All Scripture references are from the New Revised Standard Version (NRSV).

15. Sharon Betsworth, *The Reign of God is Such as These: A Socio-Literary Analysis of Daughters in the Gospel of Mark* (New York: T&T Clark International, 2010), 127.

16. Ibid., 127.

17. Fernandez, *Reimagining the Human*, 135.

the privilege that he has denied others, that healing begins to take place. She "causes Jesus to reconsider and concede that she and her daughter are indeed a part of his mission."[18] In a story in which the woman's hopelessness is expected to be the ultimate outcome, Jesus has a change of mind and "declares that the kingdom he has offered ... is so astoundingly wonderful 'that even the least in the kingdom of God'"[19] are invited.

These two examples help clarify the idea that one racial group can represent both sides of the same coin. While Jesus and his Jewish followers were being oppressed by the Roman Empire, they also were oppressing all those who were not part of their ethnic group. When this type of systemic racism occurs, we often focus only on the fact that the system oppresses one group, and we forget to acknowledge that the oppression keeps being passed along to others. It is important to recognize that systemic racism can oppress and benefit the same group of people.

The Jewish Struggle Through a Mexican-American Lens

Just as Jesus brought both inclusivism and exclusivism to the Jewish community, Mexican-American communities across the country have viewed the *Virgen de Guadalupe* in the same manner: "On the surface, these practices and traditions ... are fundamental to the identity of people who have often wandered in exile, and whose identity has sometimes been denied by the dominant culture."[20] Much like the Jews, who experienced many trials and tribulations as they were conquered and re-conquered, so too is Mexican heritage embedded in that experience: "Forced from one region of the valley of Mexico to others, the Mexica [later known as Aztecs] in 1322 ultimately came to the location that had been prophesied to them by Huitzilopochtli through the priestly class."[21] In that prophecy, this group witnessed an eagle devouring a serpent on a cactus in a place called Tenochtitlan, signifying the location in which they were to settle.

These events marked the beginning of a struggle between the

---

18. Betsworth, *The Reign of God*, 128.

19. Horsley, *Jesus and Empire*, 109.

20. Justo Gonzales, *World Religions in America: An Introduction*, 3rd ed., ed. Jacob Neusner (Louisville: Westminster John Knox Press, 2003), 86.

21. David A Sanchez, *From Patmos to the Barrio: Subverting Imperial Myths* (Minneapolis, MN: Fortress Press, 2008), 59.

natives of Mexico and the Spanish conquistadors. Among them was the "spiritual conquest" of Mexico.[22] According to legend, about ten years after the Spanish arrived in the Americas, a miracle took place just north of Mexico City in Tepeyac: "On an early December morning, the Virgin Mary first appeared to a lowly Mexica man named Cuauhtlatozin (Juan Diego) and greeted him in a familiar and loving manner."[23] The message she brought was one of compassion for the struggles of Mexica people.

To this day, Mexican-American communities still relate and connect to the message of the Virgin of Guadalupe. She, like Jesus, brought the outsider group relief from oppression. To outsiders, there is a sense of freedom found in her: "For that reason, among Catholic Hispanics, especially those of Mexican or Mexican American descent, the Virgin of Guadalupe ... has been a sign of empowerment and vindication for the oppressed native inhabitants of these lands, and in general for all the poor and the downtrodden."[24] The Virgin of Guadalupe, much like Jesus, gave people hope that their situation would get better. The struggles, deportations, conquests—they would soon be in the past. As with Jesus and the Jewish community, the outsider had become the insider.

> This is a strong example of a research paper that explores the topic of systemic racism by looking at it from several perspectives: the author's personal experience; the first-century context of the Jews, and the story of the Syro-Phoenician woman in the Gospel of Mark.

This new identity is important for many Mexican Americans in the United States because, for many, there is an ongoing sense of oppression. Immigration issues, high walls dividing the border, and the constant fear of racial stereotypes all play a role in the oppression of Hispanics. As a Mexican-American student in an Anglo world, I constantly wonder and worry about the role my race plays in everything I do. When others make comments or do certain things, I am quick to wonder if my race has any role to play in it. Every coin has two sides though. Whether one believes it or not, others are consciously and unconsciously wondering if their actions are offensive to me because of my race. I cannot count the number of times people around me have corrected or re-worded their statements out of concern that I have been insulted.

22. Ibid., 61.
23. Ibid., 61.
24. Gonzalez, *World Religions in America*, 87.

The Syro-Phoenician woman is an example of healing taking place. The systemic racism that both benefits and oppresses the Jewish community finds healing after the woman brings the issue to light. I would argue that Mexican-American communities must understand the pericope of the Syro-Phoenician woman and the story of the Jewish community in order to find healing in their oppression. It is important to understand that, as oppression is fought, we must be careful to not subject others to the same oppression we ourselves faced; we must refuse to perpetuate the oppression. Most importantly, however, we must continue to bring the issue to light and stop oppression from going unnoticed. We need to talk openly about oppression and, if one wants to be heard, one must be willing to listen to the experience of others: "If we do not allow all to bring their contributions, we shall all be the losers."[25] The oppressed and the oppressor must see that their stories are connected and that suffering is dualistic. Only then will the oppression of systemic racism be eradicated, and only then will healing be found between social groups.

> *This is an excellent concluding section, in which the author ties together all three examples, suggests new insights for understanding systemic racism, leaves the reader with a vision of hope, and concludes with an argument for healing and reconciliation.*

Works Cited

Anderson, Victor, et al. "Racism and Christianity." In *The Cambridge Dictionary of Christianity*. New York: Cambridge University Press, 2010.

Betsworth, Sharon. *The Reign of God is Such as These: A Socio-Literary Analysis of Daughters in the Gospel of Mark*. New York: T&T Clark International, 2010.

Fernandez, Eleazar. *Reimagining the Human: Theological Anthropology in Response to Systemic Evil*. St. Louis: Chalice Press, 2004.

Gonzales, Justo. *World Religions in America: An Introduction*. 3rd ed. Edited by JacobNeusner. Louisville: Westminster John Knox Press, 2003.

Horsley, Richard A. *Jesus and Empire: The Kingdom of God and the New World Disorder*. Minneapolis: Fortress Press, 2003.

Levine, Amy-Jill. *The Misunderstood Jew*. San Francisco: HarperCollins Publishers, 2006.

McIntosh, Peggy. "White Privilege: Unpacking the Invisible Knapsack." *Independent School* 49 (Winter 1990): 31–36.

Sanchez, David A. *From Patmos to the Barrio: Subverting Imperial Myths*. Minneapolis: Fortress Press, 2008.

---

25. Gonzales, 90.

* * *

Research Paper: Exploratory (#1)
Sin, Evil, and the Human Condition
Christology and Theological Anthropology
Jean Engel

What to make of suffering. Suffering has been part of man's existence since the beginning of humanity when Adam and Eve were expelled from the Garden of Eden. What is the connection between sin, evil, and suffering? Why, after all these years, do we seem to have no less suffering? This paper will explore sin and evil in relation to suffering, noting that some suffering is quite visible to all; other suffering is more systemic, with causes harder to determine; and finally, what should our response as Christians be to suffering?

| *This is a clear statement of the purpose of the paper.*

Sin and evil together contribute to the lack of proper relations in the individual, social, and natural worlds in which we live. From the Christian perspective, these two terms are inseparable, but they are different, with sin having a more individual emphasis and evil a more systemic emphasis. Peter C. Hodges argues that evil is greater than a consequence of sin, as it reinforces and intensifies sin. Evil both precedes sin as individual acts and is a consequence of sin as individual acts.[1] Mary Potter Engel considers evil to be systemic. There are structures of oppression that are bigger than individuals and groups, that tempt them toward injustice and wickedness, be it political, social, or economic arrangements, that distort how they see things or hold back their capability, so that it becomes hard to choose to do good. Engel further states that sin "refers to those free, discrete acts of responsible individuals that create or reinforce these structures of oppression."[2]

| *The delicate difference between sin and evil is well stated here.*

In addressing the subject of evil, it is important to keep aware of both sides of systemic evil: lament and blame. From the view

---

1. Peter C. Hodgson, *Winds of the Spirit: A Constructive Christian Theology* (Louisville: Westminster John Knox Press, 1994), 222.

2. Mary Potter Engel, "Evil, Sin, and Violation of the Vulnerable" in *Lift Every Voice: Constructing Christian Theologies from the Underside*, ed. Susan Brooks Thistlethwaite and Mary Potter Engel (San Francisco: Harper & Row Publishers, 1990), 154–155.

point of "victim as innocent sufferer," lament relates to our need to be in solidarity with them; blame brings attention to the structures having power over the victim. When victims realize they are not singly, ultimately, or directly responsible for their victimization, it can be freeing. While it can be said that adult victims of the sins of others can have some collusion in their victimization, the blame is not focused on them. It is crucial to realize that perpetrators and victims are not equally sinful or co-responsible. Thus, even though sin and evil are inseparable, it is important to take into consideration the context. When speaking to or of the victims, one would stress evil. If one were to stress sinfulness, one could invite their feelings of over-responsibility and self-blame. When speaking of perpetrators, one would stress sin, accountability, and individual responsibility; one would not stress evil or co-responsibility as that allows the perpetrator to avoid responsibility. The above describes what should be stressed, but in neither situation should the opposite side of sin or evil be forgotten.[3]

| *Good thesis statement to introduce this paragraph.* |

| *Clarity is important: is the writer indicating that victims may be in any way sinful or co-responsible?* |

Wendy Farley, dissatisfied with the theological traditional ways of looking at theodicy, presents a different view. She suggests there are twin faces of evil, namely sin and suffering. Where sin was the main focus of evil, she shifts suffering to the center of the problem. Specifically, she speaks of radical suffering and states "the distinguishing features of radical suffering are that it is destructive of the human spirit and that it cannot be understood as something deserved."[4] This type of suffering goes against any effort to incorporate it into standards of justice. We do not appear to live in a just world, but a tragic one. Tragedy lies between the desire for justice and the reality of suffering. Tragedy acknowledges that some kinds of suffering are utterly unjust, providing no justification. A response to

| *Again, the thesis of the paragraph is introduced with a strong, clear statement.* |

| *This is a strong point with which to end the paragraph. The argument is flowing through the document.* |

---

3. Ibid., 155–156.

4. Wendy Farley, *Tragic Vision and Divine Compassion: A Contemporary Theodicy* (Louisville: Westminster/John Knox Press, 1990), 21.

this type of tragic suffering is indignation that cannot be appeased and compassionate resistance.⁵

If those who suffer from evil are to be liberated, we must confront the people, institutions, and economies that are the oppressors. They are powerful against the vulnerable, those our society judges to be "appropriate victims" or "wrong." Especially, we who call ourselves Christian must choose to be resistance fighters with the oppressed; if not, we actually collaborate in the profanation of the vulnerable. Engel argues that both Christianity and the North American culture, through their apathy and participation in the "conspiracy of silence," have chosen to be passive and active partners in these evils against the vulnerable. We must also be aware of the interlocking oppressions of racism, classism, sexism, and ageism, compounding oppression. We must discover how they reinforce each other and not settle on one as the root cause.⁶

| *It is a good idea to identify who "we" is, instead of using the impersonal pronoun too often.* |

Sin and evil contribute to suffering in this world. Few people would disagree that suffering due to oppression needs to end. It causes a break in relationship to each other and to God. Although humankind may have the capability to do both good and evil, where do some find justification for actions viewed as sinful or evil? Will we enter into alliance with those who suffer from such things as hunger, oppression, or torture, or are we going to remain uninvolved? We are capable of suffering with those who suffer and to participate with them in their struggle. But through our involvement, we must not only address the causes and seek the eradication of suffering; we must also ask the question about its meaning and function.

| *This comment must lead to a discussion of the subject in the following paragraph.* |

Those who suffer from hunger, oppression, or torture frequently have no hope that things will change. The term "suffering" for this discussion needs to be clarified. This type of suffering has three components: physical, psychological and social. All three components must be present for this type of suffering to occur. It is more than the scientific diagnosis of "pain." There is an intensity and duration of pain being compounded by aspects in the psychological

---

5. Ibid., 11–23.
6. Engel, "Evil, Sin, and Violation of the Vulnerable," 152–154.

and social spheres. All three aspects are present in true suffering. There is no true suffering without social degradation or fear of it, which leads to isolation: fear of social rejection. "Lack of solidarity with the afflicted is therefore the most natural thing in the world... It is natural for us more or less to despise the afflicted, 'although practically no one is conscious of it.' "[7] This leads to a feeling of powerlessness. This consciousness of being powerless is a basic element of suffering. Dorothee Soëlle believes that "every attempt to humanize suffering must begin with this phenomenon of experienced powerlessness and must activate forces that enable a person to overcome the feeling that he is without power."[8] Related to powerlessness is another aspect of suffering, which is meaninglessness. This occurs when an individual does not know what to believe and thus lacks clarity for decision making. By not deciding, whatever the person is suffering will continue. Meaninglessness in one aspect of life will affect most other parts of life.[9]

| *This question forms the basis for exploration in the paragraph.* |

How are we to respond to evil? We have seen the horrific results of evil. Religions have not satisfactorily explained the origin of evil or given a suitable plan and praxis with which to respond, particularly when it comes to the suffering of the innocent. In the Christian tradition, we have the story of the fall, the doctrine of predestination, and the questions around theodicy. Felix Wilfred[10] proposes we use the ying-yang response to respond to evil. By this he means "prophetic anger" and "sapiential compassion." In the Bible, Yahweh is depicted as an angry God and a God of compassion. These two aspects of God unite in a divine mystery. Jesus' life demonstrates these two sides of the divine. Jesus expressed prophetic

| *This sentence is an excellent point, and the author has made it well.* |

anger at the evils of society and sapiential compassion in the Sermon on the Mount. Thus, Jesus is defined as showing both prophetic anger and sapiential compassion. How humanity reacts and responds to evil defines us as individuals and a people. The origin and manifestation of commonplace evil "is mostly committed by

---

7. Dorothee Soëlle, *Suffering* (Philadelphia: Fortress Press, 1975), 14–15.

8. Ibid., 11.

9. Ibid., 11–13.

10. Felix Wilfred, Head of the Department of Christian Studies, School of Philosophy and Religious Thought, University of Madras, Chennai, India.

ordinary men and women who go about their daily lives, and are, by no means, moral monsters... Thoughtlessness can be more dangerous than malice; we are more often threatened by self-serving refusal to see the consequences of conventional action than by defiant desires for destruction."[11]

In responding to evil, our first feelings should be that of indignation and outrage at the suffering and injustice inflicted on the victims. That type of response is very important. However, we live in a world that is becoming insensitive to evil. Evil has become expressed through statistics, the evening news, codification, etc. The human response is often missing. People conform to the status quo, following standards of what is socially acceptable and promote political correctness. They consider the usefulness of an action and its practical consequences. Frequently missing are confrontation, questioning, and rejection of established social practices. Wilfred gives an example that we fear arms may fall into the hands of terrorists, but there is no compelling will to eliminate arms and the arms-race. He points out that what we need is to be angry at a system that permits the increase in deadly arms. He states "terrorism is nothing but the by-product of a world which is not angry enough with the production, marketing, and accumulation of deadly arms and lethal weapons."[12] Great leaders like Martin Luther King became angry with the situation of the oppressed and foresaw a different possibility. This anger was directed at redeeming society from the results of evil oppression, rather than destroying or punishing the enemy. With all the evil in the world, we need to ask why people do not rise up to fight the evil that has not diminished.

> *This is the point that will be developed in this paragraph.*

> *Question your own assumptions: one could argue that the spirit of MLK does still exist through various organizations and movements and, thanks to those who are prophetic, they have maintained the tradition of resistance.*

Theologically, our response to evil would begin by listening for God's call and the guidance of the Holy Spirit, enabling us to respond with both anger and compassion. These two perspectives become unified when we remember God is both an angry God

---

11. Felix Wilfred, "Prophetic Anger and Sapiential Compassion: Grappling with Evil Today," in *Evil Today and Struggles to be Human*, ed. Regina Ammicht Quinn, et al. (London: SCM Press, 2009), 28–29.

12. Ibid., 29.

and a God of compassion and that Jesus gave us an example through His life. It is required of humankind that we be sensitive to God's call and discern it every moment anew. This is a way of acting and respond-

| *This is a strong beginning sentence for the paragraph and a good follow-up to the last paragraph. This next sentence continues to tie the essay together.*

ing in light of the example of Jesus. Our response to evil will be an insight of revelation, even though it remains a mystery. This usually does not come through reason and the powers of the mind, but is revealed to us.

In responding to evil, myth is important. Myth can contradict itself; it does not systematize and rationalize its contents; it is open-ended, allowing us to add to it or subtract from it. Myth is our com-

| *Again, good beginning sentence— and all others flow from it.*

panion as we move forward. Myth includes our demands and expectations, and we develop it as we proceed. Myth also plays a role in offering hope for the future, by giving strength and courage against despondency or defeatism when facing evil. Another way of understanding evil is through mystical language. Through contemplation, we can acknowledge the overwhelming greatness and unmerited love of God, which gives new horizons of hope. Mystical language has prophetic implications. The victims express their language in prophetic voice. Often the language is of a lamentation nature, not implying loss of hope but a way of coping with the evil they are suffering. It also has a cathartic effect.[13]

Following is clarification concerning prophetic anger and sapiential compassion. We must remember that the anger we are talking about is the anger of the victim. They are the persons who experience the suffering caused by the various types of oppression. Those

| *This is an important point that the writer makes clearly.*

who are in solidarity with the victims also express anger at the injustice of the suffering. Prophetic anger is about justice. In the anger of the victims, the whole being reacts. There is room to express the torment from the oppression, but to have strength still to imagine something different. Prophetic anger is healing. The wounds of society are fully exposed with the aim of healing them. This

| *This paragraph on prophetic anger is powerfully written.*

anger comes about through an encounter with an experience of

---

13. Ibid., 30–33.

something magnificent and beautiful beyond the present distortion of how things are now. The power of prophetic anger lies in the fact that it speaks of evil with real facts and feelings in a specific context. By placing it in a specific context all of the horror of evil stand out and cannot hide behind convenient pretexts. As Wilfred writes:

> Prophetic anger is directed at awakening people from their slumber, their numbness. People do not want to face the suffering of others in everyday life. There is an attempt to put up a brave front and convince oneself that everything is fine. The reality all around is lulling people to numbness. Prophetic anger provokes people out of their complacency, their situation of being lulled by the manipulative techniques of the empire, of the dominant powers. There is anger because there is a violation of human dignity and rights, and a distortion of the vision of something beautiful. Loss of vision is the cause of the perpetuation of the present as the optimal situation. It works to the advantage of the powerful and causes suffering to the victims.[14]

Compassion responds to evil understood as suffering and, as expected, to the suffering of the innocent. One is moved to compassion through the wisdom to see how the whole of reality is linked together. The cosmic family is composed of human beings, sentient beings, and all of nature. We are all linked together as part of the whole. With this holistic approach, it follows that suffering to any part of the whole becomes one's own suffering, as we are all connected. Sapiential compassion that is the result of evil-doing involves a predicament: there is the evil-doer whose personal history calls for compassion; there is, also, a proper demand for retribution to defend justice and moral standards. Mercy and compassion could become leniency and arbitrariness. What prevents this from happening is the genuine practice of compassion through an encounter with something beyond us; we are motivated by something beyond customary ways and manners. Theologically, this is the practice of reflection on the divine. God sends rain to the just and the unjust and Jesus, our example, enjoined us to show mercy, as God is merciful. "Those who experience this gratuitousness and abundance of God's love and mercy approach evil with great wisdom and compassion."[15] Through this compassion we experience the divine more deeply, as well as the human mystery. By being merciful and compassionate, those we interact with are not humiliated; their dignity

---

14. Ibid., 34.

15. Ibid., 35.

can stay intact. They have hope that they will be accepted. Through compassion, good can be drawn from the evil that exists in the world. Wilfred writes of sapiential compassion:

> Sapiential compassion involves also a self-critique and reflectiveness. It is confession of human limitations and judgment. It is a realization that the task of discerning good and evil is fraught with risks and that deciding one way or the other has serious consequences. Sapiential compassion, however, needs to be understood in an active and dynamic sense. It would simply be a cover-up of evil if it does not lead to a sense of repentance, readiness for expiation, and transformation of the self of the evil-doer or the group that is instrumental in bringing forth a particular evil. Here is the real struggle to be human in responding to evil.[16]

It is not easy when responding to evil, and even more difficult to be human in our response. However, when we go to the center of what it means to be human, we begin to understand that motives and attitudes of people are not black and white. Through prophetic anger and sapiential compassion, we mirror the divine response, for which there are no clear-cut definitions or boundaries.

This paper is compelling, well developed, exploring the meaning of being human in situations of sin, evil, and suffering, and offers a way of responding to sin and evil through what the author calls "prophetic anger and sapiental compassion."

Works Cited

Engel, Mary Potter. "Evil, Sin, and Violation of the Vulnerable" in Thistlethwaite, Susan Brooks and Engel, Mary Potter, ed. *Lift Every Voice: Constructing Christian Theologies from the Underside.* San Francisco: Harper & Row Publishers, 1990.
Farley, Wendy. *Tragic Vision and Divine Compassion: A Contemporary Theodicy.* Louisville: Westminster/John Knox Press, 1990.
Hodgson, Peter C. *Winds of the Spirit: A Constructive Christian Theology.* Louisville: Westminster John Knox Press, 1994.
Soelle, Dorothee. *Suffering.* Philadelphia: Fortress Press, 1975.
Wilfred, Felix. "Prophetic Anger and Sapiential Compassion: Grappling with Evil Today." In *Evil Today and Struggles to be Human,* edited by Regina-Ammicht Quinn, et al., 27–35. London: SCM Press, 2009.

* * *

---

16. Ibid., 36

Research Paper: Exploratory (#2)

Christus Victor vs. James Alison's Understanding of Atonement Christology and Theological Anthropology
Mary Jane Huber

The atonement theory has always caused some difficulty for me as I have explored my theology. I found it difficult to understand how Jesus' death upon the cross did anything to reveal the salvific nature of God. How could a death bring life and love? Death is a separation, an end, a destruction of life, and the resurrection was not enough for me to look past, especially as a mother, past the death of a son. Sacrifice, substitution, and the taking on of sin, of somehow being part of a penal system, did not seem to line up with the way of life that Jesus lived. To care for the weak, the outcast, the downtrodden, those cast aside by the powers of the world—that was the way of Jesus' ministry. One of the challenges in exploring theories of atonement will be to find the peace and justice of Immanuel, God with us, in the atonement.

Here is the thesis statement of this difficult and personal introductory paragraph.

A starting place for the exploration of the history and development of this theory is to look at the definition of atonement. Per the Oxford dictionary, atonement is defined as the condition of being at one with others, a unity of feeling, harmony, concord, agreement. The second definition is the restoration of friendly relations between persons who have been at variance; reconciliation.[1] For me, the sense of reunification, of at-one-ment, is important. To be at one with God is the key to life.

In the Christian faith, the atonement is understood to be the action through which Jesus' death and resurrection reconciles humanity with God. This was understood by the apostles after the resurrection, and they shared stories and testimonies to this fact with the communities they encountered. These stories, now contained in the Gospel accounts, along with the Pauline and pseudo–Pauline writings, seek to elucidate their testimony as to the salvific nature of Jesus Christ. Salvation was needed

The opening statement to this paragraph states what will be developed in the rest.

---

1. J. A. Weiner Simpson, E. S. C., *The Oxford English Dictionary*, 2nd ed., vol. I (New York: Oxford Clarendon Press, 1989), 754.

because of the separation between God and humanity. This, for some, was due to original sin, for others the influences of Satan. For the early church, Christ's victory over death proclaimed the power of God.

Gustaf Aulén, in his landmark book, *Christus Victor*, posits that there are three basic theories of the atonement that have informed the Church through the ages. These three theories are the Classic, Latin, and Subjective theories. Each attempts to show how the actions of the death and resurrection of Christ reconcile God and humanity. Aulén takes the reader through the development of the theories of atonement and attempts to show how the Classic theory is more valid than the others. In this work, all the theories of atonement are understood to have developed with the knowledge of Augustine's notion of original sin. Because of the Fall of Adam and Eve in the Garden of Eden, all humanity is separated from God. The atonement, effected by the cross event, is understood to provide the redemptive act and reconcile God and humanity.

> Remember that each paragraph in your writing should have a thesis statement that it will develop. This statement will be developed through the following paragraphs.

The oldest theory, put forth by the early patristic fathers, including Origen and Irenaeus, is the Classic theory, or Christus Victor. This understanding of the atonement declares that Christ has been victorious over death, thereby reconciling all creation to God. Humanity was created in God's image but, because of their human deeds, they have lost favor with God. For Irenaeus, life is compromised by sin; "disobedience to God is essentially death."[2] As one begins to explore Irenaeus' work on the atonement, it is helpful to comprehend what he thought about the nature of Christ, sin, and Satan in light of the death and resurrection of Christ. For Irenaeus, Christ came from heaven to defeat Satan. The power of Satan to keep people in bondage and out of a full relationship with God is an integral part of Irenaeus' understanding of the need for the atonement.

Irenaeus maintains continuity in the nature of God in his work. This is established by linking the incarnation and atonement together. "The incarnation is essentially the indispensable basis on which the subsequent work of redemption rests."[3] The incarnation

---

2. Gustaf Aulén, *Christus Victor: An Historical Study of the Three Main Types of the Idea of the Atonement*, 1st Macmillan paperback ed. (New York: Macmillan, 1969), 25.

3. Ibid., 28.

is intimately linked to the atonement because only God is capable of overcoming the powers of Satan and evil. A human could not do it. This causes a bit of a problem because the sin is caused by man's separation from God, but God's action in Christ provides the reconciliation. In other words, God, in Christ is the sacrifice, and God is simultaneously the reconciler. God reconciles the world unto God's self by overcoming, victoriously, the powers of sin and death. Christ must be understood to be fully divine in order to be a worthy sacrifice, and fully human in order to reconcile the human sinful nature to God.

> *This entire paragraph gives a very good summary of the theory put forth by the author she cites.*

One of the images that Irenaeus puts forth is that of ransom. He suggests that Jesus' death was a ransom paid to the Devil to release humans from captivity. "It cannot be too strongly emphasized that when this has been done, atonement has taken place; for a new relation between God and the world is established."[4] This new relationship is free from the powers of sin and death. The conflict between good and evil has been completed in the death and resurrection of Jesus Christ. This classic view of the atonement was the dominant view of the Western and Eastern Fathers of the church.[5]

The nature of God and Christ was a primary focus of the early church Fathers. They struggled to articulate Trinitarian doctrine, but nevertheless had some writings about the atonement. The orthodox consensus was that Jesus was fully divine and fully human, allowing him to be the medium for reconciliation. Aulén's commentary on the work of the early church fathers is less than favorable. "Many features in the patristic teaching should awaken disgust, such as its mythological dress, its naïve simplicity, its grotesque realism."[6] These teachings dealt inconsistently with the concept of Satan, but in the long run, there was a sense that Satan had taken control of humanity and that he could be paid off. Satan was tricked into believing that Jesus' death was Satan's victory. Once Satan believed, the resurrection snatched the power from Satan and returned it fully to God. Therefore, one can see that the classic theory of atonement "sets forth God's coming to man, to accomplish His redemptive work; incarnation and redemption belong indissolubly together; God in Christ overcomes the hostile powers which hold

---

4. Ibid., 30.
5. Ibid., 39.
6. Ibid., 47.

man in bondage. At the same time these hostile powers are also the executants of God's will."⁷

Both Tertullian and Cyprian offered another understanding of the atonement of Christ. The question Tertullian raised was how could there be forgiveness of sin and reconciliation with God if there were no penance?⁸ The penance, done by humans in the form of spiritual disciplines, would earn them merit in God's eyes. One can earn merit that is then used to pay the price for sin. If someone has more merit than sin, there is an excess of merit. Christ, in this view had no sin but earned great merit in his sacrificial death. This over-abundance of merit is then transferred to others. This is the beginning of the Latin theory of atonement: "Its root idea is that man must make an offering or payment to satisfy God's justice; this is the idea that is used to explain the work of Christ."⁹

Anselm of Canterbury develops this theory in his writing, *Cur Deus homo?* What he puts forth is a theory of the atonement dependent upon the idea of penal substitution. In Anselm's understanding, the human affront to God was so great that there was no possible way that humans could ever make enough of a sacrifice to make the appropriate apology. It is impossible for humans to apologize sufficiently. It was for this reason that Jesus was born, lived, and died. He was the ultimate apology, a sacrifice to atone for the great offense of humanity. God becomes man so that the sacrifice, on behalf of man, will be satisfactory. Thus, Christ comes from divine into human form, which seems like a weakness, but is the only way that reconciliation can happen. In Anselm's theory, there is no need for a ransom to be paid. Christ, on behalf and as man, is offered up freely as sacrifice for the sins of humanity. The penalty is paid by man to God through Christ who is of God. Divine justice is served. Aulén sums up the Latin theory of atonement thusly: "the payment of satisfaction is treated as the essential element in atonement and as accomplished by the death of Christ; the payment is primarily the work of Christ's human nature, but it gains increased meritorious value on account of the union of human nature with the Divine nature in Christ."¹⁰ Aulén's critique of the Latin theory was that because

| *Again, what we have is a very clear summary of an ancient church father.* |

7. Ibid., 59.
8. Ibid., 81.
9. Ibid., 82.
10. Ibid., 93.

Christ was human, his sacrifice did not have enough merit to reconcile all of humanity. It was not of infinite value and, therefore, this understanding of the atonement falls short of explaining the power of the resurrection to take away sin.

The theory of atonement continued to be revised and reinterpreted. Abelard, a contemporary of Anselm, responded vehemently to the Latin theory of the atonement. He refuted any connection between the Devil and the atonement. The love awakened in man through the life and ministry in Christ caused a change in the nature of humanity. According to Aulén, Abelard did not advance the understanding of the atonement because he did not assign any "special significance to the death of Christ."[11] Luther and the Protestant church were not able to fully separate themselves from the Latin theory of atonement. The sin of man deserved punishment, the justice of God. Christ endured the punishment instead of man. Christ's obedience and sacrifice is acceptable because of God's grace.

In Aulén's work, the latest theory to be developed is the subjective theory. This theory, developed during the period of the Enlightenment, stressed the eternal and consistent nature of God. God, they reasoned, did not need humanity and, therefore, did not need any atonement. Humanity, on the other hand, did need God and did need to have a change of heart based on the life, death, and resurrection of Jesus Christ. For Schleiermacher, salvation, as understood as a change in the attitude and actions of man, comes before atonement.[12] This is different than either the Latin or Christus Victor theories, which postulate that atonement is prior to salvation and salvation and atonement are simultaneous and analogous respectively. This last theory has an emphasis, not on the work of Christ on behalf of humanity, but of humanity for humanities' sake.

Atonement theories are just that, theories. In contemporary society, there is a desire to have a rational and definitive answer to the questions of life. Science, the guiding light of the modern world, operates as if a theory were fact until such time as the theory is disproven. It is from this mindset that many Christians enter into the exploration the atonement. Thinking along these rational, scientific, Enlightenment-based lines can limit the imagination. New ideas are much more difficult to come by,

Now, the author posits her own argument, exploring contemporary theologians.

---

11. Ibid., 96.

12. Ibid., 136.

because they first have to go through the sieve of existing structures. In the case of the atonement, any imaginative exploration is seen as a threat to the positions of power that exist within the Church.

There are, however, contemporary theologians who continue to explore the issues surrounding theories of the atonement. James Alison is one such theologian. He suggests that people learn, not from the head, but through the heart, through experience, through participation in the story. In his writing on atonement, Alison makes the case that when "we come to look at how we are saved, is that in the first place, we are looking not at a theory at all, but at a gradual induction into a set of practices."[13] Christus Victor and the Latin theory of the atonement articulate the action of the atonement as that of vengeance and retribution inflicted by God on God's Son; violence perpetrated, violence allowed, violence condoned. Alison questions how this is to be reconciled with the greatest power, the power of God's love—not violence. Just the name of the theory championed by Aulén, Christus Victor, is challenged by Alison. "Victory is the language of the near rival who triumphs over a near rival. But from the point of view, if we may use such terms, of the power that is not part of the same universe, a victory *over* someone is not a victory at all. It is in fact a sign that there is in the universe is conflict and comparative strength."[14] Alison's work in *Being Liked* and *Undergoing God: Dispatches from the Scene of the Break-in,* endeavors to lay out an alternative way to see how the power of God interacts in the world. Key to his articulation of atonement are Rene Girard's mimetic theory and understanding that atonement is liturgy.

In a nutshell, mimetic theory contends that we know who we are by imitating others. We learn what we like by seeing what others have. When we see what others have, we desire the same. This desire creates conflict between two people, families, villages, or countries. In order to reconcile, the two parties find a third party to whom blame can be shifted. The tensions and anxieties and conflict are projected on the "other" who is determined to be guilty of causing the original conflict. The third party is sacrificed and thereby becomes the scapegoat, so that the two con-

> If you have been following the author's argument in this paper, you will have seen how each paragraph flows into the next. Her last sentence in the above paragraph has introduced the first sentence in this paragraph.

---

13. James Alison, *On Being Liked* (London: Darton Longman & Todd, 2003), 21.

14. Ibid., 45.

flicted parties can reconcile. Now that the third party is gone, so is the conflict. In reality, what happens is the tension, which has been arbitrarily blamed on the scapegoat, and is not relieved but harbored by all parties below the surface.

In ancient Jewish atonement practices, animals were sacrificed on behalf of the people. Anthropologically, it is understood that the more sophisticated the society, the further its sacrificial system is from human sacrifice. Yet a human sacrifice is still at the core of the system. In the death of Jesus, this substitutionary sacrificial system is undone. The human is reinserted into the sacrifice and the core of human violence is exposed for what it is, human violence. Other scholars, such as Mark Heim, assert that "God breaks the grip of scape-goating by stepping into the place of a victim and by being a victim who cannot be hidden or mythologized. God acts not to affirm the suffering of the innocent victim as the price of peace but to reverse it."[15] From this point of view, God's "mercy has been changed from something which covers up violence to something which unmasks it completely."[16] Mimetic theory helps us understand and recover the power of life when our violence is exposed and can then be dealt with. It must lead to atonement.

Atonement, as Alison sees it, is liturgy. "Treating the atonement as a theory means that it is an idea that can be grasped—and once it is grasped, you have 'got' it—whereas a liturgy is something that *happens to and at you.*"[17] Sacrificial liturgy is often considered to be performed to on the part of humanity to satisfy a divine being. Humans must make amends, sacrifices, and acts of penance and repentance in order to garner the favorable actions of the deity. According to Alison, the First-Temple atonement liturgy was "understood that it was not about humans trying desperately to satisfy God, but God taking the initiative of trying to break through for us."[18]

Alison reflects on the liturgy of the First Temple period and compares the actions of Jesus to the actions of the High Priest. It is during the atonement liturgy that the high priest sacrifices a bull for his own sins. At this point, the priest dons a white robe and

---

15. Marit Trelstad, *Cross Examinations: Readings on the Meaning of the Cross Today* (Minneapolis: Augsburg Fortress, 2006), 217.

16. James Alison, *Raising Abel: The Recovery of Eschatological Imagination* (New York: Crossroad, 1996), 35.

17. James Alison, *Undergoing God: Dispatches from the Scene of a Break-In* (New York: Continuum, 2006), 52.

18. Ibid., 54.

becomes an angel, "the Son of God."[19] The High Priest then takes two goats into the Holy of Holies. One of the goats is the Lord and the other is the Azazel (the devil). The Lord is sacrificed and its blood is sprinkled on the Mercy Seat. This action restores the balance of creation. The sins of the people are then put on the head of Azazel, the scapegoat, and it is killed. "The rite of atonement is about the Lord himself, the Creator emerging from the Holy of Holies so as to set the people free from their impurities."[20] This is liturgy, something that doesn't just happen once, but repeatedly, each time providing us an opportunity to receive from God grace, forgiveness, and restoration.

Alison goes on to describe how he sees the passion and resurrection events as a new creation through the liturgical action of atonement. He claims that:

> the early Christians who wrote the New Testament understood very clearly that Jesus was *the* authentic high priest, who was restoring *the* eternal covenant that had been established between God and Noah; who was coming out from the Holy Place so as to offer himself as an expiation for us, as a demonstration of God's love for us; and that Jesus was acting this out quite deliberately.[21]

Per the Gospel of John, Jesus is crucified on Thursday at the same time as the sacrificial lambs for the Passover were being sacrificed. There is a definite connection between the time of death, the means of death, and the understanding that Jesus was the Lamb of God, the human reinserted into the sacrifice. Alison further interprets the tomb as the Holy of Holies with the two angels seated at the foot and head of the bed on Easter morning as the cherubim of the Mercy Seat. As the High Priest, Jesus comes out of the Holy of Holies to provide the act of reconciliation with humanity, just as did the high priest in the First Temple.

This understanding of the atonement does not have any conquering of death, payment to the devil. It contends that God does not have "to have innocent blood to solve the guilt equation."[22] Instead, it is a movement by God, as witnessed through the actions of the High Priest, Jesus Christ, which reconciles the world. This action is one that unmasks the violence of humans as strictly human

---

19. Ibid., 52.
20. Ibid., 53.
21. Ibid, 55.
22. Trelstad, *Cross Examinations: Readings on the Meaning of the Cross Today*, 218.

and not divine. The resurrection moves people to understand God as only love and this requires believers' actions to be different, to be based on love that has nothing to do with the powers of death. "Behind the death of Jesus there was not violent God, but a loving God who was planning a way to get us out of our violent and sinful life."[23] Being in the world, but not of it, and living out of, and into, the power of God's love, death no longer has any power. This is what the action of the atonement does. It releases the power of love into a world, allowing it to live as if death were not. Jesus did this "not in the Temple itself, using animal substitutes, but had come through the Veil as he revealed himself in his dying on the cross, such that his tomb, with the stone rolled away, where there was no body, was now the frontier-less Holy of Holies, because the Creator had come out into the world so as to reconcile it with himself, make it forever a sharer in the creator's inner life."[24]

> Notice how well she works in this good long quote.

This action ushers in a new reality, in which the old games of domination and preservation are not in play. This action in which God moves toward humanity in love changes everything. "It completely relativizes all anthropological structures and ways of being together which depend on identity derived over and against each other, on comparison, on rivalry, and ultimately on death."[25] This understanding is one that frees people to be in relationship with one another based on love, not domination or judgment or so-called moral behavior, which is an inherent element of Christus Victor or the Latin theories of atonement. The power of God's love, unleashed in the world through the atonement, is transformative in that, by being released from the powers of death, people are able to engage in life-giving relationships regardless of what others around them do.

> This is a good summary of her argument against Christus Victor.

Death is what limits humanity from being all that it was intended to be as the creation of God. The fear of death, the power of death, restricts people from interacting compassionately with one another. It drives people toward consumption and greed and selfishness, as if human actions can somehow ward off death. Once the internal workings of the sacrificial system are exposed and

---

23. Alison, *Raising Abel: The Recovery of Eschatological Imagination*, 46.

24. Alison, *Undergoing God: Dispatches from the Scene of a Break-In*, 108.

25. Ibid., 110.

death had lost its power, people are free to "take part in the power that brings into being, causes to be, and knows no vanity, no futility, no violence, no deception."[26] It is with the eyes and heart of faith that we are able to perceive the new reality into which Christ's death has opened the door. Jesus says "I am the resurrection and the life. Those who believe in me, even though they die, will live, and everyone who lives and believes in me will never die."[27] Jesus tells his followers that death has no power. They are to live as if death were not.

When we look at atonement as an act of liturgy, we are invited in to participate, to be engaged in a new reality that is exposed in the action of liturgy. It is a repeated act, an act in which there is no violence, only love. It is an act that is reconciling in that it offers a place where death has no power and therefore all can live without fear of retribution, shame, or defeat. Love has been shown, a love so great that it has the power to overcome death. Those who become part of this great love are able to recreate it, in a way they are compelled by the magnitude of the love they feel to recreate it in the world.

| *This paragraph is her argument, strongly put.* |

This liturgical articulation of the atonement brings into question the idea of needing merit, either personally gained through spiritual discipline, or received through superabundance of Christ's merit. There is no merit needed because God's justice is not at stake. The ability to receive the love, which has been offered unconditionally from God, is what is at stake. Humanity has fallen short of God's expectation and God comes, incarnate in Christ, to offer an alternate way of being, a way that is based only on love, not the fear of punishment and death. Victory, if it is to be described this way, comes in the form of reconciliation in which both I and my neighbor are made whole. Alison speaks of the generosity of God and states that "this generosity, the same generosity which occupied the place of shame so that we should learn not to flee that place, begins to incite in us the strange sensation that a victory of mine over someone would be, in fact, a defeat for me."[28]

Alison's articulation of the purpose and action of the death and resurrection of Jesus is one that stretches the imagination and under-

---

26. Ibid., 113.

27. *New Revised Standard Bible* (New York: Oxford University Press, 1994), John 11: 25–26.

28. Alison, *Undergoing God: Dispatches from the Scene of a Break-In*, 118.

standing if one begins with the traditional theories of atonement. These earlier theories were predicated on the notion of a need for sacrifice for the sins of humanity. God needed something from humanity in order to restore the full relationship. Christus Victor, the Latin theory, and the subjective theories of the atonement all require action on the part of humanity to restore the relationship with God. Alison advocates for a different understanding all together which moves from theory to liturgy. In his articulation of the atonement, the love of God and the action of God through Jesus Christ is what makes reconciliation possible. God's love and peace unmask the powers of human violence. "The gospel, then, is not ultimately about the exchange of victims, but about ending the bloodshed."[29] This opens up the possibility of a new way of understanding the world, one in which we will be able to realize the peace and justice of Immanuel, God with us that embraces all and empowers all to respond to each other as if death were no longer in control. This means we are to see each and every person, and for that matter all of creation, with eyes focused through the love of God.

> As she develops her conclusion, she has been able to weave the theories of the ancient church fathers with a contemporary theologian like Alison and with her own ideas to reach a satisfying answer for herself, and, she hopes, for others.

Works Cited

Alison, James. *On Being Liked*. London: Darton Longman & Todd, 2003.
_____. *Raising Abel: The Recovery of Eschatological Imagination*. New York: Crossroad Pub., 1996.
_____. *Undergoing God: Dispatches from the Scene of a Break-In*. New York: Continuum, 2006.
Aulén, Gustaf. *Christus Victor: An Historical Study of the Three Main Types of the Idea of the Atonement*. 1st Macmillan paperback ed. New York: Macmillan, 1969.
New Revised Standard Bible. New York: Oxford University Press, 1994.
Simpson, J. A. Weiner, E. S. C. *The Oxford English Dictionary*. 2nd ed., Vol. I. New York: Oxford Clarendon Press, 1989.
Trelstad, Marit. *Cross Examinations: Readings on the Meaning of the Cross Today*. Minneapolis: Augsburg Fortress, 2006.

> Note that it is not necessary to include Bibles or dictionaries in your bibliography.

---

29. Trelstad, *Cross Examinations: Readings on the Meaning of the Cross Today*, 219.

Five. Research Papers   151

* * *

Research Paper: Exploratory (#3)
Journeying Towards One Church in Christ:
A Study of Multicultural Worship
Christian Public Worship
Laura Harris-Adam

Introduction

As the diversity of the United States increases, it is becoming more and more important for the Church to learn to be "multicultural." While there are some churches that are not open to other cultures and therefore choose to stay homogenous, many churches in the United States are opening their doors to the changing communities around them, to immigrants and to refugees. However, multicultural community, and especially worship, is a difficult and complex task that demands intentional thought and study. It is important that we understand what worship is and what "multicultural" means before we move on to discuss what multicultural worship can and should look like.

> This is an example of an analytical research paper in which the author is exploring new ways of understanding a topic, hoping to add something new to the existing conversation.

> Instead of a thesis statement, the author states the questions she will be exploring.

What Is Worship?

There are countless discussions based around the question of what is Christian worship. Susan White gives some helpful theological understandings of worship in her book, *Foundations of Christian Worship*. There are two understandings that are especially helpful in the endeavor of multicultural worship. White states, "worship is a way of forming and sustaining essential relationships (both divine and human), and for this reason the word 'communion' is often used to describe what happens in Christian worship."[1] This understanding of worship as foundationally relational, both within

---

1. Susan J. White, *Foundations of Christian Worship* (Louisville: Westminster John Knox Press, 2006), 7.

the community and with God, is a helpful focus for multicultural churches that must work especially hard at maintaining the community and sense of unity among all their differences. Also, White's description of "worship as the arena of transcendence"[2] brings to light the power of God to act in and through worship: "This emphasis on divine transcendence leads to an equal emphasis on the activity of the Holy Spirit, who acts as the mediator between the 'wholly-otherness' of God and the 'this-world-ness' of humanity."[3] It is important to remember as we discuss multicultural worship that it is the power of the Holy Spirit that makes all of this possible. It is not by our efforts that God is present in multicultural worship but by the grace of God and the power of the Holy Spirit.

What Does "Multicultural" Mean?

Culture is one of those difficult topics that we all think we know what it means but can be understood in many different ways. C. Michael Hawn offers a good definition of culture: "Culture consists of a matrix of complex symbol systems that provide a means for people to participate in society."[4] All of the pieces in our communications and relationships with others that help us to make meaning of the other person's actions, speech, etc., make up our culture. This includes even our most complex symbols like language. However, having the same language as another does not automatically mean you will have the same culture. For example, I speak English and so does someone from London, but our cultures are distinct. It is important to note here that I will be using the term "multicultural" to address not only various "cultures" but also to discuss communities that include multilingual, multiethnic, and multiracial participants. This is not to say that these different kinds of diversity should not be distinguished from one another, simply that they often go hand in hand.

> *The author begins with a clear definition of the term "culture" and clarifies how she will be using the term "multicultural."*

Hawn explains that in all cross-cultural encounters, our cul-

---

2. Ibid., 11.

3. Ibid., 11.

4. C. Michael Hawn, *One Bread, One Body: Exploring Cultural Diversity in Worship* (Bethesda, MD: The Alban Institute, 2003), 11.

Five. Research Papers

tural biases and prejudices become apparent.[5] He states that we will always have cultural biases because it is impossible to get rid of our cultural background.[6] Hawn explains the difference between bias and prejudice:

> A healthy bias acknowledges other worldviews and presupposes other equally valid cultural ways of making meaning. Cultural bias becomes prejudice when it assumes an exclusive posture toward other cultural perspectives—when there is only one right way to view the world.[7]

While it is impossible to eliminate our biases, we can either be self-aware and open to other cultures or prejudiced and closed to other cultures. Those persons who choose to be closed to other cultures will not likely feel comfortable in a multicultural church where all those present are validated and even celebrated.

What Is Multicultural Worship?

Culture has always been a factor in worship; as Kathy Black reminds us, "Throughout history, most worship services have been 'multicultural' to some degree in that they contain elements from diverse cultures, including roots in Jewish worship."[8] In our globalizing world, there are increasing numbers of congregations that are welcoming diversity and are coming to the realization that multicultural worship is difficult even while it is fruitful and rewarding. The relationship between culture and worship is often referred to as "inculturation." White discusses the move from inculturation in the mission field to inculturation happening everywhere:

| *The use of subheadings is helpful for guiding readers through the various sections of the paper.*

> Inculturation has been a process by which the insights, attitudes, and practices of indigenous cultures and traditional patterns of worship are creatively combined to give birth to new forms of Christian liturgical expression.[9]

| *Another clear definition of terms.*

---

5. Ibid., 10.
6. Ibid., 11.
7. Ibid., 11.
8. Kathy Black, *Culturally-Conscious Worship* (St. Louis: Chalice Press, 2000), 2.
9. White, *Foundations of Christian Worship*, 159.

For example, while visiting a church in India, I experienced inculturation when the traditional Hindu oil lamp was used in a Christian worship service along with cultural symbols and practices; this usage was given new meaning for its Christian context. Inculturation is the use of symbols or practices from one's wider culture for the purposes of worship, and in that use the meaning of the symbol or practice is changed.

There are some who are uncomfortable with this idea of inculturation. Some assume that their own cultural way of doing worship is the only true and right way. Therefore, bringing in different cultural practices is not truly "Christian" and looks like worship of a different god. However, Hawn responds in a helpful way by describing worship as transcultural, contextual, countercultural, and cross-cultural.[10] Hawn appeals to the transcultural aspect of worship to address the issue of inculturation: "The transcultural significance of worship focuses on those qualities and theological assertions that should be present in Christian worship regardless of cultural context."[11] This is the answer to the question, "What is distinctly Christian in worship?" For example, most Christian communities would agree that proclamation of the resurrected Christ is one of these beliefs that Hawn describes.

In this section, the author is critically engaging her research sources—Hawn being the first—to arrive at a new understanding of the topic.

Hawn goes on to discuss that worship is also contextual. Just as Jesus was born into a time and place, so we live in a specific time and place, and the culture of that space defines much of what we do.[12] However, we must be careful to be aware that we do not begin to make our cultural practices into transcultural ones.[13] Hawn also proclaims worship as countercultural, evidenced by Romans 12:2. "Each culture has its own manifestations of sin… The incarnation was a countercultural corrective to the prevalence of evil in all cultures."[14] Finally, Hawn also describes worship as cross-cultural: "elements of cultures should be respected when used in other places in the world."[15] The nature of cross-cultural worship

---

10. Hawn, *One Bread, One Body*, 13–18.
11. Ibid., 13.
12. Ibid., 14–15.
13. Ibid., 15.
14. Ibid., 16.
15. Ibid., 18.

Five. Research Papers

is the focus of the rest of Hawn's book. All of these ways of viewing worship as it relates to culture are important to understand as we move forward into a world of multiculturalism.

Theological and Biblical Reasons

Are there theological and/or biblical reasons for seeking multicultural worship? Donald H. Juel discusses Galatians 3:26–28 as one of many biblical supports for multicultural worship. In Galatians, Paul envisions a new world order in which the distinctions that humans create between peoples have fallen away. Juel states: "The small passage, this baptismal formula, has potential

| *Juel is the second source the author analyzes as she explores new understandings of the topic.* |

to enable us to re-imagine Christian worship. It offers a vision of a Christian community characterized by diversity and hospitality."[16] Juel later reminds us that Paul does not mean that we should erase all of our differences, but simply that our differences do not separate us from one another.[17] One of the major issues when discussing multicultural worship is how to not demand that the minority group(s) assimilate into the majority culture. This will be addressed later in the analysis of North Shore Baptist Church (NSBC).

Black also addresses some biblical backgrounds for multicultural worship, highlighting the story of Pentecost in the Acts of the Apostles.[18] This example in Acts 2 of the whole community speaking in tongues so that all could understand each other is a profound witness to the power of multicultural worship. Black states,

> The story of Pentecost is about a multicultural, multiethnic, multi-class, intergenerational community that, to some degree, held things in common, spent time together in the temple, ate together, broke bread in various homes, and praised God—they worshiped together.[19]

This witness is an example of what Black calls the "kin-dom vision"[20]; this is a living out of the new heaven and the new earth

---

16. Donald H. Juel, "Multicultural Worship: A Pauline Perspective," in *Making Room at the Table: An Invitation to Multicultural Worship*, ed. Brian K. Blount and Leonora Tubs Tisdale (Louisville: Westminster John Knox Press, 2001), 43.

17. Ibid., 55.

18. Black, *Culturally-Conscious Worship*, 36–39.

19. Ibid., 39.

20. Ibid., 35–62.

that we are called to work towards in hope. Black is not only using the biblical text to support multicultural worship but also offering a theology of multicultural worship. Juel pushes this theology even further by reminding us that it is not only about the coming of the eschaton but is also incarnational: "Particularly in a multicultural, pluralistic setting, worship may offer the possibility not only of announcing the dawning of a new age, but of experiencing a fellowship within the body of Christ."[21] Pentecost was a relational event among diverse peoples. The miracle of speaking in tongues was a celebration of the diversity that is present within Christian community and worship.

There are many more places one can find theological and biblical support for multicultural worship but there is not room in this paper to address these further. Therefore, we now turn to some of the difficulties of multicultural worship and how NSBC has addressed those issues.

Multicultural Worship at North Shore Baptist Church

North Shore Baptist Church in Chicago is a unique church that is working to embody the mission of Christ within a multicultural church. NSBC has four language congregations: English, Japanese, Spanish, and Sgaw Karen (the language of a Burmese hill tribe). The history of NSBC is long and complex, including various language groups that began at NSBC and then moved on to become their own separate churches.

This paper explores the topic in a specific context, so in addition to being an exploratory research paper, it also is a case-study of a particular church.

However, now there are four congregations that have different stories regarding their founding. The Japanese congregation began in 1954 during a period of history when Japanese Americans were suspect and many European American churches were unwilling to welcome them. The Spanish congregation began in 1978 and has grown in its membership to include a wide range of congregants with many ethnic and national backgrounds of the Spanish-speaking world. Throughout the history of the church, the English congregation, which began in 1905, has welcomed various minority groups, including a substantial Filipino Fellowship and refugees from many places, most recently from Burma. The Karen Fellowship

---

21. Juel, "Multicultural Worship," 44.

began a separate worship service in 2009, but continues to participate in English worship every Sunday. It is important to note that NSBC considers itself to be one church with multiple *equal* congregations. In 1989, the Constitution of the church was changed to reflect this equal partnership and, in 1996, the pastoral team was established so that there was no longer a senior pastor with subordinates, but pastors from each language congregation who are also pastors of the whole church.[22]

Three times per year, all of these groups come together for a joint worship service: to celebrate Stewardship in the Fall, for Healing and Anointing in the Winter, and for the Annual Meeting Celebration in the Spring. These services always incorporate all four languages of the congregations, as well as the musical leadership from all congregations. I will examine the makeup of these services in light of the research I have done on the topic of multicultural worship.

First, I would like to address the issues surrounding assimilation, especially when it comes to language. Kathleen Garces-Foley makes quite a few claims about multicultural worship in her essay "New Opportunities and New Values." She states, "Churches that succeed in forming a single community for both worship and fellowship do so by being English-only."[23] This is simply not the case at NSBC; the Karen Fellowship participates in English worship, which includes the Scripture reading in Karen, and the Karen pastor leads at least one prayer every Sunday and occasionally presides over the communion table in Karen. While these additions to the English-language service do not fully accommodate the Karen Fellowship, they are evidence of an effort for inclusion. The Karen Fellowship is able to have a full service at another time on Sunday. Garces-Foley goes on to say:

> Perhaps the strongest argument against multicultural churches is that they push members to assimilate to a common cultural center. This requires them to reject their distinctive cultural and linguistic heritage—at least while participating in the church—and to adopt 'American' cultural norms, which are inevitably those of middle-class Anglo-Americans.[24]

---

22. Most of these dates can be found at: http://www.northshorebaptist.org/DesktopDefault.aspx?tabid=38.

23. Kathleen Garces-Foley, "New Opportunities and New Values: The Emergence of the Multicultural Church," *Annals of the American Academy of Political and Social Science* 612 (July 2007): 213, accessed May 3, 2012, http://www.jstor.org/stable/25097937.

24. Ibid., 214.

This understanding of multicultural worship does not take into account the complexities of multicultural churches. *All* are asked to give up some comfort in multicultural worship. It may be true that the immigrants or the non-dominant cultures are asked to give up more, but there can be elements of worship in multiple languages and cultural manifestations. For example, during joint worship at NSBC, the Scripture reading and prayers are done in all languages, music is available in all languages, and the sermon is usually in English but sometimes includes other languages. It is not as clear-cut as Garces-Foley makes it seem. Overall, her argument is very binary: multicultural worship is either one way or another, not taking into account that a church can do all of these things. Meeting the needs of a diverse group and worshiping in multiple languages is hard work but, with dedication, it can be done.

> *Here, the author challenges one of her sources.*

Tools for Multicultural Worship

Therefore, let us move towards some practical tools that can help churches like NSBC do the difficult work of multicultural worship. I was surprised to find that NSBC has already engaged many of the tools in the resources I consulted. Many of the suggestions from both Black and Hawn are tools that have become widespread in the multicultural church world and are focused not just on worship but also on multicultural community in general. Hawn highlights four areas that need to be addressed when navigating multicultural communities: "sense of time, nonverbal cues, role of written versus oral traditions, and relationship between the leadership and the congregation."[25]

> *By exploring Hawn's four areas in the context of this church, the author is able to arrive at an in-depth understanding of the challenges and opportunities.*

Different cultures have different understandings of time. Black describes these as "monochromatic time," which is linear and therefore can be wasted or saved and so on, and "polychromatic time," which is cyclical and places emphasis on relationships and the event, rather than on the need to start and end an event on time.[26] It can be difficult to bridge the gap between these two

---

25. Hawn, *One Bread, One Body*, 20.
26. Black, *Culturally-Conscious Worship*, 68–69.

different understandings of time. A European American may feel that it is frustrating when the Latino community shows up late to worship. This is a prominent issue at NSBC that has been addressed in some different ways. First, it is important to simply be aware of the different understandings of time and be able to not place judgment on either side. Second, a community can tailor its events towards these different understandings. During joint services at NSBC, the Japanese organist almost always plays the prelude because this is an important time of gathering for that community, and the Spanish praise music that is most important for the Spanish-speaking members comes later in the service to accommodate their late arrival.

The issue of nonverbal cues covers many issues in the multicultural church community. Hawn discusses that European-Americans are less attuned to nonverbal cues and pay attention to verbal and written communication, while African-Americans and Latinos (and I would argue Asian-Americans) put much more weight on nonverbal cues, especially in regards to inclusion and welcome.[27] It is important for European-Americans to be aware of the nonverbal signals that they are giving to those of other cultural backgrounds.

Black also discusses these issues; she brings to light "indirect speech," which is the cultural phenomenon of a member saying "yes" to participating in an activity or leadership role when face-to-face with the requesting party, but then not showing up at the event.[28] This is because, in many cultures, it is more important to "save face" than to be upfront about one's inability to be present at a given event. Black suggests that it is helpful for the leadership in the church to have a "Plan B" in case this occurs.[29] NSBC has also addressed this by following up with a phone call or a secondary conversation and encouraging the members to participate when they can, but to also let the leadership know when they cannot. I have experienced this in NSBC's youth group when we plan an event and very few youth respond, so we do not know how many young people to expect. It is most important to be flexible and adjust the activity to the group that is present.

The differences between written and oral traditions are common among multicultural communities and can impact the worship

27. Hawn, One Bread, One Body, 21–22.

28. Black, Culturally-Conscious Worship, 67.

29. Ibid., 68.

experience. Black mentions that this often comes up in the announcements during worship.[30] At NSBC, we have found that it is important to provide announcements in written form and orally during the service, and to extend individual invitations for those most likely to be involved in the most culturally appropriate format. Since members are so varied in the kinds of announcements they will respond to, it is important to provide all of these types where appropriate.

The issue of power dynamics within a multicultural church is the most important to address. Since European-American culture is so different from most other cultures on this issue, it is extremely important for all members of the community to understand the dynamics at play. Both Hawn and Black use Eric Law's work with "high-power-distance" and "low-power-distance" cultures to understand these dynamics:

> People of high-power-distance cultures often perceive themselves as relatively powerless in the face of a powerful elite group that controls decisions and wealth ... Low-power-distance cultures, by contrast, usually have an upper class and a larger middle class ... and, as a result, believe that they have access to power and decision making.[31]

This manifests itself most commonly in church committee meetings when European-Americans dominate the conversation and leave Asian-Americans and Latinos with no voice. Hawn suggests a model called "mutual invitation,"[32] which NSBC has used in various meetings to be sure that all voices are heard.

Concluding Suggestions for NSBC

After research into theories of multicultural worship and some applications that NSBC is already doing very well, I have a few suggestions for NSBC's joint worship services. First, in light of Hawn's appeal to "select worship leaders who reflect congregational and neighborhood diversity,"[33] I think it is important for NSBC to

| *The author now moves to her synthesis—how the research informs her thinking about the reality of multicultural worship.* |

---

30. Ibid., 73.

31. Hawn, *One Bread, One Body*, 25.

32. Ibid., 26.

33. Ibid., 146–148.

continue to include more diversity in the leadership of worship, which is already done by having all the pastors participate, but should be increased by giving more responsibilities to the "minority" pastors and allowing joint worship to look more like their worship than English worship.

Second, Hawn mentions that it is important to "permeate the worship space and worship rituals with inclusive nonverbal forms of communication."[34] One way this could begin to be included more fully is in the artwork and visuals of the space. Currently, the main sanctuary and most of the common spaces are filled with Anglo-centric artwork and décor. As NSBC moves towards renovations of both the Spanish congregation's worship space and the English congregation's worship space, it is important to be thinking about incorporating the church's diversity into decisions about the décor, the beauty, and the artwork of the space.

Third, in Black's discussion of various kinds of multilingual worship, she suggests "learning the language of another" as an option for multilingual worship.[35] Understanding that learning another language is extremely difficult and uncomfortable for some, I think it is an opportunity in joint worship to support one another by teaching even very small amounts of language to our sisters and brothers. Even just learning a word here and there would be an exciting challenge for the church.

This is an excellent example of an exploratory research paper that integrates theory and practice.

Finally, in my research I was struck by how much NSBC has done effectively over the years toward living out multicultural worship and community with awareness of the various issues and with effective problem solving. I would highly commend both Black and Hawn's texts to the leaders of NSBC as informative texts for further growth in being a multicultural community. In the words of Kathy Black, "multicultural congregations are prophetic witnesses to our world, taking the lead in creating community despite the tremendous diversity among us."[36] NSBC is a church on the journey toward the banquet table of God that is set before all and where all are welcome. Let us embrace this journey with grace when we stumble and rejoicing when we dance!

---

34. Ibid., 149–153.

35. Black, *Culturally-Conscious Worship*, 33.

36. Ibid., 115.

Works Cited

Black, Kathy. *Culturally-Conscious Worship*. St. Louis: Chalice Press, 2000.

Garces-Foley, Kathleen. "New Opportunities and New Values: The Emergence of the Multicultural Church." *Annals of the American Academy of Political and Social Science* 612 (July 2007): 209–224. Accessed May 3, 2012. http://www.jstor.org/stable/25097937.

Hawn, C. Michael. *One Bread, One Body: Exploring Cultural Diversity in Worship*. Bethesda, MD: The Alban Institute, 2003.

Juel, Donald H. "Multicultural Worship: A Pauline Perspective." In *Making Room at the Table: An Invitation to Multicultural Worship*, edited by Brian K. Blount and Leonora Tubs Tisdale, 42–59. Louisville: Westminster John Knox Press, 2001.

White, Susan J. *Foundations of Christian Worship*. Louisville: Westminster John Knox Press, 2006.

* * *

CHAPTER SIX

Sermons

The very first thing I tell my new students on the first day of a workshop is that good writing is about telling the truth.—Anne Lamott, *Bird by Bird*

Sermon-Writing and Delivery—Two Sides of the Same Coin

Some of you may already have experience in writing or preaching sermons before coming to seminary, and those who haven't no doubt will have heard many sermons preached over the course of your lives. The goal of this chapter isn't to teach you how to become an excellent preacher; you'll learn to write and deliver dozens of sermons in beginning and advanced preaching courses. Our goal is to provide a basic introduction to the *process* of sermon writing—how to make the most of your own gifts and the tools available to you to craft the best sermons you possibly can.

Keep in mind, though, that sermon writing and sermon delivery are an integrated whole—rather than two separate activities, they are two dimensions of preaching. Both involve the ability to connect with listeners, share personal experience with them, and help them enter deeply into the text. Both dimensions require a unity of thought and expression, authenticity, spontaneity, and an engaging communication style. Perhaps most importantly, both call for being open to the Spirit, being present emotionally, and having an attitude of awe, humility, and expectancy.[i] If you approach sermon writing in this way, the words on the page are not just a message about the biblical text that you read aloud or speak to a congregation; instead your words become a compelling and inspiring means for bringing the text to your listeners through your own experience—your experiences in life, with the Bible, and with God.

Many pastors, both seasoned preachers and beginners, prefer to preach using only notes or with no manuscript at all, and you may decide to do this as well. For preaching classes in seminary, though, you'll be asked to write at least a couple of sermon manuscripts. Writing out a sermon is good practice for crafting sermons in the future—because the process is the same whether you're developing a full manuscript, preaching notes, or a sermon you'll preach from memory.

Types of Sermons

Because each of us brings a different combination of gifts to preaching, there are as many different types of sermons and approaches to preaching as there are individuals. If you're reading this chapter, you're probably taking an introductory preaching course right now, and your professor will outline the types of sermons you'll be called upon to write and preach. Many preaching professionals identify three basic types of sermons:

- *Expository sermon.* This type of sermon is designed to do three things: expose what the text says; explain its "meaning" to the original listeners; and apply it to our lives today.
- *Textual sermon.* A textual sermon uses stories from our own lives to illustrate a biblical text.
- *Topical sermon.* A topical sermon is built around one topic that is then illustrated with different biblical texts in order to help listeners understand the topic in their own lives.

In beginning preaching courses, your professor will provide guidelines for different types of sermons and various sermon structures. But, regardless of the type of sermon you're writing, you'll use the process of exegesis in order to uncover deeper meaning in the biblical text.

Exegesis for Sermon Writing

Using exegesis in preparation for writing a sermon is very similar to the process for writing an exegetical paper. You'll *analyze* the text to understand it in its own context (*explicatio*), and you'll *synthesize* what you've learned to contemporize it for a community of faith in the present (*applicatio*).[ii] In writing an exegetical paper, however, you'll complete these steps in a linear fashion, conducting an analysis first, then synthesizing your research to identify a common thread or a new interpretation of the text. Exegesis for sermon preparation tends to be less linear and more organic; it begins with your own deep reflection and engagement with the passage, then moves to an in-depth study of the text. Throughout the process, however, you're likely to alternative between reflection and study, moving back and forth as you discover what the passage has to say to your audience. Every preacher finds her or his own approach to sermon writing, but here's a simple process to get you started.

REFLECT ON AND ENGAGE THE TEXT

1. *Select a text.* For a preaching class, your professor will most likely assign a text or provide a choice of texts on which to write a sermon—or you may choose to focus on a lectionary passage that you plan to preach in the future. Most often, your sermon will be textual (based on the text), but if the professor gives you free reign to write a sermon on anything you want, you may decide to choose a topical approach. This means you'll have to identify several biblical texts that illustrate your topic; a Bible Concordance can be helpful for identifying passages related to certain key phrases or topics (see "Appendix B: Research Sources").

2. *Read the text.* Read the text aloud several times—different versions, if possible. Note its organization and layout, and outline how the thoughts flow. Summarize in your own words what happens in this passage. Write it out by hand, word for word, several times. Immerse yourself in the text so you are thoroughly familiar with it and can tell the story without the aid of the text itself.

3. *Note your impressions.* After you've fully immersed yourself in the text, jot down your initial impressions, any questions the passage raises for you, and preliminary sermon ideas that come to mind.

4. *Experience the text.* Meditate on the text, engaging all of your senses and emotions as you do. What feelings do you experience as you sit with and immerse yourself in the text? As you try to imagine the world of the text, what do you see, hear, feel, smell, and taste? How might it have felt for the original audience to hear and understand the words of the text? How might it help your listeners to have a sense of this?

5. *Consider your audience.* What are primary concerns facing your congregation? What are key issues in the world today? What is a real problem that the biblical text addresses? Read the text again through a variety of lenses, considering what it might be saying about you, your community, your nation, and your world. What themes in the world of the text—such as justice or inclusion—resonate for your community today?[iii]

Analyze the Text

After you've spent time reflecting on the text, you're ready to study it; you also have a reason to do so because your encounter with the passage will have raised some questions. Keep in mind that if you skip the earlier steps and do the analysis first, you won't encounter the text personally and instead will fill your mind with information you'll feel compelled to share with your listeners.

In analyzing the text, you'll use the same approaches as you do for exegetical papers, but exegesis in preparation for preaching is different in several ways. First of all, you won't be including most of your findings in your sermon; instead, you'll be using the steps of exegesis to help you discover the main proposition or idea for your sermon. Second, exegesis for sermon preparation is different in that you have to decide not only *what* is relevant to your listeners, but also *how* it's relevant. What information will help listeners apprehend the text in their lives today, and how can it open up the text to new understandings? Third, exegesis in sermon preparation is *not* the end, but the means. Once you've done the exegetical research, the challenging task still remains: to create a bridge between the world of the biblical text and the world today. A sermon is not a summary of your research on the text.[iv]

Be sure to refer to "Steps for Exegetical Analysis" in Chapter Two as you begin your analysis; also check out the resources listed in Appendix B—Research Sources, under "Liturgy, Preaching, and Worship." Remember to save all of the exegetical papers that you've written in separate, labeled file folders. They will serve as great resources for your sermons, and part of your work already will be done.

WRITE THE SERMON

Now, you're ready to write a sermon outline, a rough draft, or even notes to guide you when you deliver the sermon.

1. *Discover the proposition.* This is where you discover the big idea that will drive your sermon. What is the idea that forms the bridge between the world behind the text (the historical context), the world of the text (the form, key words, and ideas in the text), and the world in front of the text (your audience)? What is the significance of the text for the world today? How can the message of the text be transformative for your listeners?

2. *Make it relevant.* Consider a real problem or issue we are all facing right now, and allow your listeners to consider the implications in their lives. Don't give solutions, but help your audience discover how the text speaks to the issue. Your goal is not to talk about the text, but to let the text itself speak about the community, the nation, and the world.[v]

3. *Identify your supporting points.* Your sermon may have several supporting points, but the fewer you have, the more powerful and memorable it will be. Supporting points help explain the text, illustrate it, compare and contrast it in order to reinforce your proposition. Your sermon will be more powerful if you stick with one main point, one memorable idea rather than several. This does not mean over-simplifying or speaking down to your audience; it means focusing on one powerful idea.[vi]

4. *Write a conclusion.* A powerful and persuasive conclusion will make your sermon memorable.

Following this process will help you avoid the two extremes: on the one hand, a sermon that is merely a "report" on your research and, on the other hand, a sermon that is simply your own subjective interpretation of what the text means.

QUICK TIP: WHAT MAKES A GREAT SERMON?

If you think about the sermons that have had the most impact on you—the ones that have stayed with you the longest—chances are they share similar qualities. Certainly the preacher's speaking ability, presentation, and personal charisma all influence the effectiveness of a preaching experience, but there also are qualities of the sermon itself that contribute to your ability to persuade and inspire.

1. *Communicational excellence.* A sermon must be well-organized, clear, and easy to follow. It also must be engaging; preachers today must compete with a variety of media that communicate powerfully and persuasively, so you must use images, stories, and language that engage people's imaginations and hearts.

2. *Biblical faithfulness.* Good sermons are designed to help listeners understand the biblical text in a new way and, as a result, must be rooted in the Bible itself. An effective sermon is not about your personal opinion, interpretation, or experience—which is why homiletical exegesis is extremely important. Without this step, a sermon can easily become the preacher's message rather than an exposition on the biblical text arrived at through careful analysis, spiritual preparation, prayer, and reflection.

3. *Transformational power.* Good sermons allow listeners to be challenged, stretched, and changed, opening them to deepen their faith and move closer to God.[vii]

Tips for Sermon Writing

- Keep in mind that the Bible commentaries—as well as much of the research you'll do on a biblical text—express various scholars' interpretations about what the passage means. These interpretations can be very helpful for seeing the historical context or for knowing how the text has been traditionally understood. But many of these ideas (particularly those of white male European scholars) are presented as normative and universal, and they are not necessarily so. Always remember to ask yourself the question, "Whose perspective is this?"[viii]

- Avoid trying to harmonize diverse parts of the biblical text in an effort to find a unified message. Keep in mind that the different books of the Bible emerged out of a variety of times, locations, and circumstances, which means that it does not speak in one unified voice; instead, it is a living document reflecting the diversity of life. Acknowledging this is honest and more relevant to members of a congregation than trying to force a unity that isn't there; it will help them as they seek to understand the Christian "inheritance in light of the present, changing experience of faith."[ix]

- Keep in mind that the meaning of a biblical passage lies not only in the text itself, but also "behind" the text in the world of the author *and* "in front" of the text in the world of today's reader. In preaching, you bridge these three worlds, making all three meaningful and relevant to your listeners.

- Use transition statements to tell listeners what's coming, to indicate where you're headed, to reiterate an important point you've just made, to show how one point relates to another, and to remind listeners of the primary theme or topic of your sermon.[x]

- In most seminary writing, you'll choose language, style, tone, and voice suitable for an academic setting (see "Style Guidelines" and "Academic vs. Personal Voice" in Chapter Four). In writing sermons, you'll use a style that is much more personal, anecdotal, evocative, inspirational, and even poetic. You can use rhyme, alliteration, and metaphor to reach your listeners on many levels. You'll also be writing for speaking, which means using a less formal style than you would employ for writing (for example, "can't" instead of "cannot," etc.).

- Avoid talking about ideas such as mercy, justice, love, or discipleship in abstract terms. Instead, illustrate these ideas with concrete examples—stories or images that translate these larger concepts into real-life examples that have meaning and impact.[xi]

Using Inclusive Language

An important element of writing in the seminary is learning to use inclusive language. The goal is twofold: to avoid being insensitive and to speak to as diverse an audience as possible by paying attention to the terminology you use. Following these guidelines will help you with inclusive language:

1. *Eliminate gender bias.* There are several acceptable alternatives to the default pronoun, "he." One option is to use "she and he" or "hers and his" in place of the masculine pronoun. Another is to recast the sentence in the plural and so that "they" and "their" can take the place of "he" and "his." A less awkward solution is to vary the pronouns, alternating between "she" and "he" throughout a paper, but being consistent within a sentence or a paragraph. Rewriting the sentence to avoid pronouns altogether is another possibility. Watch out for terms like "man" and "mankind" and replace them with non-sexist language such as "person" or "humankind."

2. *Avoid masculine images for God.* When referring to God, many students choose to repeat the name rather than use "he" and re-inscribe a masculine image: "God is the creator of the universe, and God existed before time began."

3. *Stay away from labels.* Watch for labels that unintentionally disparage a person or a group. When referring to various racial, ethnic, and other cultural groups, use the names preferred by the members of those groups. Avoid indicating an individual's gender, race, ethnicity, or age unless those details are relevant to the topic—and when you do choose to include information about these factors, make sure you do so for *all* individuals you're discussing.

4. *Avoid making people "other."* Do not assume that your demographic group is the "norm" and everyone who is different from you is "other." In your writing, be careful with sentences such as "when we invite others into this country…" Statements like this imply that there is a group of people ("we") who are making decisions for everyone else.

5. *Be careful with biblical metaphors.* The biblical text is full of images of light and darkness, and unconsciously using these oppositional ideas to represent goodness and sin can be offensive to people of color. The same goes for sight and blindness and other images that may unfairly depict certain qualities as negative.

* * *

Sermon: The Book of Revelation

Rivers, Robes, and Mothers
Revelation 22: 1–5, 12–14, 16–17, 20–21
Rebecca Wilson

Then the angel showed me the river of the water of life, bright as crystal, flowing from the throne of God and of the Lamb through the middle of the street of the city. On either side of the river is the tree of life with its twelve kinds of fruit, producing its fruit each month; and the leaves of the tree are for the healing of the nations. Nothing accursed will be found there any more. But the throne of God and of the Lamb will be in it, and his servants will worship him; they will see his face, and his name will be on their foreheads. And there will be no more night; they need no light of lamp or sun, for the Lord God will be their light, and they will reign for ever and ever.

'See, I am coming soon; my reward is with me, to repay according to everyone's work. I am the Alpha and the Omega, the first and the last, the beginning and the end.' Blessed are those who wash their robes, so that they will have the right to the tree of life and may enter the city by the gates.

'It is I, Jesus, who sent my angel to you with this testimony for the churches. I am the root and the descendant of David, the bright morning star.' The Spirit and the bride say, 'Come.' And let everyone who hears say, 'Come.' And let everyone who is thirsty come. Let anyone who wishes take the water of life as a gift.

The one who testifies to these things says, 'Surely I am coming soon.' Amen. Come, Lord Jesus! The grace of the Lord Jesus be with all the saints. Amen.

Christian life is a journey and the story of our collective journey begins in Genesis. As creation unfolds, we find ourselves in a garden. Lush and green. Beautiful and fruitful. The garden is watered and sustained by a river flowing out of paradise. For early cultures a river was considered a gift and a giver of life. A source of blessing and nourishment.

> The sermon begins with vivid visual imagery to draw listeners in and prompt them to use their imaginations in hearing the message.

If we enter the river in Genesis and navigate its course, we will pass through Exodus, where the young daughter of a pharaoh rescues a baby floating in a basket alone. Passing through the Psalms, we see poetic prayers comparing God's love to bountiful streams. We read of people coming to the river's edge in search of peace and comfort. Simply wanting to be in the presence of the holy. In Lamentations, the river is said to be the tears of people crying out over injustice and destruction.

As we reach the New Testament, rivers become a place of baptism. Jesus is lowered into the waters of the Jordan by his cousin John. He rises from the river with increased power and passion to do the will of God. His willingness to enter the river challenges his followers to do the likewise, *immerse yourself in living water and never be the same again.* If we dock long enough in the Gospel of John, we hear Jesus remind those who believe that even from their own hearts living water flows.

> *Listeners already know that "river" is a primary theme of the sermon. Here, the river motif is used as a metaphor for journeying through the biblical story but also as a reminder of baptism.*

Finally, if we stay the course for all sixty-six books, we find ourselves in Revelation. Today's reading not only takes us to the final book, but to the Bible's final chapter as well. Revelation can be a scary place to anchor if you do not have maps and other nautical tools. Many of the images are frightening. If the image of a calm river brings peace, then images of beasts bring panic. Many interpretations of Revelation draw on our fears, lifting up violence and destruction. But reading today's text, I hear and see hope. The final chapter of the final book takes us back to the beginning of the Bible's first book. It takes us back to the river.

Revelation is a letter written to the seven churches regarding the following of God's commandments. Those who stay strong in the face of persecution and temptation are encouraged to remain faithful. Those who follow society's commands rather than God's are given a stern warning.

> *The sermon includes just this one brief section on the background of the text. Most sermons include too much background. Whenever you include any exegesis you have done, it is important to make it relevant to the topic and to listeners.*

Revelation is full of vivid symbolism. Some take the symbols literally and use them to point to the coming destruction of the earth. I am more in camp with those who see Revelation as a revealing of God's heavenly vision here on earth. Love, peace and justice here and now.

We left Genesis on a river, which is the water source for an abundant garden. We are now standing at the riverbank of Revelation. An angel tells us that this river is as bright as crystal. It is the watering source for the tree of life. This tree is the nourishment and the healing for the nations.

Let us paddle a little farther up the river. There are some women I want you to meet.

Do you see those women? Near the tree? Gathering food and water? Caring for their children? Washing their robes? | *This is an excellent use of questions to help listeners visualize the scene.*

There is hope in Revelation. There are seven pronounced blessings, the final one right here. Blessed are they that wash their robes that they will have the right to the tree of life. These women, as do women all over the world, labor hard to care for and to feed their families. The tree gives them fruit. The river provides drink and a place to bathe and wash their robes.

We might not all walk around in robes, but we wear clothes and those clothes need washing. Literally speaking, laundry, especially without a washer and dryer in your home, is hard work. Figuratively, washing robes means that these women keep the commandments of God. That they are diligent and faithful. They press on even when life is hard. They journey to the river, despite the obstacles and challenges to getting there. Their hands are blistered. Their feet are calloused. Yet they continue traveling to the river: filling their buckets, picking crops and washing their robes.

Do not forget what you have seen here, but there are a few more places I want to take you.

The river flowing out of Eden divides out into four branches. Pishon flows toward a land of sweetness and gold. Gihon flows around Cush, modern day Ethiopia. The Tigris flows east and the Euphrates west of Mesopotamia. From these four rivers, other rivers have formed. And this is where we are headed.

Traveling the African Nile we see women of immense courage. Washing robes. Keeping the faith in the middle of famine, war, and religious violence. Wondering how they are going to care for husbands and children with Malaria. With HIV or AIDS. | *The river motif now connects listeners to a present-day context.*

Traveling the Yellow River in the north of China we see women of incredible determination. Washing robes. Keeping commandments in the face of persecution and oppression. Many still valued only for their ability to conceive and birth male children.

Traveling the Amazon in South America we see women of strong character. Washing robes and keeping commandments even though their land has been taken over by developers. Even though it is cheaper to buy corn from another country than to grow it for themselves.

And close to home, traveling the Detroit River, we see women that much of society has forgotten or ignored. These brave women get up every day to wash robes and keep the commandments. Trying to maintain their dignity while looking for work where there is none. Searching for water that is not contaminated or food that is not spoiled. Breathing air that is some of the most polluted in the country. Trying to educate their children in a system where the drop-out rate is greater than fifty percent.

I know this is not an easy river ride to take, but my hope is that in seeing these women along the banks, you will remember your own experiences with the river of life and be inspired to get back in and to bring someone else along with you.

> *The sermon interprets symbols and imagery of the text, but at the same time opens listeners up to going deeper with their own understanding of it.*

Maybe you know what it is like to have a never-ending pile of robes to be washed or challenges to be faced. **Come to the river!**

Maybe you want to help someone with their washing. Maybe you have a robe to spare. **Come to the river!**

Maybe you feel outside of God's love. Unworthy of God's grace. **Well, come to the river!**

Maybe you have encountered God's love and grace in a way that changed your very being. And you want to share it with others. **Well, please come to the river!**

> *This sermon does not assume all listeners to be in the same place, but speaks to them wherever they are at this moment.*

Some see Revelation as a warning of the chaos and devastation to come. I see Revelation as a glimpse, a pre-screening of the coming kingdom of God. A world centered on the river of life. Where everyone has access. Where the water is clean and crystal. Where no one is thirsty. No one is hungry because the river is irrigating the crops of the field. There is no fighting. No violence. No war. The calm of the river serves as a reminder of the peace that God has instilled in our hearts and our relations. The river is not owned or controlled by anyone. There are no fees or dues to pay. No forms to sign for entry. **One and all come to the river!**

> *The repetition is powerful and memorable; it is a form of "verbal poetry." Here, it is used as an invitation and a call to action.*

I had my own come-to-the river experience years ago. I was part of a group that traveled to Nicaragua. Affectionately known as the land of lakes and rivers. Most of our time was spent at the Casa Materna. A place for rural women with high-risk pregnancies. The

Six. Sermons

Casa was birthed by women who sought to address the high rate of maternal death in the country. The Casa's work is twofold. They deal directly with pregnant women just before and after delivery. They also do outreach and education in the rural, mountain communities from where the women come. Our group traveled to one of these communities.

We were not on a riverboat, but rather we were crammed in a small pick-up truck. The roads were rough. At times it seemed we were not even on a road. The rainy season was nearing an end. Flooding made many roads impassable. It poured for the last half of our ride.

Yet, as we arrived at the village of Samulali, the rain stopped, the sun appeared, and we were met by about thirty children, all of who were born to mothers served by the Casa. These children accompanied us up a large hill to a small brick home, with open holes where windows might be, and with a dirt floor. We were welcomed by the whole community. The mothers very proudly introduced and showed off their children. Everyone cleaned and dressed in their best robes. The women told stories of how the Casa had not only helped with the delivery of their children, but also with the betterment of their lives. They received health education. They learned how to grow and prepare healthy food and how to purify water for drinking. They were taught about their rights as women. And about the signs and dangers of domestic abuse.

Inside the small house, they shared with us their corn and beans and some sweet treats. As it was nearing time to leave, I passed through the kitchen where a young mother was holding her baby. I asked if I could take a picture of her and the baby. She said yes, and I did. Then the mother pointed at my camera. Motioned that she wanted it. Then she pointed to her baby and motioned that she wanted me to hold her. In a moment of holy and life-giving exchange, she took a picture of me holding her baby girl.

At this time in my life, I was very unsure of who I was and where I was headed. I was not really sure where I belonged. I was struggling with God and with the idea that maybe I was not quite worthy of God's love and grace. I was still a passive participant of life. Sitting on the river's edge. Fearful of fully getting in.

> *The preacher relates a touching personal story and ties it beautifully to the sermon topic and to Mother's Day, when this sermon was preached. The story also is a concrete example of the hope she mentioned earlier.*

In that moment, holding that baby, I was literally holding the gift of life. And I felt more connected to the source of life than I ever had. That this mother trusted me, a stranger, with her baby and wanted a picture of her baby and me together was like the experience of stepping into a cool, calm river on a really hot day. Refreshing and renewing. That this little baby looked up at me and laughed as I held her was a reminder that we do not get to the river of life alone. The river of life flows for us all, but sometimes we need someone who has already encountered the current to lead us from the banks to the center.

So, on this day set aside for honoring mothers, let us also honor those women and men and babies that we have encountered along the way that have led us to the river. Those who have shown us the love of God. That have inspired us by their commitment to following the commandments and their faithfulness to the washing of robes. That have challenged us to live like Jesus. To embrace the power and passion of our baptismal vows.

> *This is a good example of what Paul Scott Wilson refers to as a "four-page sermon"—(1) trouble in the Bible; (2) trouble in the world; (3) grace in the Bible; and (4) grace in the world.*

I do not believe that journeys end. They change in course and direction, but they do not end. The book of Revelation, it may be the final book of the Bible, but it is not the end of the story. There is still much to be written. As children of the river, we are called to be active participants in the writing of this story. God calls us to share our experience with the river. To share what we know about the experiences of the women we have seen on the river today.

> *By prompting listeners to travel this journey with her, the preacher helps them experience the sermon rather than just hear the words she speaks—so that hearing the sermon is an act of worship.*

Come to the river. Drink the water of life. Eat the fruit that heals, that you may be a source of blessing and nourishment for the world.

Amen.

* * *

Sermon: The Gospel of Matthew

Seismic Love: A Sermon Based on Matthew 21:1–10
Advanced Preaching
Mary Jane Huber

The earth shook under her feet and the building around her began to crumble. In a few minutes, Emma's world came crashing in around her. Things that were high were brought low, things that were low were raised up. The city was in turmoil.

> *Interesting beginning that keeps the listener in suspense.*

Emma waited for six hours, wondering if she would live to make her wedding day. Listening for signs of help; shouting out, "save me! Save Me!" Then it came. Her rescue; one by one the pieces of the building were removed and she was brought out into freedom. All this time, her fiancé, Christopher, was waiting on the street. Holding his breath, hoping against hope for a chance of a new life. His focus was on love, love for Emma and also love and compassion for all those who were searching, or being searched for, in the aftermath of the recent earthquake in New Zealand. Stories like Emma and Christopher's have been played out around the world over the past year, the past month and even more so this week, most notably in Japan. The earth itself seems unsettled during our Lenten journey to the cross.

> *This now sets the sermon in contemporary times, although up to this point, listeners were not sure the topic was biblical.*

We have news reports from another time and place—we know it as Palm Sunday. Have you ever wondered about those reports—are they part of a 24-hour news spin? The amazing thing is that the report that gets told annually is one that has children jubilantly shouting Hosannas and waving palms. This is a day, in many congregations, when children have free rein to make noise and shout in the sanctuary for a few moments—moments that are an attempt to re-create the events of Palm Sunday—events, when we look closer, that were really anything but joy-filled—hopeful, yes—but joy filled? I am not so certain.

> *This opening sentence leads into an excellent passage that sets a vivid scene of what we now know is Palm Sunday.*

The Scriptures tell us that the whole city of Jerusalem was in turmoil when Jesus entered, humbly on a donkey (or two). The people, adults with the children, shouted hosanna—hosanna—blessed is he who comes—A shout of praise from the Psalms—the Hallel Psalms that were used by pilgrims on their way up to Jerusalem for Passover. Hosanna was already on their lips—Hosanna was already in the air—but, as Christ comes, Hosanna is now in their hearts—in their hearts as, perhaps, they lay claim to an ancient meaning of the word. In ancient Hebrew, the word meant "Save us! Save Now!" How this changes the tenor of the event. From a joyous blessing to a cry for salvation! Salvation from the bondage and oppression of being just barely tolerated—Did the Roman soldiers or authorities understand that what was being shouted this year was very different than what had been shouted the year before? The people shouted Hosanna, they waved their palm branches, but things were not as they had been. They laid their garments on the road to prepare the way for the victor—they prepared the way of the Lord! "Hosanna—blessed is he—Hosanna Save us!"

The whole city was in turmoil. This turmoil was a churned up, anxious, excitement about not only the situation, but it was a turmoil that meant an overturning of the way things were. It was a turmoil that would shake the foundations of power and structure of the religious authority, the city, and the world. It was a seismic turmoil. Those in who were in high positions would be brought low and the lowly would be raised up—The shouts proclaim Jesus as the Son of David! The Messiah—the one who saves! The words echoed off the walls of Jerusalem. The city was in turmoil because what was happening was more than an exchange of power—empire for empire—it was a transformation of power. The power of love, a power of the value of each person, the power of shalom was now the victor.

| *This is the subject sentence.*

| *This final sentence leads well into the next paragraph.*

Shalom, justice and peace is what sustains us when all else seems to fall away. And it is this desire for peace, not just the absence of oppression or fighting, but peace that lives out the vision of God's kingdom here on earth—that is a time and space, a way of being, that values each person and sees the God-given gifts in each person free from need, free from want; a vision that challenges us to consider how we are in relationship to one another.

This Palm Sunday our world is being shaken by seismic activity not unlike the kind that shook Jerusalem 2,000 years ago. People throughout North Africa and the Middle East are calling out "Save

| *Good tie-in to today's world.*

us!" and seeking to claim the power that transforms their lives and brings real justice. The act of one man, Mohamed Bouazizi, in Tunisia, stated boldly that he, and those like him, have value. His act, crazy or inspired, has touched the hearts and minds of many. The oppressed in Egypt, Iraq, Oman and Yemen, and Syria have found their voice, they have cried out to the powers that be—"Save us!" "Save us!"—and have heard back that the power for the transformation does not reside in the existing power structures. These voices seek leaders, new governments, not transitional governments, but transformational governments that will have a greater vision for the people and that will guide their country to a way of living that sees how valuable each person is.

God not only promised such a way of being, a kingdom on earth as in heaven, but it has been delivered. It is already present—the power that says "yes, you are of value, the empire cannot crush you—the power is the power of God's love for all people." Hosanna! Save us!

For many of us, living out of, and into, transformational love is a challenge. It can go terribly wrong when the powers of this world, the power of power, when power itself is made into a god. The actions of Libya, the actions in Sudan, the actions in Ivory Coast, and even actions in local business and politics, show us that, when these powers of the world are in charge, when people do not matter, when ideology and self interest are the guiding factors, there is oppression, destruction and loss of life.

| *Another transitional sentence that then opens up the paragraph to contemporary times for listeners.* |

This Palm Sunday is our opportunity to think again about what it means to be a follower of Jesus. One who cries out for God's saving grace. A follower of the way that is the way of love, a way that will not "other" anyone, but challenges and confronts systems, persons and powers that do. It is the hope of faith that all those who struggle for justice, all those who believe in the saving grace of God, will have all the courage they need, the strength they need, all the patience they need, all the wisdom they need to seek God's shalom, to honor the neighbor and to love the enemy.

| *Here, the author returns to the main theme.* |

Let us raise our palms, raise them, and call out to God to save us.

- From financial concerns, personal and institutional—Save Us!
- From the pain of broken relationships—Save Us!
- From our own desire for security—Save Us!

- From the dis-ease in the world—Save Us!
- From concern about our future ministry—Save Us!
- From the limited way we love our neighbors—Save Us!
- From our blindness that prevents us from seeing Jesus in our midst—Save Us!

> *This is a very good use of the repetitious poetic refrain.*

Save us—but you and I know that it doesn't matter what we say, so much as it matters whether we allow the seismic activity of God's transforming love to take place in our heart—to shake our foundations and realign them with God's purpose in this world—love of neighbor, love of enemy, love eternal that cannot be stopped.

So let us open ourselves to the presence of God so we can shout and know that God will not forsake us, that God will not let our cries go unheard! Save us so that we may be released from the bondage of fear, racism, prejudice, anxiety and insecurity—so that in the freedom of God's love our lives our lives can be lived differently—lived in grace, and the responsibility that comes with it—the responsibility to love God and our neighbor, no matter what.

The Lord that is present in this sanctuary tonight was also present a few weeks ago when Emma and Christopher were married in a town outside of Christ Church, New Zealand, in borrowed suits, in a still standing church, in the presence of a still speaking God, whose love embraces not only the newlyweds, by the newly widowed, the newly childless, and the newly liberated—valuing each, loving each beyond measure and inviting us to shout, "Save us!" to the world that needs to hear, and experience, the seismic turmoil of God's love made real.

> *The author has come full circle to her opening. This is the strength of a good sermon.*

May the people of faith be a living witness to God's love—the greatest power in the world—Love which cannot be constrained by borders, politics, race or clan. Love that is freely given to all. May this love and the hope it inspire make the seismic action of Palm Sunday be felt in our communities, and around the world. Hosanna!

> *Strong repetition of the refrain to close.*

Blessed be the one who comes in the name of the Lord! Hosanna! Save us!

* * *

CHAPTER SEVEN

Journal Articles

Half of my life is an act of revision.—John Irving

It is not possible to generalize about writing for an academic journal, even in theology. Obviously, each professional journal has different requirements and the wise writer checks those requirements before attempting to offer an article for publication. However, we hasten to add here that one does not have to be a full-fledged Ph.D. graduate with a teaching position in an elite institution, or a world-renowned pastor with televised preaching skills, in order to have an article considered for publication. Both of us had articles published in well-regarded journals when we were master's students, papers sent in by professors with whom we were studying, unbeknown to us at the time. Imagine our surprise when we were contacted by the journals, asking permission to publish our articles. To say we jumped at the chance is an understatement.

So don't sell yourself short—or underestimate your abilities. If an assignment for a class happens to fit the type of work that a journal publishes, and if a professor sees promise in your writing, you may have to do some revision, or you may not, but nonetheless, you are on your way. Some of you, like me (Diane), may come from a background in English literature; I combined my literature work, upon occasion, with the study of theology or ethics, which was one of the fields of study for my doctorate. I also had a concentration in feminist theology for my doctoral exams, which led me to study theology and history, leading me to look at the life of Frances Willard. The journal article was actually a final paper written in a course in religion and gender studies which my professor, Rosemary Radford Ruether, sent off to the journal in the United Kingdom without my knowledge (for which

I am very grateful). This is also a reason to keep all your papers in separate labeled files; you never know when they'll prove useful, either as sermon topics or for later adaptation for submission to journals.

A word about publishing and journal "quirks": *Feminist Theology*, for example, the journal in which the Frances Willard article appeared in the U.K., required relatively little changing from the original course paper. As with most journal articles, I was required to write and include an abstract, something you should learn how to write. An abstract is simply a short, usually one paragraph summary of your piece of writing, whether it is an article, a master's thesis, or even a dissertation. Obviously, it will be somewhat longer for a dissertation, but people are often fooled into thinking they can write pages for their abstract for their dissertation and they cannot. This is an exercise in learning to be concise and accurate, in learning to think clearly and sum up an elaborate idea in a relatively small space. After the abstract, *Feminist Theology* asks for footnotes, but does not want a "Works Cited" or "Bibliography" page at the end of the article. It also does not want "Endnotes." This made for easy writing. A proof copy was sent to me by email to check over, and that was that.

Other journals may require more intense labor; each is different. I didn't solicit this consideration of publication. If you and a professor or a mentor think something you've written is worthy of publication, spend time looking through all the journals or magazines in your seminary or divinity school library and see which one looks like a good fit. It's not a good idea to submit the same article to multiple places all at the same time. Consider what you are going to do if they all accept you. Or if two or more accept you. Remember, you are not being paid for this writing. Later, when you become famous, they, perhaps the most famous of them, will call upon you to write and then you may be paid, but not as you start out.

A word about length:

If the journal specifies, as they do, number of words, or something like "between 1500 to 2000 words," they mean it. Publishing is all about keeping within the borders and pages in a journal. If your piece is too long, they will either not consider it at all, or if they think is worthwhile to ask you to edit it down, they will give you a chance to cut and crop. This is very difficult for many of us to do—this is, as Jane Austen once said, "our own darling child." I once submitted an article to the Journal of American Literature in England that I knew was too long when I sent it. But I just couldn't get myself to cut anything. The publisher sent it back, telling me it was twice as long as could be considered, but if I would cut it in half, they would publish it. I wrote back and, arrogantly I think in retrospect, asked if they would consider publishing it over two issues. You can imagine the response I received. The publisher was kind enough still to give me a chance to chop the article in half for publication, but three years later, it still sits languishing, unpublished, because I can't see what I can possibly take out. Thus, the dangers of not keeping to the word count in the first place.

These articles, of course, are copyrighted and must not be used again in another publication or book without the express permission of the journal. That information is printed on the inside cover of the journal itself. To familiarize yourself with the types of articles a journal publishes, read through a number before you think about submitting something for publication.

Writing for Publication

If you, or your professor, believe you have a piece good enough to be submitted for publication in an academic journal, it's a good idea to revise it before you submit it. Certainly you'll revise it according to the journal's specifications, length requirements, and citation style guidelines, but you may want to consider looking at other aspects as well.

1. Note how other scholars shape their arguments, and think about revising your article to follow some common organizational patterns. You'll notice in reading articles in scholarly journals that they often include the following elements: (1) statement of a question, problem, or issue to be explored; (2) brief background on conventional approaches to the question or ways of understanding the problem; (3) presentation of the author's argument or interpretation, with support to illustrate how it disproves or enhances earlier interpretations; (4) a response to potential objections to the new idea; and (5)

a summary or conclusion that restates the argument and discusses the broader implications in the field.[i]

2. Following blogs is another way to gain a sense of writing for a general audience. Although each blogger has a unique voice, you'll notice patterns that can help you find your own style. (An excellent blog for theology, religion, and the Bible is *Faith and Theology*, http://www.faith-theology.com/; see also the comprehensive list, "100 Exceptional Websites for Christian Theologians," at http://theology-degreesonline.com/christian-theology/ or "Top 100 Theology Blogs" at http://www.christiancolleges.com/blog/2009/top-100-theology-blogs/). You also may want to contribute an opinion or editorial piece as a guest blogger as a way to gain practice in writing for the public square (sites such as ABC's *Religion and Ethics* allow guest contributions, http://www.abc.net.au/religion/).

3. Writing for a general academic audience differs from the writing you do in seminary. When writing for professors, you assume a certain level of knowledge of the subject, but when writing for publication in academic journals, you must target both knowledgeable and less informed general readers. Whether you're writing for theological journals, religious TV or radio programs, blogs, news weekly columns, general magazines, websites, or books, when writing for a general audience, you write clearly and purposefully, with confidence and authority, in a voice that is uniquely yours.[ii]

* * *

Journal Article: Feminist Theology
Imagining God in Our Ways:
The Journals of Frances E. Willard
Diane N. Capitani

Abstract

This paper examines the journals of Frances W. Willard, founder and organizer of the Woman's Christian Temperance Union in the United States, and their revelations about the gender battle that raged within the psyche of Willard and other young women of her day. The failure of organized Christianity to provide solace or unbiased counsel to women such as Willard is apparent in a close reading of Willard's work. Within the pages of her journals, the struggle she faced is obvious on almost every page; her struggle with what society said she should do, and what she knew she was capable of doing, is present for all to see. The paper argues that because, however, she lived in the United States within a short window of nineteenth-century time, she was able to form a "Boston Marriage" with a young

| *Note that an abstract should be no longer than one-half to two-thirds of a page; it should simply give a brief overview of the subject of the article, book, or dissertation.* |

woman who provided her with the comfort and support she needed. The Boston Marriage, arguably, was available only for relatively well-to-do, white-middle-class women of an educated class, who had attended college and, because they were able to find a "service" career of some kind, could live together in harmony. Enlightened families, like that of Henry James, were able to support female members of their class who did not "fit in" to societal norms of the day and accept their lifestyle, while negating the sexuality of it. Organized religion, however, did not, and it is the failure of her church to help her find a way of life she can tolerate about which Willard writes.

| *The article begins with two quotes, which establish the problem the article attacks—as well as the problem for the church and Willard.* |

You shall not lie with a male as with a woman; it is an abomination (Lev. 18.22)

So God created humankind in his image, in the image of God he created them; male and female he created them (Gen. 1.27).

Much of organized Christian theology has struggled (and continues to do so) with these two arguably contradictory quotations from Leviticus and Genesis that concern themselves with gender issues. Genesis appears to establish a genderless religion, both male and female created equally in the image of God, a dualism that sets up a paradigm of gender equality that the Church has not followed. Male and female are interchangeable. There is no mention of sexual roles or subordination, in the two biblical passages given above. The creation of two | *Here is the thesis of the article.* |
humans with separate gender roles seems to come after the Fall. It is impossible to create genderless religion without deconstructing religious hierarchy and sexual constructs. Organized religions of all types have always chosen to ignore any Bible passage that conflicts with the established orthodoxy because all are built upon a hierarchical pyramid with a white, male patriarch at the top. "Weaker" members of humanity occupy successively less important

roles in the structure. What one has, then, in Christian religious structure, is a selective choice of meaning in the use of the Bible, a deconstructing and reconstructing of the Word of God to make it fit the need of the moment.

| *The paragraph goes on to unpack the contradiction in Genesis.*

Organized Christianity has failed, and continues to fail, to address the issue of same-sex relationships in any constructive way. It has also failed to address the position and needs of women within Church and society. Those inroads for women or the gay community that have been made have been small ones.

| *This is the topic sentence of this paragraph.*

The Church has continued with patronizing attitudes toward women, particularly in leadership roles, where the idea of a genderless God has not caught on. But the congregations within the Churches have not accepted it either, which allows the problem to continue and worsen. The idea of a totally accepting God is controversial; yes, God forgives, but... The Church, one can argue, pays lip service to the idea of a God tolerant of same-sex relationships. I would argue that mainline denominations do not really see God as all-inclusive. Whatever adherence is given to the abstract ideal emotionally, people do not seem to want to believe God is inclusive.

A variety of contemporary explorations of the subject, like Larry Graham's *Discovering Images of God*,[1] attempt to assure us that wise leaders exist within the clergy to minister to the gay and lesbian community, for example; he relates narratives of the way this could

| *Again, here is a topic sentence that introduces the topic to be explored in the paragraph; it cites a well-regarded book.*

work by constructing a theology based on the image of God that is all-inclusive and reassuring. I would argue, however, that the Christian Church has not done this historically, nor is it currently doing this in any broad way. Reflecting on the narratives Graham gives us, after having just explored the journals of Frances E. Willard, leader of the WCTU, gives one pause. Willard expresses the same concerns as the contemporary gay and lesbian community of Graham's work and struggles with the same vision of self that people such as a young white man named David Wilkinson hold, who saw himself as deviant because the message the Christian

---

1. Larry Graham, *Discovering Images of God* (Louisville: Westminster John Knox Press, 1997).

Church had given him was that same-sex feelings were unnatural and sinful. Willard would not have sought counsel from a minister; in her day and time, late nineteenth-century North America, were not to have sexual thoughts at all, let alone deviant ones. She was forced to confide in her journals instead. An examination of these journals is illuminating because of the picture of the failure of both God and Church to make her comfortable with her own identity. A close look is telling: the same struggle goes on for women of the gay and lesbian community when they face their Church today. Condemnation with the words of Leviticus has not moved on much since the 1800s.

| *The paragraph turns to the main subject—Frances Willard.* |

Willard participated in several unofficial "Boston Marriages" (as these relationships between women were called then). They were common among educated, career-oriented, comfortably provided for young women of the white middle class in the mid-to-late nineteenth century. Within the bonds of these relationships, women of Willard's type found the support, understanding, and acceptance that the Church could not or would not provide. Within their circle of friends and colleagues, these friendships were accepted, as women today find acceptance in support groups and friendships and the gay community finds such support within itself. Important is the place of the Boston Marriage as precursor to gay and lesbian relationships today and the exploration of the historical struggle of women like Frances Willard to find a place within religion and society present in contemporary life stories.

| *The author introduces the "Boston Marriage."* |

"I love women so curiously—I am *sorry* that I do. I am so careful of them—feel as if no one had the right to be familiar with them—I'm so ashamed to put it down but there it is, part of the great Deep in Me"[2]: the voice of Frances Willard in her personal journal of 1861, her entry penned on 28 January. Willard, like a number of other young, intellectual, educated women of her day, struggled with her inability to "love" men in the way that she found she

| *This paragraph begins quotes from Willard's own journals that will continue throughout the article and provide strength for the position the paper is taking: that these were real feelings Willard harbored all through her life, that her church refused to help her with.* |

---

2. Carolyn DeSwarte Gifford, ed., *Writing Out My Heart: Selections from the Journal of Frances E. Willard, 1855–1896* (Urbana: University of Illinois Press, 1995), 25.

loved women. Willard's diaries and letters are full of references of this kind, detailing the struggle that she engaged in, not just in the realm of "career," but in the more personal realm of human male-female relationships. Willard eventually engaged in a number of close relationships with other young women, entering into several Boston Marriages over the years. These close "affairs" between women of the late nineteenth century, impossible to find acceptable in North American society of the day, flourished during a short space of time in the nineteenth century for a variety of reasons.

| *The end of this paragraph leads into the beginning of the next.* |
| *Here the author begins the discussion of the Boston Marriage and its particular place in American history.* |

The idea of a Boston Marriage came about at exactly the right time and place. The Boston Marriage:

was used in late nineteenth-century New England to describe a long-term monogamous relationship between two otherwise unmarried women. The women were generally financially independent of men, either through inheritance or because of a career. They were usually feminists, New Women, often pioneers in a profession. They were also very involved in culture and in social betterment, and these female values, which they shared with each other, formed a strong basis for their life together.

Faderman finds that "late nineteenth century America, and even (or rather, especially) proper Boston, believed that there was [a] potential [for the development of a fine and sensitive character] in love between women."[3] She argues that in those days, "it was assumed (at least by those outside the relationship) that love between women was asexual, unsullied by evils of carnality."[4] Consequently, a possibly sex-hating Victorian society of more intellectual leanings could find it acceptable that some women, higher-minded perhaps, devoted to a life of the mind rather than the flesh, could live at a different level than others. These were women who took the cult of true womanhood to its extreme, creating the perfect picture of devotion to others by removing themselves selflessly from the "normal" pleasures of the hearth of the Victorian mother. Their families eventually became those they came to rescue: the unloved, the alcoholic, the widow, the orphan, and the immigrant. Charity cancelled out sex.

Frances Willard occupied the same sort of position as the

---

3. Lillian Faderman, *Surpassing the Love of Men* (New York: William Morrow, 1981), 190.

4. Ibid., 190.

women of East Coast Boston Marriages. She was intelligent (although her diaries indicate that she never really thought so), educated, able to pursue teaching so that she could be self-supporting, eventually the power behind the Women's Christian Temperance Union (saving the alcoholic). While her family was not as wealthy as those of some of the other women discussed in this piece (Annie Fields, for example was the widow of the publisher James T. Fields when she embarked on her Boston Marriage with Sarah Orne Jewett, the writer), Willard was able to live comfortably. This seems to have been a prerequisite to most types of freedom. Both of Willard's parents valued education, so she grew up, like most of the others who favored Boston Marriages, in a house that valued books. Born in New York Frances moved with her family to Oberlin, Ohio at a young age, then, due to her father's ill health, to Wisconsin, where she lived an isolated childhood, with none but her siblings for companionship. The Willard children were educated through their mother's efforts; their father, Josiah Willard, placed more importance on the education of his son Oliver, of course, than on the education of his daughters. Frances was a tomboy; life in a rural setting allowed her freedom to be one, another characteristic she shared with other women of the Boston Marriage. Her mother did not discourage her interest in non-feminine things, a fact Frances appreciated all her life in her continued closeness to her mother. She hated "women's work" and the way women were forced to dress, even though, at age 16, she was forced to finally adapt to the norm for females. Her mother, however, had allowed her to grow and believe in freedom for women as well as men, her greatest gift to her daughter. Eventually Frances and her sister Mary were allowed to attend the Milwaukee Female College in 1857; her Aunt Sarah was instrumental in this, as she possessed enough education to be a history professor there.[5] Aunt Sarah was to prove a staunch supporter later in Frances's life when Frances turned down her opportunity to marry Charles Fowler, an action deeply lamented by the rest of the family, even her mother.

| *This paragraph develops a picture of Frances Willard as fitting the profile of the woman who was socially able to be part of the Boston Marriage group.* |

| *Willard's family history, developed here, is similar to those of other women who will have Boston Marriages.* |

5. Ibid., 203.

Perhaps important to note in Willard's case is that her father discouraged shows of affection from children after the age of two years. How dreadful it must have been for a small child to be refused a bedtime hug! The picture of the stern male, holding and controlling the purse strings, that Willard talks about in her writings comes out of her relationship with her father, and her emotional crippling that was partially responsible for her later struggle to show any sort of affection to men. There is no question that her father disliked her thread of independence and her desire to be self-supporting and control her own money.[6] The family's eventual move to Evanston, Illinois allowed her even more freedom to pursue her teaching career at the Female College (at what is now Northwestern University) than she had before (even though she did not really like teaching).

| *Note that the end of this paragraph flows into the beginning of the next.* |

In Evanston, Frances Willard fell in love with Charles Fowler, a young Methodist minister and a member of her brother's class at the seminary. At least, she felt that she must be in love, but a reading of her journals tells us that what appealed to her was Charles's intellect, his way of speaking, his willingness to listen to *her*. At this point in her life, at the age of 22, Frances struggled with following the correct female path, which many of these women did try to follow. Charting her relationship with Charles Fowler through her journals of 1861 reveals that it was not physical attraction that Frances felt for Charles Fowler, but intellectual equality, or the feeling that he gave her that intellectual equality was possible between men and women. When she met Fowler, she was struggling with illness—common enough among young women of this time who chaffed at female roles and wanted a career instead. She had also formed a close, strong friendship with a young woman named Mary Bannister, for whom she later admitted a real attraction, one that she could never feel for "Charlie."

This section introduces Willard's life in Evanston and her first attraction for a young man—fueled by interest in his intellect.

On 30 March 1861, Frances Willard had met Charles Fowler, and wrote in her journal that he was "a very fine scholar, thought by some persons the best student and orator in the Institute [the Methodist training ground at what is now Northwestern University]. He is fine looking (in an intellectual 'point of view') and gentle-

---

6. Annamary Horner Dewitt, *The Many Faces of Love* (Master's Thesis, Garrett-Evangelical Theological Seminary, Evanston, IL, 1987), 4.

manly." She liked him "well enough."[7] Later journal entries comment on his "eloquence," his "brilliance," his "strength of character," but never on any feeling of Frances's that one could label "excitement." They had much in common; often, she notes that she could sit and talk with him for hours, and eventually she allowed herself to think that this was love, and to become engaged to him. But she is never happy in the engagement even though her family is delighted—even her beloved mother felt that Frances had finally found her proper place. In a journal entry of 8 May 1861, Frances expresses what is perhaps the key for her in her supposed attraction to Charles Fowler: "Mr. F. 'paid' my intellectual abilities a compliment that I shall not forget which may nerve me for something more than I've put down—who knows?"[8] This may be the secret: for the first time in her life, a man was acknowledging her intellect. In the male-dominated nineteenth century, this would surely be enough to make a woman feel wanted and even perhaps to cause her to feel that she could spend her life with a person like this. She learns to value his words, "more highly than all the words of all other men."[9] After they kissed, she allowed herself to think that she was in love, but there was confusion ahead.

> *Again, this reinforces the idea of Charlie's intellect, not an emotional attachment.*

> *The end of this paragraph explains why Frances allows herself to become engaged—a man admires her intellect!*

On 13 June 1861, France expressed very explicitly that the person she truly loves is Mary Bannister, whom she refers to as "My Darling."[10] It is telling to examine her excitement at receiving a note from Mary:

> Received a letter from *Mary.* Oh Darling—Darlin! One week from this disconsolate evening I hope to lay my head upon your arm and have you say the Sacred, beautiful *Three Words* that I do not care to hear from any lips save *yours* and his.[11]

> *The article introduces her first real love for a woman, which will be the subject of most of the rest of the text.*

---

7. Ibid., 23.
8. Ibid., 28.
9. Ibid., 30.
10. Ibid., 30.
11. Ibid., 30.

One may question why she would want to hear the same words from Mary as from the young man she supposedly loves, but at this point, Frances is unsure as to what and how she really feels.

By August, when an encounter with Mary has left her knowing that she has wanted to kiss her and has not, that she feels "sinful" and wishes she were more religious, Frances is growing unhappy and begins to suffer assorted bouts of ill health. She comments that she will repay Charlie for his devotion "cost what it will." The woman who must take care of the suffering no matter what it costs is beginning to make herself known. But in September, she is able to write in her journal that she now knows that what she feels for Mary "is not right or natural" and she goes on to add that:

The subject of ill health will crop up now and then, as it does for many of the participants in a Boston Marriage.

> They say that you and I should love each other as we do for it is in the present and in my wretchedness and conflict, be it right or wrong, I *will* say that I am *glad*. Ours is such a love as no two women ever had for each other before. It is wild and passionate, deep and all-pervading. It is 'abnormal.' Will God damn us for it? Did he send this Friendship which I thought my choicest Blessing only to poison it and turn it to a curse? What can I do? What must I do? I get no light—no answer. I have the keen belief that God is angry, that I am very Wicked—that Charlie and I are estranged.[12]

The subject of "unnatural love" is broached.

The problem, however, is that Mary is to marry Frances' brother Oliver, which she does, leaving Frances both happy (because she loves them both and wanted them happy) and despondent. Of course, ill health follows. Note, however, that there is a turning away from religion present in all these stories from these unhappy young women, because the Church is teaching them that what they feel is unnatural, and that as women, they must accept their proper place on earth.

Frances decides to tell her mother; how much she tells her is unclear, but she does find support in her mother's care. It is clear that her mother cries when Frances decides not to marry Charles; one supposes that strong friendships between women are fine because

A slight change of topic is important here, to show surprising support from her mother.

---

12. Ibid., 36–37.

no one expects them to be sexual, and because many of these, like Mary Bannister's with Frances, still give way to traditional marriage. One would guess that Mrs. Willard hoped that eventually, Frances would take the marriage road as well. Mrs. Willard, though, is unusually helpful and understanding; Frances writes on 11 September that "She [mother] don't think it mean or bad—we must both know it is abnormal."[13] Her mother has reassured her that if God thought it wicked, he would not have allowed the friendship with Mary to happen—an interesting argument.

One of the worries that many of these young women had was that if they refused marriage, they would become a burden to their families, a very valid concern in the nineteenth century, and indeed, up to the present. Frances continued to vacillate between feeling she should marry Charlie, and feeling that she was not good enough for him because she could not feel toward him like a woman should. At one point, she notes that, "I cannot let myself be a dead weight on Father's hands, now that I am so old, so well able to care for myself."[14] One wonders how many women, feeling exactly as Frances Willard did, allowed themselves to be prodded into marriage for just such a reason—arguably a higher percentage than a male-dominated culture would choose to think.

| *Another topic introduced to show that the worry about what will happen to them if they don't marry is necessary.* |

In a long explanatory passage written on 15 October, Frances finally decides that she really does not love Charlie enough to be able to follow through on the engagement:

| *Frances opts for the single life, a brave choice in her day. But is it because she is not poor, a prerequisite for a Boston Marriage?* |

> I thought I loved Charles Fowler six months ago. I admired him, honored him, sympathized with him—loved him—yes, I will say I loved him. He met all my requirements, he realized my idea of an upright, noble, educated, gifted man. I liked to be with him and talk with him ... I was excited and frightened.[15]

Frances has allowed herself to say, "I love you," but:

> ... after that—his [sic] caresses were irksome, *always,* they never aroused an emotion in me. His presence gave me no pleasure, except as I felt

---

13. Ibid., 39.
14. Ibid., 43.
15. Ibid., 47.

him to be a companion—appreciative, refined, and noble-hearted. His absence did not trouble me—his return after weeks spent at Home [sic] gave me not a thrill of pleasure.'[16]

How very telling all this is! She goes on to note that:

> His kiss wakes no feeling in [her] heart ... [but she] is capable of more, for a *kiss*, a caress—a loving word from *Mary* will send the blood hurrying along ... veins and give that peculiar sensation, so delicious, so rare, that people call a 'thrill.'[17]

These are strong words indeed; Frances realized that throwing everything away was going to lead her into a difficult situation. She would be the disappointment of her family, and thought "of the scandal and gossip involved, the putting away from myself of a nobleman's devotion."[18] She was right. When she returned home on 16 October, even her beloved mother was disgusted with her conduct, although, as usual, mother came to her rescue, trying to offer some support. Needless to say, more ill health followed.

Refusing Charlie costs even her mother's support and, of course, Frances becomes ill.

Like many other young women who wished not to follow the nineteenth-century domestic path, Frances was attracted to men who treated her as an equal and admired her intellect as she admired theirs. If the relationship could have been maintained on this level, she, and others like her, might have chosen to follow through and enter marriage. It is the "culture" (e.g., kissing) that she objects to:

> The 'culture' has always been the great 'bone of contention.' I have often wondered what my nature is in this. I have no other experience to compare it with. I know that with Mary I frankly like such things. That is all. It don't seem 'nice' to me from C...[19]

Later, still reflecting on what others might see as 'unnatural,' Frances notes that even religion (or perhaps, especially religion), fails her and is no source of solace:

> I have "leaned" on my own nature and found that it suffices for all it's [sic] needs"—exclusive alike of humanity and of Divinity. It is not "nice"

---

16. Ibid., 48.
17. Ibid., 48.
18. Ibid., 49.
19. Ibid., 55.

as Mary said. It isn't natural or right. It is not Christian—it is not the Spirit that will be at home in the pure land beyond above all the lands that human eyes have seen.[20]

A few days later, she writes that "Never yet, on this subject, have I had word of help or counsel—the slightest indication of attention from Heaven." Religion did (and still does) leave these women outside the walls. A later discussion of Sarah Orne Jewett will reveal the same struggle with, in Jewett's case, a turn to Nature as the true religion, because Nature is maternal. Willard, like others in her time, realizes finally that she is different than other women, "stronger than most women" and writes that "I am unlike them in many ways—I do not cling like them; I do not reverence like them; I am not swallowed up in another's love like them; why should I be?"[21] Of course, Willard, like Jane Addams, Sarah Orne Jewett, and others, went on to accomplish great things in the world, either in the world of charity or the world of letters. In nineteenth-century North America, leaving behind "normal" relationships was one of the only ways to accomplish this. One did have to be strong to accomplish much, because society was against it, the family was against it, and the Church was against it. Love of a man complicated the effort because it was demanding; it led to children and the responsibilities of home and hearth. A relationship with another woman allowed a freedom unheard of within most marriages of the day.

> *Here is Willard now addressing the issue of the failure of religion to offer anything to these women as solace. This will continue all through her life.*

> *This becomes a main point in favor of non-marriage, IF one had the means to support oneself.*

On Thanksgiving Day, 1861, Frances Willard finally penned one of her most direct declarations of her feelings:

> Tormented with the abnormal love and longing of a woman for a woman—one never so lovable and sweet as now. Open to ridicule from this, to censure from the Other side. Not very good—not very near to God.[22]

The struggle and torment of this finding of the true self is obviously intense. Her father was ill at the time and she struggled with

---

20. Ibid., 55.
21. Ibid., 57.
22. Ibid., 59.

that, and the need to be available for care on the home front as well. With no God to turn to, Willard had to struggle within herself and find the strength there. She toyed with the idea of using Christ as a model for awhile, but that simply was not possible; one assumes that she means as a model of celibacy, but she was too passionate a creature for that.

| *This will become Willard's answer.* |

What Willard realizes is that she has "no need for" Charlie.[23] What she needs she finds within herself or with other women. On 30 January 1862, she finally writes Fowler a letter, breaking off the understanding, taking all the blame upon herself. To herself, on paper, she admits that losing Mary was far harder to bear than giving up Charles. The word "unnatural" is sprinkled throughout her journals at this time: "So strange that a *woman* should love another woman as a man would love her."[24] Aunt Sarah knows, she reveals, and is "dear" and "kind," though Willard herself cries about her "nature alone at night."

By September 1862, Willard is installed at the Female College, where she develops a friendship with a young student named Ada, "nearest of all-and without family, nearer than any others—has been my Gift."[25] On 6 January she ponders her "nuisance" (Ada):

> She will go away from me—it will be best and the inevitable thing, Mary B. went. It was right ... God forgive me my sins in it. Why do I love women so? It is a *nuisance*. It don't pay—they are sure to go off and leave me lamenting.[26]

| *Note that the development of this article is flowing smoothly because it is chronological—moving through Willard's life as it unfolds.* |

Mary's marriage to Frances's brother Oliver had deeply wounded her; in this hurt, she turns to Ada, even while realizing the wrongness of it, her too-great need that Ada will be unable to fill:

> You, Ada, dearest of them all—your heart will want a stronger one than mine when you're a woman ... you'll want a manly head to bend low while you say those dear words 'I love you Darling!' that you are content to give me for awhile yet.[27]

---

23. Ibid., 67.
24. Ibid., 79.
25. Ibid., 82.
26. Ibid., 82.
27. Gifford, *Writing Out My Heart,* 191.

Seven. Journal Articles

Writing Out My Heart, the 1995 collection of Willard's journals from 1855–1896 by Carolyn Gifford, presents a clear picture of Willard's early struggle with her "nature" and her use of the name "Philip" to refer to any man her female loves would eventually turn to, leaving her behind: "I've never loved a woman who was not intensely feminine—and such women are *bound to find Philip*. I would like to *be Philip!*"[28]

> *Here is one of the most direct statements of her desire to be male.*

Willard formed a series of these attachments to women, beginning with Mary Bannister, continuing through Ada Brigham, Kate Jackson, Delevan Scovillle, Isabel Somerset, but enduring with Anna Gordon, who was to prove her lasting companion, friend, organizer, confidante, and true love. Willard's need for achievement was strong and she accomplished it as educator, social reformer, struggler in the battle to give women the right to vote, as well as president of the WCTU.

> Frances' greatest contributions to women were to show that a woman could be complete without a husband, that she could earn a living for herself ... and that she could run the largest woman's organization in the world and do it well.[29]

Willard commented on the number of female friendships she saw around her, so it may be argued that this lifestyle was not uncommon among educated women of a certain social class:

> *This paragraph points out that these relationships seemed to be accepted, in part, in a certain, more comfortably well-off and educated social class.*

> The love of women for each other grow more numerous each day... That so little should be said about them surprises me, for they are everywhere... In these days, when any capable and careful woman can honorably own her own support, there is no village that has not its example of 'two heads in counsel' both of which are feminine.[30]

These were women who held several things in common: ill health, before they found their emotional partner and left the marriage track, a desire for career or achieve-

> *This is a good description to close the paragraph.*

---

28. Ibid., 191.
29. Ibid., 191.
30. Dewitt, *The Many Faces*, 103.

ment denied them in the traditional family role, education, religious struggle, a bent toward social reform, working physically for it and/or writing to support it and most importantly, financial independence.

Significantly, most of the partners of the Boston Marriage were financially independent women, an important point. Education alone was not enough to give these women the freedom to break out of the mold of the true woman. In fact, as Jane Addams complained, education simply opened the door to a world filled with possibilities and then slammed it shut. Well-trained to think for herself in college or young ladies' seminaries, there was then no outlet to use a mind to well-developed to be content with homemaking, having children, subjugating oneself to a man.

| *A key issue is introduced in this topic sentence.*

And if the young woman knew herself to be unsuited to marriage (and this could be for a number for reasons, among them an inordinate fear of childbirth), her options were narrowed even more. Now she was left with the task of caretaking invalid relatives, helping out in married siblings' families, being the spinster. But financial independence freed the woman from this worry, as long as these young women could find a suitable outlet for their energies.

| *Note again how this closing sentence leads into the beginning of the next paragraph.*

The most acceptable outlet for their energies was social betterment. One could argue that in a century of social reform movements and attempts to train the lower classes in the way of middle-class values, there was no more acceptable outlet for the unmarried, educated comfortably well-off young woman than the world of organized, structured, female benevolence. This world gave the unmarried lifestyle sanction, approval; women who chose to stay unmarried, and who chose to leave their own family circle, could remain socially acceptable by devoting themselves to helping others. Such kindness and concern for others removed them from the sins of the flesh; therefore, their close same-sex friendships were non-threatening. These friendships could only have flourished in a certain milieu, before they were pathologized by the psychoanalytic theories of the late nineteenth and twentieth centuries. There was only a small window of opportunity for this type of freedom to flourish.

Friendships between women that were close and intimate have always existed. But those that came to exclude men from the intimacy seemed to form in the years most of these young women attended all-female colleges. There, they were able to express themselves completely with those with whom they were intimate. When | *This paragraph summarizes the subject well.*

forced to leave this world, return to their family home and take up the traditional roles intended for women, most seemed to become ill, suffered depression , experienced what Freud would term "hysteria." Finding a soul mate with whom they could correspond helped; finding a life together in pursuit of a common goal was sometimes harder. In Boston circles, an outlet was found earlier than in some parts of the country: Henry James modeled his novel *The Bostonians*[31] on "one of those friendships between women which are so common in New England."[32] In this novel, he treats the relationship between the two heroines, Olive and Verena, as a Boston Marriage. Olive, he says, found "what she had been looking for so long—a friend of her own sex with whom she might have a union of soul." James did not see this relationship as the twentieth century might, as "sick" or "unnatural" but rather as "constructive and fulfilling,"[33] one in which each woman could realize her full potential, use her abilities and not be stifled. His own sister Alice had finally found health and happiness in her relationship with Katharine Loring, and he saw nothing strange in this, but rather, called it an "American phenomenon."[34] The two women, of course, devoted themselves to working for Boston charities, giving their choice legitimacy, and allowing them acceptance by their contemporaries.

Sarah Orne Jewett, author of *The Country of the Pointed Firs*, among others, was another bright talented woman of the era, who formed a lasting relationship with widowed Annie Ticknor Fields after the death of James Fields. Due to James Fields' successful publishing business, there was plenty of money, which allowed Jewett to continue her writing and allowed | *Here is a good example of an author who had this type of relationship followed by mentions of others.*

the two of them to spend their lives together. Annie Fields showed no desire ever to remarry, and Boston culture society had no difficulty with the friendship between the two.

31. Henry James, *The Bostonians* (Toronto: Bantam Books, 1984).
32. Faderman, *Surpassing the Love*, 190.
33. Ibid., 198.
34. Ibid., 198.

Frances Willard, like Jane Addams, Sarah Orne Jewett, Willa Cather and others, continued as members of mainstream religious denominations, which did give sanction to their work because charity was defined by the nineteenth-century Christian Church as the appropriate place for women's energies if they did not have a husband and family. But these women did not seek counsel or support from it. They were fortunate to be economically secure, to be educated and to have lived in that small space in time that allowed their friendships to develop into life-long, commitments because society would not have imagined that they were sexual relationships. Historically, we do not really know if they were. Their support, like many of those in the narratives Graham gives in her book, came from without the institutions of organized religion, not within it. The work environment provided support and satisfaction; like Katherine Bowen, who story appears in Graham's book,[35] these working women of the nineteenth century got their strength from the women around them and were able to accomplish great things. Willard struggled with the idea that God could not love her, because the Church had taught her so; it was her mother who said that God created her as she was, so she must be loved. One of Graham's interviewees, Diana, comments that "anger at the church is very high because so many of my friends had to struggle with this false belief that God didn't accept them ... that I had to choose between love of a woman and love of God."[36] A look through Willard's journals and letters reveals the same feeling, until the love she finally finds convinces her that she is a whole person, and an accepted one.

> Lillian Faderman, in her excellent study, *Surpassing the Love of Men*, tells us that Later nineteenth century America, and even (or rather, especially) proper Boston, believed that there was such potential in love between women. Perhaps because it was assumed (at least by those outside the relationship) that love between women was asexual, unsullied by the evils of carnality, a sex-hating society could view it as ideal and admire, and even envy, it as the British had admired and envied ... it.[37]

Whatever the case, the Boston Marriage slipped into a small slot in time when a new group of educated young women with money could find an acceptable role through some of the tradi-

---

35. Graham, *Discovering Images of God*, 55.
36. Ibid., 48.
37. Faderman, *Surpassing the Love*, 203.

tional ways (charity, benevolence, social improvement) and still have their own brand of intimacy, romantic or otherwise. They created a new kind of family, but one that fit the traditional definition of a family as a place where one is at home, is loved and supported and can grow; it is the twentieth century and beyond that has seemed to have difficulty accepting this definition. While we seem to be a culture obsessed with sex, we cannot deal with it sanely, nor can the Church. In fact, one could argue that the Church and its teachings are still the cause of discomfort and pain for many who choose a different path, because it cannot decide whether to be Christ-like and accepting, or patriarchal and condemning.

| *This is a strong concluding paragraph.* |

Works Cited

Dewitt, Annamary Horner. *The Many Faces of Love.* Master's Thesis, Garrett-Evangelical Theological Seminary, Evanston, IL, 1987.

Faderman, Lillian. *Surpassing the Love of Men.* New York: William Morrow, 1981.

Gifford, Carolyn DeSwarte, ed. *Writing Out My Heart: Selections from the Journal of Frances E. Willard, 1855–1896.* Urbana: University of Illinois Press, 1995.

Graham, Larry. *Discovering Images of God.* Louisville: Westminster John Knox Press, 1997.

James, Henry. *The Bostonians.* Toronto: Bantam Books, 1984.

* * *

Journal Article: Moral Theology

Does Suicide Exempt the Deceased from the
Hope of Future Redemption?
Michele Watkins-Branch

Introduction

Thesis

In order to address the question of whether suicide exempts the deceased from the hope of future redemption, it is crucial to understand that the Bible does not contain any explicit moral declaration against suicide. It does, however, contain several accounts of its practice. Given the lack of biblical foundation to declare the moral condemnation of suicide, it is the interrogation of the practice

| *In this succinct opening paragraph, the author tells the reader exactly what to expect in this article.* |

of Christian theologians who have adopted such a concept that has such profound implications on our doctrinal formulations about the nature of both God and humanity. A Christian theologian *par excellence*, Augustine is posited as a formidable conversationalist on the issue of suicide. This work explores Augustine's theological method in order to explicate the process by which suicide *becomes* known as a sin within Christian discourse. By examining Augustine's contribution and the varied appropriations of this "sin-talk" in the work of John Calvin, Jacobus Arminius, and John Wesley, this work questions whether suicide can be understood as a moral offense, and contends with the moral arguments that exempt those who die by suicide from the hope of future redemption. In an effort to complicate the condemnation of suicide, this essay intends to make a positive intervention into the practices of damning those who have died by suicide through suggesting ways in which we draw from Reformed understandings of grace in order to affirm the sacred worth of individuals who die by suicide, reaffirming the hope of their eternal security.

How Suicide Becomes A Theological Dilemma

First and foremost, scholars must acknowledge that the condemnation of suicide is not an ideological invention of Christianity, but a stance that many early theologians and faith communities appropriated from ancient philosophy. The acclaimed medieval historian, Alexander Murray devotes the majority of his work entitled *Suicide in the Middle Ages: The Curse of Self-Murder* toward making this point. Murray historically excavates the centuries of desecrated bodies of those who died by suicide from antiquity throughout the Middle Ages in order to locate the theological arguments behind these rituals of condemnation. Murray's excavation leads him beyond the medieval period to the suicide doctrine of the Stoics and the oppositional stances to such doctrines held by Plato and Aristotle, which he argues as the leading driving forces behind the early church's suicide rhetoric.[1] Murray continues by arguing that this Greek philosophical tradition

> *This section gives an amazingly comprehensive, yet readable, overview of the history of this issue.*

---

1. Alexander Murray, *Suicide in the Middle Ages: The Curse on Self-Murder*, vol. 2 (New York: Oxford University Press, 2000), 123–142.

was, in actuality, more instrumental than the Bible in shaping early Christian stances on the issue of suicide.[2]

The dialogues of the middle period substantiate this argument, particularly in Plato's *Phaedo, The Laws*, and Aristotle's *Nicomachean Ethics*—each containing colloquies on the morality of suicide. Echoing the Pythagorean prohibition of suicide, Socrates asserted to Cebes in the *Phaedo* that philosophers should be ready to die, but not willing to take their own lives because human beings 'belong' to the gods.[3] Socrates reflected on his own impending death when building upon this thought in his endorsement of divine punishment and wrath against those who die by suicide:

> Well if one of your belongings were to kill itself, without signifying that you wanted it to die, wouldn't you be vexed with it, and punish it, if you had any punishment at hand? ... So perhaps, in that case, it isn't reasonable that one should not kill oneself until God sends some necessity, such as the one now before us.[4]

Comparably, Plato added in the *Laws* that the bodies of those who die by suicide have lost their sanctity to the extent that he states confidently the following:

| *The use of quotes is skillful—and also very helpful for the reader.* |

> For him [the suicide] what ceremonies there are to be of purification and burial God knows... They who meet their death in this way shall be buried alone, and none shall be laid by their side; they shall be buried ingloriously in the borders of the twelve portions of the land, in such places uncultivated and nameless, and no column or inscription shall mark the place of their internment.[5]

Aristotle, a student of Plato, contributed to the ancient conversation on suicide in his *Nicomachean Ethics* in which he qualified courageous death and cowardice death. Aristotle argued that courage is expressed when one bears the threat of death as an aspect of his or her endurance, but cowardice being the antithesis to courage when death is an individual way of breaking free of suffering.

> The reckless are impetuous, and though prior to the dangers they are willing, in the midst of them they withdraw, whereas courageous men are keen in the deeds but quiet beforehand. In accord with what has been said, then, courage ... inspires confidence and fear ... and it

---

2. Ibid., 108–11, 116–117.

3. Plato, *Phaedo*, trans. David Gallop (New York: Oxford University Press, 2009), x, 6; 61c-62c.

4. Ibid., 7.

5. Plato, *Laws*, trans. Benjamin Jowett (New York: Cosimo, Inc, 2008), 220; 874.

chooses and endures what it does because it is noble to do so, or because it is shameful not to. But dying in order to flee poverty, erotic love, or something painful is not the mark of a courageous man but rather of a coward.[6]

So what we have in these perspectives of a few of the leading philosophers of the ancient Greeks are a primer of sorts on what will become markers of Christian discourse on suicide. It is a representative interpretation of suicide as the cowardice seizure of divine power to choose one's death that incites the wrath of God and sanctions communities to affirm this divine punishment of the soul through the desecration of human bodies. These are arguments that Greek philosophers used against the Stoic defense of suicide as an expression of the "self-preservation will," which philosopher and historian, John Sellars, describes as the desire "to pay more attention to the preservation of oneself as a rational being, even if this might lead one to suicide."[7]

Demonstrating the point that these condemning perspectives pertaining to suicide were not invented by Christian theologians but existed even prior to the common era is not sufficient for the objective of this work. It is more fruitful to note the ways in which Christian theologians integrated these perspectives as sources in their formation of what would become written and customary doctrinal stances of the Church. Acknowledging the fact that the Bible does not contain any explicit moral declarations condemning suicide, one is further compelled to consider the validity of Murray's argument that Christian theologians, such as Origen, Jerome, and Augustine, relied upon their knowledge of the Greek philosophical tradition and its tenets as a source for Christian moral deliberation.[8]

| *This writer is covering a great deal of information, but her writing is clear and easy to follow.* |

Given the brevity of this work, it would be sufficient to explore the arguments of Augustine as representative of the early church's stance on the issue of suicide. Though Augustine did not know Greek as a language, but became acquainted with Greek philosophy through the Latin dialogues of Cicero and Plato, he was extensively educated in the ancient classics in Thagaste with the intention to learn the skills of master

---

6. Aristotle, *Nicomachean Ethics*, trans. Robert Bartlett and Susan Collins (Chicago: University of Chicago Press, 2011), 57; 1116a 9–13.

7. John Sellers, *Stoicism* (Los Angeles: University of California Press, 2006), 110.

8. Murray, *Suicide in the Middle Ages*, 99–100.

orators.⁹ It is for this reason that it comes as no surprise that Augustine flourished under the tutelage of Ambrose in Milan. Ambrose was a master rhetorician who was educated in Rome and an expert in Greek literature.¹⁰ Within just a few years under Ambrose's mentorship, Augustine became a priest in AD 391, and ordained Bishop of Hippo in AD 396 where he demonstrated his own competency in philosophy and theology, not as a Professor, but in the fight to unify an intensely divided North African Church.

By the time Augustine became the Bishop of Hippo, the North African church had been separated into two different churches for nearly a century between the Catholics and the Donatists, who each had their own resident bishop.¹¹ The Catholics were clearly those who were aligned with the Church of Rome, its sacramental theology of one baptism, and its ecclesiology of the unified church. In stark contrast, the Donatists claimed to be the chosen church of purity and strict adherence to law and ritual. Donatist re-baptized its membership and engaged in what ritual suicides, which were argued not to be Christian but an inherited practice carried over from their Numidian traditional religious practice of worship of the High God of Africa named Saturn.¹²

The ritualization and valorization of suicides among the Donatists warranted a formalized condemnation of suicide from the Roman episcopacy, and Augustine assumed this responsibility. Historians have identified the Donatists as the historical impulse behind Augustine's fervency to construct a sound and official moral declaration against suicide.¹³ It is because of the Donatist controversy that Augustine becomes the most influential Christian theologian in the shaping of the early church's doctrinal stance on suicide.

---

9. Peter Brown, *Augustine of Hippo: A Biography*, Revised Edition (Los Angeles: University of California Press, 2000), 24–25.

10. Ibid., 25.

11. See W.H.C. Frend, *The Donatist Church: A Movement of Protest in Roman North Africa* (New York: Oxford University Press, 2003), 1–25 and Erika Hermanowicz, *Possidius of Calama: A Study of the North African Episcopate in the Age of Augustine* (New York: Oxford University Press, 2008), chapters 3 and 4 for more on the origins of the century-long controversy between the Donatists and the Catholics of North Africa that resulted largely in the repeated persecution of the Donatists by Roman emperors Constantine and Honorius. Frend and Hermanowicz note, in the aforementioned sections, the excessive violence of the Donatists that included vicious physical attacks on Catholic and frequent suicides among their own group.

12. Brown, *Augustine of Hippo*, 21.

13. See Murray, *Suicide in the Middle Ages*, 106–107 and Hermanowicz, *Possidius of Calama*, 34–35.

Accordingly, Augustine responded aggressively against the Petilian and Gaudentius, the Donatist Bishops, and by expressing his outrage about the "daily suicides" and "false martyrdom" of the Donatists.[14] Most exceptionally, it is in Augustine's *The City of God* that Augustine devoted several chapters to the specific issue of suicides. In our examination of these particular writings, one can note the 'improvisional' nature of Augustine's method for the biblical and theological interpretation of suicide and the presence of inconsistencies within that method. Utilizing these writings as a collective source of evaluating Augustine's praxis and theological assumptions that undergird his praxis, one can argue that his soteriology of the 'elect' is appropriated here with dire implications on theological anthropology. I argue that it is Augustine's soteriology and its subsequent adoption by Thomas Aquinas and John Calvin that propagates and legitimates the *desacralization* of those who die by suicide.

> *Note how each paragraph has a topic sentence, making the content easier to apprehend.*

In the first book of *Contra Gaudentium*, Augustine devoted much of chapters twenty-seven to thirty-one to the use of scripture and civil law to argue against what became the common practice of suicide in Hippo. In chapter twenty-seven, Augustine argued incoherently that suicide is the work of the devil and damnable by God. This is an argument that he later contradicts in his suggestion that, at times, God commands us to be ready to kill ourselves and others, and even in those cases the killing is an immoral action. In order to elucidate Augustine's contradictions it is important to consider his method of biblical interpretation.

Augustine noted the parallels between demonic possessions as witnessed in scripture and the temptation to do harm to oneself. Augustine argued that the devil is behind the demon possessed boy who often fell in fire and water, the herd of pigs who threw themselves in the sea after receiving the Legion of demons, and Satan's attempt to get Jesus to throw himself off the pinnacle of the temple.[15] Characteristic of patristic biblical interpretation, Augustine employed the allegorical method exemplified by that of his predecessor Origen, who believed that biblical passages that appear to be indirect or vague should be interpreted by comparing these texts with other passages of Scripture that are more

---

14. Augustine, *Contra litteras Petiliani libro duo.*

15. Augustine, *Contra Gaundentium Donatistarum Episcopum libri du,* 1.27.30.

straightforward.[16] However, Augustine did not continue interpreting scripture in this way. He departs from this method in his refutation of Gaudentius' argument that the Bible does not condemn suicide, but in fact, valorizes it.

Gaudentius cites the account of Razias, the Jewish elder who fell upon his sword in order to 'die nobly rather than to fall into the hands of sinners' (2 Maccabees 14:42).[17] In response, Augustine used the aforementioned Platonist understanding that suicide is excusable only when 'God sends some necessity,' and denotes the account of Razia's readiness to kill himself as a demonstration of human courage to execute divine command such as the case of Abraham who was ready to kill his own son, and Samson who tore down the wall to defeat the Philistines.[18] Without any notations of divine command present in the passage, Augustine assumes this must be the case—an invention that is referred to as such by Alexander Murray in his analysis of Augustine's theological method.[19] Murray describes Augustine's intertextual methods of biblical interpretation as 'inventive inconsistencies' given that soon after Augustine's assumes that divine command is a factor in Razias' suicide, he concludes that his suicide is in actuality wrong.[20]

What becomes even more self-contradictory is Augustine's argument in the same chapter that suicide is both immoral and damnable. Augustine stated:

> Quomodo enim vindicetur, nisi qui eum ausus est trucidare damnetur? In hac ergo voce non estis nisi accusatores vestri, quia vos estis rei sanguinis vestri. Nec Deus nisi vos damnabit, quando a vobis vel collisum, vel suffocatum, vel exustum, vel quocumque pacto trucidatum, vel si hoc elegeritis, effusum sanguinem vestrum vindicabit.[21]

Note Augustine's usage of disparaging phrases such as *Nec Deus nisi vos damnabit*: 'Nor would God have, but will damn,' in the same sentence with the term *vindicabit*, which means to avenge

---

16. David Dockery, *Biblical Interpretation Then and Now: Contemporary Hermeneutics in the Light of the Early Church* (Grand Rapids: Baker Book House, 1992), 94.

17. Jacques Bels, "*La mort volontaire* dans l'oeuvre de Saint Augustin." In *Revue de l'histoire des religions*, tome 187 (1975), 161–162.

18. Augustine, *Contra Gaudentium*, 1.31.39.

19. Murray, *Suicide in the Middle Ages*, 109.

20. Ibid., 108.

21. Augustine, *Contra Gaudentium Donatistarum Episcopum libri du*, 1.27.31.

or punish.[22] It is clear that Augustine wishes to express that suicide is the work of the devil as well as an offense against God that necessitates and foresees the enactment of God's retributive justice. What is most observable in Augustine's argument is the lack of biblical justification and abundance of Greek philosophy upon which he bases his argument.

Just in a short passage, one can become aware of the operational framework from which Augustine develops a formal Christian declaration against suicide. Though Augustine did not quote Plato or Socrates here, he clearly withdrew upon their expressed beliefs that suicide is a damnable offense in such a way that it becomes definitive "sin-talk." It is important to state that Augustine was not the first to engage in this philosophical–Christian dialectic, but other Christian rhetoricians like Lactantius discussed the abominable nature of suicide in the eyes of God and God as the avenger of such an offense.[23]

> *It is clear that the author spent a lot of time writing, revising, and editing this article; the information is so clearly presented, and paragraphs flow from one to the next.*

However, distinguishable from Lactantius, Augustine's writings occur during a pivotal period in the development of the Christian church as an institution evidenced by the Roman Edict of Milan in AD 313 and the Council of Nicea in AD 325 As an Episcopal leader of the church during such a formative time, Augustine's perspective stigmatizes suicide within Christian religion in an unprecedented fashion to the extent that this stigma becomes the definitive position of the church.

Problematic Dimensions of Suicide as "Sin Talk"

What makes Augustine's formidable contribution to Christian discourse on suicide so problematic is the degree to which he relies on philosophical ideas as well the staggering observations of *discretionary grace* and contradictions within the style and form of his

> *Heads and subheads help break up this long article but, most importantly, they provide a "map" to let readers know what to expect in each section.*

---

22. Francis E.J. Valpy, *An Etymological Dictionary of The Latin Language* (London: Balwin & Co, 1828), 511.

23. Lactantius, *Divinae Institutiones III*, trans. Mary F. McDonald in *The Fathers of the Church* (Washington: Catholic University of America Press, 1964): 214: 3.18.30–35.

argumentation. These 'inventive inconsistencies' fail to demonstrate a sound moral declaration against suicide. They bear witness to the reality that Augustine wrestled with the convergence of his abstract theological and philosophical ideals and the tangible lived realities that complicate the practical application of those ideals.

AUGUSTINE'S DISCRETIONARY GRACE

The convergence of the theoretical assumptions and the practical implications of Augustine's sin talk here on suicide can be better understood if one considers the relationship between Augustine's theological anthropology and his soteriology as expressed in his doctrine of grace. In Augustine's aforementioned language of damnation as the divine punishment for suicide, it is clear that it is his understanding of limited atonement that allows his doctrine of grace to be susceptible to exclusive interpretations of salvation. Augustine demonstrated a disconcerting form of *discretionary grace*, specifically when he addresses whether suicide is permissible in order to retain honor or avoid punishment.

Leaning in the rhetorical arguments expressed by his mentor St. Ambrose in *De Virginibus,* in the *City of God,* Augustine sympathized with the Christian virgins who commit suicide in order to avoid being raped, or the dishonor of having been raped. Though these virgin suicides lack the ability to repent like all other suicides as he notes in the case of Lucretia, Augustine made the claim that the Christian virgins must have been commanded by God (a claim he does not suppose or propose in defense of Lucretia) and argued that with divine command these Christian virgins are to be forgiven.[24] Augustine exonerated Abraham and Samson as justified by the "special intimation from God Himself."[25] Augustine also absolved the Christian virgins whom he references earlier by pronouncing that they are to be granted forgiveness for their incurrence of guilt even by what he suggests must have been by divine command. Readers quickly become aware that Augustine did not appear to have a sound perspective on suicide fully developed. This was expressed in his rendition of a kind of discretionary grace by way of pardoning sins to some and not others who commit the "sin of suicide.

The most indicting incident of Augustine's practice of discre-

---

24. Augustine, *City of God,* trans. Marcus Dods (Peabody: Hendrickson Publishers, Inc., 2011), 1.17.

25. Ibid., 1.21.

tionary grace can be observed in his commentary on Judas Iscariot in his *Exposition of the Psalms* and *Tractates on the Gospel of John*. Augustine commented on Psalm 94, which describes God as an avenger against the wicked. He utilized Judas as a biblical example of the abominable upon whom divine punishment was rendered to avenge the betrayal of Christ. Augustine stated:

> ... and we execrate Judas, through his deed God hath confessed so great a blessing upon us; and we rightly say, God hath recompensed him after his iniquity; and in his malice hath He destroyed him. For he delivered not Christ up for us, but for the silver for which he sold Him.[26]

We find continuity in Augustine's thoughts on Judas later in his remarks on Psalm 109, where he writes to encourage his parishioners to use the Psalms in their prayer life, and to 'pray in Christ.' Again, Judas was used as a negative example of an individual who did not 'pray in Christ,' and who indicated such by virtue of his suicide. Speaking hypothetically, Augustine believed that if Judas did pray that he would have received forgiveness and would have expressed hope to live instead of choosing to die.[27]

It is in the *Tractates on the Gospel of John* that Augustine provided a declarative statement on Judas' damnation. Theologian, Anthony Cane properly notes that Augustine complicated Jesus' admission in John 6:71 by suggesting that Judas was not chosen as a part of God's elect, but for another purpose within God's plan.[28] Understandably, Augustine was not expected to be a fan of Judas Iscariot; however, the argument here is that he erred in his use of speculation to justify condemnation. Augustine interrogated Judas' hope for future redemption by downplaying the probability of Judas being forgiven, even if he did confess his sin. For Augustine, it was Judas' betrayal of Christ *coupled* with his suicide that excluded him from being a recipient of God's redemptive grace but a target of God's wrath.

Augustine's Doctrine of Predestination & Perseverance of the Saints

Scholars of Augustine have come to understand the rationale behind his pronouncement of damnation on those who commit

---

26. St. Augustine, *Exposition on the Psalms*, trans. Rev. H.M. Wilkins (Baxter: Oxford, 1850) XCIV, 379–380.

27. Anthony Cane, *The Place of Judas Iscariot in Christology* (Burlington: Ashgate Publishing Ltd., 2005), 99.

28. Ibid.

suicide not by divine command, such as the case of Judas Iscariot, when examining his *Treatise On the Predestination of the Saints*. In this treatise, Augustine systematically outlined his thoughts on divine grace and human freedom relative to the doctrine of election. In summary, he described divine grace as the unmerited gift from God to come to faith in Christ, and argued that it could only be rejected by hardened hearts against God who are those non-elected by God.[29] Augustine believed that God chose the elect based on God's foreknowledge of who would choose to come to faith in Christ; therefore God instructed all to come to faith in Christ not because all would, but because God designed it to be impossible for humanity to be saved without doing so.[30]

In the second book of the treatise entitled *On the Gift of Perseverance*, Augustine described what he believed to be the mutual inclusivity of election and perseverance whereby the extent of an individual's endurance is dependent upon whether or not he or she has been predestined by God to be saved.[31] Augustine explained that there was no such thing as a temporal perseverance, but true perseverance was unto death, which was presumably not caused at one's own volition.[32] This makes it more comprehensible why Augustine understood suicide to be indicative of an individual's non-election, and therefore condemnation.

Demonstrated here is one of the most significant areas of discontinuity within Augustine's theology and it brings to light both his genius and shortcomings. While Augustine make a pristine contribution toward an orthodox Christian understanding of the Fall of humanity that helps make sense of sin and evil in the world, his doctrine of predestination and perseverance fails to make sense of how the elect might be able exercise their restored human freedom to determine the extent to which they allow the divine grace to sustain their human participation on earth.

Through a critical engagement of Augustine's arguments so far, we can make some crucial observations in the task of surmounting the condemnation of suicide and its exemption of the deceased from future redemption. The first observation is the presence of this

---

29. Augustine, "On the Predestination of the Saints," trans. Robert Ernest Wallace, in *Saint Augustine's Anti-Pelagian Works: A Select Library of the Nicene and Post-Nicene Father of the Christian Church*, ed. Philip Schaff (Grand Rapids: Eerdmans, 2007), 1.3 and 1.13.

30. Ibid., 1.14 and 1:34.

31. Ibid., 2.1.

32. Ibid.

convergence between the abstract and the concrete, evidenced by Augustine's practice of *discretionary grace*. In *On Nature and Grace*, Augustine states: "This grace, however, of Christ, without which neither infants nor adults can be saved, is not rendered for any merits, but is given *gratis*, on account of which it is also called grace. *"Being justified,"* says the apostle *"freely through His blood."*[33] Theoretically, Augustine believed that even in the absence of actual sin or actual repentance, all of humanity (infants and adults) shared in both sin and in redeeming grace of Christ. However, in his praxis, Augustine conditioned the extent to which individuals are worthy of this grace based on the condition of their death and genders.

The second observation is the problematic presence of contradictions or exceptionalism contained within Augustine's argument describing the sinfulness of suicide. Theoretically, Augustine believed in adherence to the commandment 'Thou shall not kill' (Exodus 20:13)–that God does not permit homicide, but in his practical interpretation of this commandment, he exercises the aforesaid discretionary grace to note Abraham and Samson as exceptions without biblical evidence to support this claim. In desperation to apply this divine command not to kill as a sufficient argument against suicide, Augustine argues that though the text does not add 'yourself' at the end, it is implied.[34] The main challenge that comes with Augustine's aim to treat this commandment as if it covers all aspects of life causes him to alter his argument with a series of exemptions that permits the killing of *irrational creatures*, or killing prompted by divine command.[35] Through what reads as impromptu exemptions and discretionary proclamations of grace and forgiveness, Augustine enters into a gridlock of practical and moral issues that are all predicated on perseverance, which becomes a criterion of worthiness.

Augustine does not invent the criterion of worthiness that is inherent in the theorization of suicide because it is visibly displayed in the assertions made in the works of Plato and Aristotle. However, it is through Augustine's integration of Greek philosophical ideas in his interpretation that allows the criterion of worthiness to be adopted in traditional Christian theological discourse on suicide. The *worthiness* criterion that Augustine adopts is a troublesome

---

33. Augustine, *On Nature and Grace*, IV.1.

34. Augustine, *City of God*, 1.20–21.

35. Ibid.

motif that is inherited in the religious doctrine of Christian theologians *par excellence* within the tradition such as Thomas Aquinas and John Calvin. This next section examines each of their respective appropriations of this moral standard.

The Criterion of Worthiness Within Christian Tradition

THOMAS AQUINAS (1225–1274)

Aquinas quotes Augustine's speculative commentary on the commandment 'Thou shall not kill' to ground his argument that suicide is unnatural, contrary to the assumption of individual responsibility within the human community, and an offense against God's power to determine life and death.[36] The most distinctive aspect of Aquinas' contribution to the Christian conversation is found in his delineation between sins that are venial (forgivable) or mortal (unforgiveable). Emerging out of this conceptualization of sin, Aquinas identified suicide as a mortal sin that was the "most grievous" and "most dangerous" of sins because one has no time left to repent.[37] This characterization of suicide as a mortal sin demonstrates a parallel between Augustine and Aquinas in that Aquinas expands upon the criterion of worthiness in Augustine's theological formulations concerning the nature of human redemption and its antithesis, which is human damnation.

| *The information is so well organized that the article will make an excellent reference for other scholars.* |

AQUINAS & MEDIEVAL LITERARY TRADITION

The influence of Aquinas during his time is unprecedentedly illustrated in the literary work of Dante's, *Divine Comedy,* which describes the eternal fate that awaits humanity. Individuals who have committed suicide are sentenced to the seventh level of hell. Suicides are forever stripped of their human bodies, dramatically changed into thorny trees from which they hang for all of eternity—maintaining an unending disposition of shame.[38] One cannot dis-

---

36. Thomas Aquinas, *Summa Theologica* (North Carolina: Hayes Barton Press, 2000), 2.64.5.

37. Ibid.

38. Dante Alighieri, *The Divine Comedy: 1: Inferno,* trans. John D. Sinclair (New York: Oxford University Press, 1969), 1.13.

miss the Aristotelian idea that suicide is unnatural that Aquinas furthers during the medieval period that is reflected here in allegorical form. The individual who commits suicide is perceived as one who has abandoned rationality, which is marker of their humanity, and therefore cursed to take on the form of an irrational creature. The individual who usurps the power of God to determine his or her own fate steals a life that does not belong to them, and is therefore condemned to bear the defilement of thieves, or 'harpies.'[39]

The most fascinating part of Dante's literal illustration of suicide and the punishment of eternal damnation can be found in his conversation with whom the reader comes to know as Pietro della Vigne. Pietro explains he killed himself to escape the contempt of the emperor:

> My mind, in scornful temper thinking by dying to escape from scorn, made me, just, unjust to myself. By the new roots of this tree I swear to you, never did I break faith with my lord, who was so worthy of honour; and if either of you return to the world let him establish my memory, which still lies under the blow that envy gave it.[40]

Given the level of religious symbolism within the *Divine Comedy*, one cannot help but consider Pietro's appeal as the author's literary depiction of a sinner's plea that wishes to express to a medieval audience the context of the human struggle not to "sin," while attempting to abide in faith. In order to make this conjecture, one must interpret Pietro's earnest request to Dante to carry this message of his abiding faith to the emperor as an effort made to redeem his honor. Pietro's situations bears striking similarities to Jesus' parable of the rich man and Lazarus in the gospel of Luke 16: 19–31.Drawing on these parallels as such, the moral principle to be grasped is that, be it pride or wealth, a perversion of either is sinful and ushers one into damnation.

In Wallace Fowlie's *A Reading of Dante's Inferno*, he interprets Pietro's condition to be a theological representation of the relentlessness of God's divine punishment toward suicides who "deny

---

39. Ibid. "Harpies" were described in the Greek mythology as the winged creatures who often stole food from Phineus, the king of Thrace. In an attempt to escape the torment of the harpies, Phineus voyages with the Greek hero Jason to retrieve the Golden Fleece for King Pelias. See Apollonios Rhodios, *The Argonautika: Expanded Edition*, trans. with introduction and commentary by Peter Green (Los Angeles: University of California Press, 2007), 85–91; Giovanni Boccaccio, *Boccaccio's Expositions on Dante's Comedy*, trans. with introduction and notes by Michael Papio (Toronto: University of Toronto Press, 2009), 529–530.

40. Ibid., 171.

the mobility of their God-given body."⁴¹ Fowlie summarizes the Catholic perspective on suicide that Aquinas carried forth in the Christian tradition—a perspective that Dante wished to elucidate in this piece of artistic literature. In such a case, there is no hope for redemption for those who commit suicide because they are not subject to the grace of purgatory, but sentenced to hell where they will never be forgiven of their sin. The criterion of worthiness that Dante illustrates is Aquinas' valorization of the Aristotelian idealization of courage. Aquinas appropriates this idealization of courage in such a way that he interprets courage to be a defining component in an individual's ability to embody the virtues of faith, hope, and charity.⁴² Otherwise stated, one is not worthy of redemption if one is not faithful enough to bear the brunt of long-suffering; hopeful enough in the power of God's deliverance; or charitable enough to have positive regard for the divine gift of human life.

Understanding the historical trajectory within which philosophical ideals are reinscribed by key formers of Christian theology is necessary to contend with the spirited history of condemnation that is associated with suicide. The brief history of ideas on suicide is an exemplar among many instances in which Christians utilize secular license in their ethical mediation. The most convincing element of this age-old argument that suicide is immoral is the intertextual interpretation that Augustine engages to support the argument that there are particular instances of suicide that are associated with diabolical motivation. However, what remains unacknowledged is how a preoccupation with the condemning of suicide impedes the consideration of how the omnipotence of God is at work even in the midst of perceived evil. How are we to affirm the intrinsic value of life and encourage the ascent of the both the soul and body into participation with the divine while at the same time resisting the urge to condemn, which arguably seeks to repel the redemptive work of Christ?

Within Christian tradition there is no escaping the groundwork of Augustine and this work of Aquinas, nor is it the intention of this work to convince one to do so. However, the criterion of worthiness must be evaluated in order to utilize the genius of their contribution without inheriting its contradiction. It can also be seen to be inadequate to dismiss the biblical revelation in a place of eternal suf-

---

41. Wallace Fowlie, *A Reading of Dante's Inferno* (Chicago: University of Chicago Press, 1981), 93.

42. *Summa Theologiae*, 2:2:64:5.

fering and punishment that is referenced in the gospels (Matthew 25:46; Luke 16: 22–28) and in the book of Revelation (14:10–11; 19:3; 20:10). Considering this reality, damnation should not be seen as a non-factor within the Christian saga of sin and redemption but as a matter that occurs out of divine omnipotence. Jesus instructs us not to be fearful of human power, but to have reverence for the power of God who determines the fate of our soul.

John Calvin (1509–1564)

John Calvin was one within the Reformed tradition who attempted to moderate the urge to damn suicides while at the same time affirm the sanctity of humanity. Calvin clearly inherited the idea that suicide was sinful from Augustine and Aquinas, and believed it to be a perversion of pride, unnatural, and indicative of demonic influence.[43] Jeffery Watt's article entitled "Calvin on Suicide," examines Calvin's condemnation of suicide and notes that Calvin believed it to be not only a sin, but the result of divine punishment for resisting the will of God.[44] Though much of what we find in Calvin is the influence of Augustine on his theology, Watt's notes that Calvin did not engage Augustine's distinction between martyrdom and suicide nor did he agree with the desecration of bodies and the disgraceful burial of suicides.[45] Though Augustine and Aquinas did not speak in favor of these practices in particular, there is no evidence that suggests that either of the two spoke against it. One can only assume that the Catholic and Protestant practices of denying Christian burial to suicides would not have become a Christian religious tradition had they spoke in any way against it. The point here is there is evidence that Calvin rejected the common idea and customary practice that held that those who died by suicide were completely devoid of sanctity.

In Calvin's sermon on Ahithophel (2 Samuel 17) he stated: "God wants our enemies to be honored even after their death… It would seem s if they were unworthy to be buried in the earth, or rather that the earth was not worthy to have them."[46] Calvin speaks against this concept of worthiness in one respect, but relies upon

---

43. Jeffrey Watt, "Calvin on Suicide" in *Church History 66:3* (Cambridge: Cambridge University Press, 1997), 466–470, 512–514.

44. Ibid., 462–465.

45. Ibid., 472–473.

46. Calvin, *Supplementa Calviniana*, ed. Hanns Ruckert (Neukirchen, Germany, 1961), 517.

it in his discourse on Judas Iscariot. Calvin commented in his *Fourth Sermon on the Passion of Our Lord*: "For there is Judas who is entirely cut off from the number of the children of God. It is even necessary that his condemnation appear before men and that it be entirely obvious."⁴⁷ The criterion of worthiness emerges consistently, and allows for the discretionary and exclusive problematized discourse on eternal security.

Augustine's doctrine of predestination and Calvin's appropriation encounters a key problem to be restated here: though they wish to stress God as the sole actor in salvation, their commentaries on suicide lack scriptural basis and are overly influenced by secular philosophy. When Christian theologians speculate on the degree to which certain things are sinful, these speculations can lay groundwork for "sin-talk" that leads to further speculation as to which sins are *worth* of exoneration and/or which sins are an indication of God's predestination.

JACOBUS ARMINIUS (1560–1609)

The practice of exempting those who die by suicide from the hope of future redemption is exacerbated in early modernity and in the Age of Enlightenment. During this span of time, Christian theologians grappled extensively with ideas on human reason and autonomy expounded upon by philosophers such as Rene Descartes, Thomas Hobbes, and John Locke.⁴⁸ On the heels of Calvinism would emerge the competing voice of Dutch theologian, Jacobus Arminius who came to develop a different perspective on human freedom and divine grace.

Arminius adopted the orthodox belief in the depravity of humanity that was formidably articulated by Augustine and that persisted to a modern height in the teaching of John Calvin.⁴⁹ Though he believed that humanity was only free to sin without the grace of God, Arminius expressed a concept of divine grace that acknowledged the importance of the human will and the *persuasive*

---

47. John Calvin, "Fourth Sermon on the Passion of Our Lord Jesus Christ," in *Sermons on the Saving Work of Christ*, trans. L. Dixon (Grand Rapids: Baker Academic, 1980), 108.

48. See Michael Losonsky's *Enlightenment and Action from Descartes to Kant* (New York: Cambridge University Press, 2007) for a thorough historical explication of philosophical ideas from classical modernity to the Age of Enlightenment and its influence on how epistemology is determined to be influenced by human society and social relationships.

49. Jacobus Arminius, *Arminius Speaks: Essential Writings on Predestination, Free Will, and the Nature of God*, ed. John D. Wagner (Eugene, OR: Wipf & Stock, 2011).

role of God that opposed Calvin's perception of a more *coercive* divine grace.[50] An understanding of divine grace to be persuasive highlighted the possibility of human beings to opt out of salvation. Arminius argued that all of humanity, the elect and the non-elect had the opportunity to experience the grace of God, but that this grace was not irresistible. Arminius held that faith would be the determinant of salvation because, for him, the doctrine of justification by faith implied divine mercy that absolved the believer and divine judgment that indicted the non-believer.[51] John Wesley came behind Arminius a century later to add that the lack of faith as well as non-repentance could cause a once believer to lose their salvation. In Wesley's "Thoughts on Suicide," he described suicide to be an expression of human resistance to grace and a crime of impatience that justified punishment and disgraceful burial in order to deter others.[52]

From the early church to the Reformation and into the Age of Enlightenment, we have observed the trend of condemnation within Christian discourse. An examination of Augustine's philosophical hermeneutics that guided his allegorical and intertextual method of theological and biblical interpretation revealed a speculative and inconsistent moral declaration of suicide as a sin of perdition that influenced his soteriological idealization of perseverance. Failure to acknowledge the moral ambiguity within his argumentation denied those who died by suicide hope for future redemption and provided Christian communities with license to posthumously imagine and physically dramatize the desacralization of human beings.

Human history has attested to the reality that human hands are far too feeble and frail to handle creation without the assistance of the divine. When left to our own devices, we conceptualize out of our misconceptions and appraise with unreliable scales that are liable to be both erroneous and misleading. An unprecedented example of such misguided measurement has been in the theoretical and material handling of the bodies and souls of our brothers and sisters who have died by suicide. This desacralization has been documented throughout European history from the refusal to extract the bodies of suicides from open doors, due to the social and religious identification of those bodies to be unworthy of proper extrac-

---

50. Ibid., 334.

51. Ibid., 140.

52. John Wesley, "Thoughts on Suicide" written on April 8, 1790. *The Works of the Reverend John Wesley A.M.* Vol. VII, (New York: J. Emory and B. Waugh, 1831), 463.

tion, to the public mutilation and hangings of bodies, and the denial of Christian burials. The first eighty pages of Alexander Murray's work provides an account of how the bodies and property of those who died by suicide were physically handled and how the fate of their souls were theorized in religious and philosophical discourse.[53]

Positive Interventions: From the Exemption of Hope to the Embodiment of Hope

IMPLICATIONS FOR THEOLOGICAL ANTHROPOLOGY

It was not until the Age of Enlightenment and the development of the social sciences that important shifts were made to consider mental illness as not merely an indication of demonic influence, but a significant public health issue.[54] This shift in Christian discourse on suicide opens the door for some positive interventions in the practice of condemning suicides in such a way that allows room within the faith tradition to lament in acknowledgment of the many men and women who have been desacralized by our "sin talk," and to express our repentance for allowing our "sin-talk" to recapitulate sin through an expressed commitment to be attentive to the need to affirm the sanctity of humanity in our processes toward suicide prevention. Lamentation and repentance in this context necessitates some constructive work within our doctrinal formulations on God and humanity.

| *Here, the author gets to the meat of the article—the implications for theological anthropology and practice.* |

Working with the poignant suggestion made by Stephen G. Ray in his work *Do No Harm: Social Sin and Christian Responsibility* where he draws attention to how some Christian theologians, in their incongruent descriptions of sin, actually impede their efforts to astutely discern the way that sin is materially experienced within the concrete reality of the human community.[55] Ray articulates a constructive theological anthropology that cautions against sin talk

---

53. Murray, *Suicide in the Middle Ages*, 10–84.

54. Anton J.L. van Hooff, "A Historical Perspective on Suicide in *Comprehensive Textbook of Suicidology*. ed. Ronald W. Maris, Alan L. Berman, and Morton M. Silverman (New York: Guilford. Jordan, John R. 2001), 119–122.

55. Stephen G. Ray, *Do No Harm: Social Sin and Christian Responsibility* (Minneapolis: Fortress Press, 2003), 75–76.

that renders assumptions about how sin affects our closeness to God. He substantiates his theological anthropology by seeking to redeem "sin-talk" by working with Augustine's understanding of human depravity without inheriting the aforementioned appraisal of his shortcomings. Ray argues that a responsible theological anthropology leans toward the Augustinian principle that all of humanity stands before God in both a state of disgrace because of original sin as well as a state of grace because of the redemptive work of Christ.[56] By leaning on this principle of participation, we are able to resist the tendency to qualify sin in a way that leads toward the development of a system of hierarchy that contains upper and lower echelons of human standing with God. The historical condemnation of suicide that is described in this work bears witness to the creation of this system of hierarchy within Christian discourse that has marginalized those who die by suicide, and this principle of participation provides a way to dismantle this oppressive discourse.

In an effort to move from the practice of articulating the exemption of hope toward the embodiment of hope, I propose for consideration Psalm 139:8. This psalm testifies to the presence of the divine even in the darkest residences of our souls. Hebrew Bible scholar, J. Clinton McCann, notes that the psalmist here wanted to emphasize the inescapable presence of God even in the bowels of Sheol, which was usually believed to be outside of divine proximity.[57] McCann cautions against reading Psalm 139 with the aim to justify the classical doctrine of predestination, but clarifies "however, the word *predestination* may be appropriately applied to Psalm 139 if it is understood fundamentally as an affirmation that our lives derive from God, belong to God, and find their true destination in God's purposes."[58]

To take McCann's observation a step further, how might we understand the work of God in the midst of our eternal state of belonging within proximity to God? The Eastern Orthodox tradition helps us to understand the divine activity that furthers the constructive work of a theological anthropology that affirms the presence of divine activity in both human life and death. Gregory of Nazianzus uses the term *perichoreo* to describe the relationality of the members

---

56. Ibid., 108–11.

57. J. Clinton McCann Jr., "*The Book of Psalms*: Introduction, *Commentary*, and Reflections," in The *New Interpreter's Bible*, vol. 4 (Nashville: Abingdon Press, 1996): 1237.

58. Ibid., 1237.

of the Trinity in which he states: "Just as the natures are mixed so also the names pass reciprocally (*perichoreo*) into each other by the principle of this coalescence."[59] In Gregory's *Oration 18*, he uses the term *perichoreo* to describe the reciprocal nature of life and death and says, "Life and death, as they are called, apparently so different, are in a sense revolved into (perichorei), and successive to, each other." Scholars like Brian Scalise interpret Gregory's use of the term *perichoresis* to describe the Trinity as well as to offer an explanation on how humanity is renewed in the image of Christ through the passing of divine properties to humanity.[60] If we apply these observations of perichoresis in our task to restore the hope of future redemption to those who die by suicide, then we are able to problematize Augustine's assertion that the perseverance of the believer can only be expressed within the realm of human life and the state of that believer's death. Demonstrated here is a departure from Western theology toward a more holistic view of life that includes a view on the continuity of life and death as integral to the renewal of life.

Continuing in this departure from traditional Western theology, it is advantageous to consider two of the tenets of Womanist theology and ethics in our conversation. For example, by considering the Womanist ethical tenet of radical subjectivity, we are encouraged to acknowledge, even within the case of suicide, the ways human agency can be used in order to 'seriously, responsibly, and audaciously' forge new possibilities in the world.[61] Acknowledgment of human agency permits believers to choose *how* they wish to participate in divine grace in a way that does not nullify divine justification just as in their human choice to have faith does not nullify God's prevenient grace that extends to them the invitation to faith. This is how we are able to construct a theological anthropology that expresses the sovereign activity of God's grace without posthumously oppressing those who die by suicide.

IMPLICATIONS ON THEOLOGICAL PRAXIS

Let us now consider ways in which we can both articulate the sovereign activity of God's grace within our theology as well as

---

59. Gregory of Nazianzus, *Epistle CI: To Cledonius the Priest against* Apollinarius, par. 4. Verna Harrison, "Perichoresis in the Greek Fathers," *St. Vladimir's Theological Quarterly* 35, no. 1 (1991): 55–56.

60. Brian T. Scalise, "Perichoresis in Gregory Nazianzen and Maximus the Confessor," *Eleutheria* 2, no. 1, (2012), Article 5, 3–5; 9.

61. Stacey Floyd-Thomas, *Mining the Motherlode: Methods of Womanist Ethics* (Cleveland: The Pilgrim Press, 2006), 8.

embody such a hopeful declaration within our communal praxis. Considering that more than ninety-percent of those who die by suicide in the United States are found to have diagnosable mental disorders, one can only reasonably deduce that humanity had a handling problem when it comes to those who have died by suicide; humanity, historically and presently, has had a handling problem with the living, and particularly those who are living with mental illness.[62] In *Testamentum Imperium's* last volume that attended to this question of redemption for suicides, Karen E. Mason attends to this reality in her proposal of a non-judgmental method of pastoral care that nurtures suicidal members in hope and galvanizes the surrounding faith community as an embodiment of that hope as intervention and method of suicide prevention.[63] Communal embodiment of hope can then be seen as the passing of divine properties of creative relationality that exists within the Trinity and the believer toward the transformative renewal of communities in the image of Christ.

Creative relationality is described also within Womanist discourse to suggest that instances of communal transformation and renewal have a soteriological dimension that is essential in the human struggle against sin and evil in the world. Echoing Delores Williams' argument that the salvific work of Christ can be found in the ministerial vision of Christ, Monica A. Coleman interprets the ministerial vision of Christ to have a communal dimension that she refers to as 'creative transformation.' Coleman describes 'creative transformation' as the discernment and action taken upon the call of Christ in particular situations where it is necessary to challenge the destructive behaviors at work in order to affirm the life giving and redemptive incarnation of God in the world.[64]

Through these considerations of radical subjectivity and creative transformation, perceptions of suicide can cease to be entrapped in speculative dialogue concerned with whether or not it is a sin. Rather, the dialogue can be opened up to consider suicide and all that influences it as an existential reality. Considering the role of human agency, the redemptive work of Christ, and the reality of systemic evil as operative factors at work, it can then be possible to see suicide not as sin, but as a way of grappling with sin and

---

62. National Institute of Mental Health. Suicide in the US: Statistics and Prevention.

63. Karen E. Mason, "Does Suicide Exempt the Deceased from the Hope of Future Redemption?"

64. Monica Coleman, *Making A Way Out of No Way: A Womanist Theology* (Minneapolis: Fortress, 2008), 89–90.

evil. Is it possible to consider suicide then, as the simultaneous stretching forth of the human soul toward divine grace and a willful turn away from a fallen world shaped largely by systemic evil and the human resistance to be conformed by grace? The systemic evil within a fallen world that I am referring to operates on a number of levels and materialize in what social scientists have identified as risk factors for suicidal behavior. These risk factors are inclusive of, but not limited to, family conflict, mental disorders, social isolation, and economic oppression.[65]

Working with the social theory of Emilie Durkheim (1897) and Shneidman (1987), a recent study has identified that when the strongest of these risk factors are present and the human need to belong and to feel valued are unmet, the risk of suicidal behavior increases.[66] Though there are more male suicides than female suicides, this study also highlights the reality that women are more likely to attempt suicide because they are more likely to experience the aforementioned risk factors.[67] Instead of debating the sinfulness of suicide, theologians should examine how such disparities on suicide are reflective of systematic oppression and the intersections of sexism, racism, and classism. Statistics on violence and rape indicate that women of color are, arguably, the most unsafe group of people in the U.S.[68] This is the question behind the question: the theological agenda should be to determine how the way we talk about sin and worthiness provides a theoretical framework that allows this to be the case. Meaning, in order to investigate the theological marginalization of those who die by suicide, we must be able to discern the ways in which theological conversations become gestures of the faith community to place or *dis*place people within the salvation narrative. The first task of the theologian is to see this *displacement* by human beings to be contrary to the gospel of Jesus Christ, and to be fortuitous enough to identify its practice as *sinful*. Secondly, theologians must help communities to be attentive to the individual, as well as the conditions within society that

---

65. Kimberly Van Orden, T.K. Witte, K.C. Cukrowicz, S.R. Braithwaite, E.A. Selby, T.E. Joiner. "The Interpersonal Theory of Suicide." *Psychological Review* 2010 Apr; 117(2): 575–600.

66. Ibid., 588–591.

67. Ibid., 591–592.

68. M.C. Black, K.C. Basile, M.J. Breiding, S.G. Smith, M.L. Walters, M.T. Merrick, J. Chen, and M.R. Stevens, *The National Intimate Partner and Sexual Violence Survey (NISVS): 2010 Summary Report* (Atlanta: Center for Disease Control and Prevention, 2011): 83–86.

shape them and their perceptions of their realities, in their care of suicidal persons. In this respect, the dialogue on the sinfulness of suicide can no longer be a distraction in our communal discernment and fight against systemic evil, as we must work to help people escape condemnation in life and in death.

This is an excellent example of a scholar presenting very detailed and complex information, but in a way that is clear, organized, and relevant.

* * *

APPENDIX A

Theological Terms

Alterity the quality or state of being other; a philosophical term that relates to "otherness"
Anamnesis a recalling to memory; in Christianity, the Eucharist recalls Christ's giving his body and blood for humanity's sins at the Crucifixion
Anthropic referring to humankind or humans
Anthropocentrism belief that humans are the center of creation, the central element of the universe
Antithesis the use of an assertion and a contrasting statement
Apocalypse from the Greek word for "revelation," a type of writing that describes a mysterious and divine vision of a heavenly world in the future
Apocalyptic writings (particularly New-Testament writings) that describe the end of the world
Apocrypha early Christian writings from the second century (intertestamental period) not accepted into the Protestant canon but included in the Roman Catholic Bible
Apostasy renunciation of a religious faith, a political belief, or even any previous loyalty
Autograph the first copy of a biblical text
BCE a notation used after a date that means "before the common era" and replaces the notation B.C. ("before Christ")
Biblical criticism a broad discipline that includes a range of interpretive activities for evaluating biblical texts
Canon from the Greek, meaning "rule" or "measure, a decree from a sacred council or an accepted list of sacred books ("canon of Scripture")
CE a notation used after a date that means "common era" and replaces the notation A.D. (Latin for "the year of our Lord")
Chiasm/chiasmus a specific textual pattern in which ideas or clauses are presented, followed by a repetition of those same ideas in reverse order; in this type of pattern, the first and last phrases or concepts correspond to one another, the second and next-to-last correspond to one another, and so on
Chreia a commentary, usually brief, on a famous event, saying or happening that Jesus used as illustration to make his point

Christophany   a manifestation or an appearance of Christ
Codex   an ancient biblical text in bound book form, rather than scroll
Concupiscence   a longing of the soul for what will give it delight (this can be sensual or sexual desire)
Dialectics   a way of arriving at truth through the exchange of logical arguments
Diaspora   the scattering of a people of a common national origin, culture or belief; dispersion
Didache   the teachings of the twelve Apostles
Ecclesiology   the part of theology concerned with the nature and function of the church and its doctrine
Eidetic   having the characteristic of essences, forms or images
Eschatology   study of the "last things" or the end of the world
Eschaton   the End Times
Exegesis   to explain, to interpret; the critical interpretation of a text or portion of Scripture; the exposition of a biblical text using specific methods of biblical criticism
Form criticism   the study of biblical texts in terms of the oral and written traditions behind them
Formula   a set of words used in a particular setting or context ("Amen, Amen, I say unto you …")
Genre   a word that, in literary theory, refers to a type of literature
Gnosis   from the Greek for "knowledge," generally refers to a type of spiritual knowledge
Hebrew Bible   the canon of writings accepted by Jews as Holy Scripture, which Christians refer to as the Old Testament
Hermeneutics   the principles, set of rules or interpretive lenses used to read a biblical text
Homiletics   the process by which the meaning of biblical texts are communicated through preaching
Inclusio   a literary device in which a passage is "bookended" between a beginning and ending that are intentionally similar
Kenosis   from the Greek, an emptying; this can be a self-emptying to become receptive to God's Divine will, as Christ voluntarily renounced his divine attributes in order to become human
Kerygma   preaching, proclamation; to preach; the proclamation of the Christian faith
Koine   from the Greek word for "common," a term describing the everyday Greek used by inhabitants of the Roman Empire; the language of the New Testament and the early Christian movement
Lacuna   a gap in a Scriptural text or manuscript
Lectionary   an arrangement of Scriptural texts organized for use in the liturgy

Metonymy the process of substituting one word or phrase for another ("Son of Man" for Jesus)
Mimesis from the Greek for "imitation," referring to the act of imitating
Mishnah from the Hebrew for "repetition" or "instruction," a term referring to the practice of Jewish interpretation of Scripture *and* to the collection of those interpretations
Ontology a science or study of being
Parousia from the Greek word meaning "presence" or "arrival," refers to the Second Coming of Christ
Pentateuch from the Greek words for "five" and "book," a term referring to the first five books of the Old Testament, known as the Torah in Judaism
Pericope a particular section of the biblical text usually defined by a story, event or parable
Polemic controversial discussion or argument; the art or practice of dispute
Process theology a theological movement that emphasizes God's participation in the evolving world
Prolegomena a preliminary essay or discussion, as in a book; a preface
Q from the German word for "source" (*Quelle*), used by biblical scholars for a hypothetical collection of Jesus' sayings that may have been a source for the Gospels of Matthew and Luke
Redaction criticism the study of the editorial methods used by biblical writers to shape materials they received from other sources
Septuagint the Greek translation of the original Hebrew Scriptures (between 250 and 100 BCE)
Sitz-im-Leben setting in life or social setting
Soteriology the theological doctrine of salvation, in particular as effected by Jesus Christ
Source in biblical studies, a word that refers to a source document that lies behind a written work
Syncretism the attempt to merge two different religious systems into one system
Synecdoche use of a part for the whole, or a whole for a part
Systematic theology an arm of theology that seeks to present theological concepts in an orderly and systematic way
Talmud the collection of rabbinical commentaries and interpretations on the Torah, including a systematic presentation of rules of conduct and moral and spiritual teaching
Tanach an acronym for the three parts of the Hebrew Bible, Torah ("law"), Neviim ("prophets") and Ketuvim ("writings")
Targum the Aramaic translation of the Hebrew Scriptures
Textual criticism a method of biblical critical that studies texts in terms of the original words or forms

Theism   belief in the existence of a God or gods, or a personal God as creator and ruler of the world

Theocentric   assuming God as the center

Theodicy   a study that attempts to reconcile the goodness and justice of God with the presence of evil and suffering in the world

Theophany   God appearing to man

Tradition criticism   the attempt to uncover the ways in which a tradition developed from the time the form originated to the latest form

Typology   a doctrine of belief that sees significant events and persons in Christian dispensation symbolized or prefigured in the Hebrew Scriptures

Vulgate   the translation of the Hebrew Scriptures into Latin (405 CE)

Yahweh   the proper name for the God of Israel, composed of the Hebrew consonants YHWH and usually translated as "Lord"

APPENDIX B

Research Sources

As you begin seminary study, you'll need to know how to access a variety of research materials, so the best thing you can do is familiarize yourself with what your library offers in both print and electronic resources. Here are some important print resources you'll be using.

Print Resources

Bible Commentaries. Bible commentaries offer interpretation and exposition to help readers gain a deeper understanding of a biblical text. A commentary can be a single volume covering the entire Old Testament or New Testament in one place, or it can consist of multiple volumes, each interpreting an individual book or set of books. Commentaries typically start with an introductory overview of a book, followed by an exposition on each chapter, within which there are often detailed, verse-by-verse analyses. Commentaries have been written by some of the most knowledgeable theologians in church history, each of whom interprets the text from a particular theological perspective. More recent commentaries generally are written by a team of scholars whose combined interpretations provide a balanced perspective. It's a good idea to begin with one of the all-purpose commentaries to get a general overview of the text before delving into the many historical commentaries available online.

- Albright, William Foxwell, and David Noel Freedman, gen. eds. *The Anchor Bible.* 120 volumes. Garden City, NY: Doubleday, 1963–2008.
- Barton, John, and John Muddiman, eds. *The Oxford Bible Commentary.* Oxford, UK: Oxford University Press, 2007.
- Friedman, Richard Elliott. *Commentary on the Torah: With a New English Translation and the Hebrew Text.* San Francisco: HarperSanFrancisco, 2012.
- Hubbard, Robert L., Jr., gen. ed. *New International Commentary on the Old Testament.* 24 volumes. Grand Rapids, MI: William B. Eerdmans, 2013.
- Kee, Howard Clark, ed. *Cambridge Annotated Study Bible (New Revised Standard Version).* New York: University of Cambridge Press, 1993.

- Mays, James L., ed. *HarperCollins Bible Commentary*, rev. ed. New York: HarperCollins, 2000.
- Petersen, David L., and Beverly R. Gaventa, eds. *The New Interpreter's Bible: One-Volume Commentary*. Nashville: Abingdon, 2010.
- Petersen, David L., and Gail R. O'Day, eds. *Theological Bible Commentary*. Louisville: Westminster John Knox, 2009.

There also are a number of Bible commentaries today that interpret the text from the perspective of a particular audience or reader. Here are some of the more common ones.

- Adeyemo, Tokunboh, gen ed. *Africa Bible Commentary: A One-Volume Commentary Written by 70 African Scholars*. Grand Rapids, MI: Zondervan, 2006.
- DeYoung, Curtiss Paul, Wilda C. Gafney, Leticia A. Guardiola-Saenz, George Tinker, and Frank M. Yamada, eds. *The People's Bible: New Revised Standard Version with the Apocrypha*. Minneapolis: Augsburg Fortress, 2008.
- Guest, Deryn, Robert Goss, Mona West, and Thomas Bohache, eds. *The Queer Bible Commentary*. London: SCM, 2006.
- Newsom, Carol Ann, Sharon H. Ringe, and Jacqueline E. Lapsley, eds. *Women's Bible Commentary*, rev. and updated, 3d ed. Louisville: Westminster John Knox Press, 2012.
- Schottroff, Luise, and Marie-Theres Wacker, eds. *Feminist Biblical Interpretation: A Compendium of Critical Commentary on the Books of the Bible and Related Literature*. Grand Rapids, MI: William B. Eerdmans, 2012.
- Segovia Fernando F. and R.S. Sugirtharajah, eds. *Postcolonial Commentary on the New Testament Writings*. London/New York: T&T Clark, 2007.
- Stone, Ken, ed. *Queer Commentary and the Hebrew Bible*. New York: Sheffield Academic, 2001.

Concordances. A concordance is a listing of key words in the biblical text (some list *every* word in the text) in alphabetical order, followed by citations of all the verses in the Bible in which the word appears. There are different concordances that correspond to different Bible translations (NIV, NRSV, etc.). These are a few of the more commonly used concordances, but your seminary library may have others as well.

- Hatch, Edwin, and Henry A. Redpath. *A Concordance to the Septuagint and the Other Greek Versions of the Old Testament (including the Apocryphal Books)*, 2d ed. Grand Rapids, MI: Baker Academic, 1998.
- Kohlenberger, John R. III, ed. *The Concise Concordance to the New Revised Standard Version*. New York: Oxford University Press, 1993.
- Marshall, I. Howard, ed. *Concordance to the Greek New Testament* (Moulton and Geden), 6th ed., fully rev. New York: Continuum, 2004.

- Strong, James. *The New Strong's Exhaustive Concordance of the Bible.* Nashville: Thomas Nelson, 2003.
- Whitaker, Richard E., and John R. Kohlenberger III, eds. *The Analytical Concordance to the New Revised Standard Version of the New Testament.* Grand Rapids, MI: William B. Eerdmans Publishing/New York: Oxford University Press, 2000.

Dictionaries. Dictionaries provide concise definitions of theological concepts and terms, important events, biblical themes, key theories, and significant theologians.

- Alexander, T. Desmond, and Brian S. Rosner. *New Dictionary of Biblical Theology.* Downers Grove, IL: InterVarsity, 2000.
- Espín, Orlando O., James B. Nickoloff. *An Introductory Dictionary of Theology and Religious Studies.* Collegeville, MN: Liturgical, 2007.
- McKim, Donald K. *Westminster Dictionary of Theological Terms.* Louisville: Westminster John Knox, 1996.
- O'Collins, Gerald, and Edward G. Farrugia. *A Concise Dictionary of Theology*, rev. and exp. ed. New York: Continuum, 2003.
- Soulen, Richard N., and R. Kendall Soulen. *Handbook of Biblical Criticism*, 4th ed. Louisville: Westminster John Knox, 2011.
- Unger, Merrill F. *The New Unger's Bible Dictionary.* Chicago: Moody, 2009.

Encyclopedias. Like dictionaries, encyclopedias explain theological concepts, but entries are much more in-depth and comprehensive. Here are a few good ones to check out.

- Byrne, Peter, and Leslie Houlden, eds. *Companion Encyclopedia of Theology.* New York: Routledge, 2013.
- Metzger, Bruce M., and Michael D. Coogan, eds. *The Oxford Guide to Ideas and Issues of the Bible.* New York: Oxford University Press, 2001.
- Rahner, Karl, ed. *Encyclopedia of Theology: A Concise Sacramentum Mundi.* New York: Continuum International, 1975.
- Stephen Bowden, John. *Encyclopedia of Christianity.* New York: Oxford University Press, Inc., 2005.

Exegesis and Biblical Interpretation. The following resources are helpful for exploring biblical interpretation in more depth and for understanding exegetical strategies and methods.

- Gorman, Michael J. *Elements of Biblical Exegesis: A Basic Guide for Students and Ministers.* Grand Rapids, MI: Baker, 2008.
- Hayes, John Haralson, and Carl R. Holladay. *Biblical Exegesis: A Beginner's Handbook.* Louisville: Westminster John Knox, 2007.
- Tate, W. Randolph. *Biblical Interpretation: An Integrated Approach.* Grand Rapids, MI: Baker, 2008.

Historical Context of the Bible. There are numerous sources for information on the history and culture of the biblical world; here are several good ones to consult.

- Coogan, Michael David. *The Oxford History of the Biblical World.* New York: Oxford University Press, 2001.
- De Vaux, Roland. *Ancient Israel: Its Life and Institutions.* Grand Rapids, MI: William B. Eerdmans, 1997.
- Malina, Bruce J. *The New Testament World: Insights from Cultural Anthropology.* Louisville: Westminster John Knox, 2001.
- Roetzel, Calvin J. *The World that Shaped the New Testament.* Louisville: Westminster John Knox, 2002.

Literary Analysis of the Bible. These resources help you explore the New Testament and Old Testament in terms of literary aspects such as form and genre.

- Bailey, James L. *Literary Forms in the New Testament: A Handbook.* Louisville: Westminster John Knox Press, 1992.
- Schmid, Konrad. *The Old Testament: A Literary History.* Minneapolis: Augsburg Fortress, 2012.
- Walsh, Jerome T. *Style and Structure in Biblical Hebrew Narrative.* Collegeville, MN: Liturgical, 2001.

Source Analysis of the Bible. Check out these resources for investigating sources of biblical passages and the relationship between various books of the Bible.

- Aland, Kurt. *Synopsis of the Four Gospels: Greek-English Edition*, 10th ed. Stuttgart: German Bible Society, 1993.
- Arnold, Bill T., and Bryan E. Beyer. *Readings from the Ancient Near East: Primary Sources for OT Study.* Grand Rapids, MI: Baker Academic, 2002.
- Beale, G.K., and D.A. Carson, eds. *Commentary on the New Testament Use of the Old Testament.* Grand Rapids, MI: Baker Academic, 2007.
- Patton, Carl S. *The Sources of the Synoptic Gospels.* Chicago: University of Chicago Press, 1915.
- Vriezen, Theodoor Christiaan, and Adam Simon van der Woude. *Ancient Israelite and Early Jewish Literature.* Leiden: Brill, 2005.

Textual and Word Study of the Bible. These resources are helpful for studying a word in the original biblical language and for exploring textual aspects such as grammar and syntax.

- Arnold, Bill T., and John H. Choi. *A Guide to Biblical Hebrew Syntax.* New York: Cambridge University Press, 2003.
- Burer, Michael H., and Jeffrey E. Miller. *A New Reader's Lexicon of the Greek New Testament.* Grand Rapids, MI: Kregel, 2008.

- Koehler, L., and W. Baumgartner. *The Hebrew and Aramaic Lexicon of the Old Testament.* Boston: Brill Academic, 2001.
- Metzger, Bruce M. *A Textual Commentary on the Greek New Testament.* Peabody, MA: Hendrickson, 2006.
- Moule, C.F.D. *An Idiom Book of New Testament Greek.* New York: Cambridge University Press, 1959.
- Pratico, G., and M. Van Pelt. *Basics of Biblical Hebrew Grammar.* Grand Rapids, MI: Zondervan, 2001.
- Rogers, Cleon L. *The New Linguistic and Exegetical Key to the Greek New Testament.* Grand Rapids, MI: Zondervan, 1998.
- Tov, Emanuel. *Textual Criticism of the Hebrew Bible*, 2d rev. ed. Minneapolis: Augsburg, 1992/2001.
- Zerwick, Max. *Analysis of the Greek New Testament.* Rome: Editrice Pontificio Istituto Biblico, 1996.

Writing and Research Help. For more help on research and writing, check out these helpful resources.

- Badke, William. *Research Strategies: Finding Your Way through the Information Fog.* Bloomington, IN: iUniverse, 2011.
- Booth, Wayne C. et al. *The Craft of Research*, 3d ed. Chicago: University of Chicago Press, 2008.
- Core, Deborah. *The Seminary Student Writes.* St. Louis: Chalice, 2000.
- Heidt, Mari Rapela. *A Guide for Writing About Theology and Religion.* Winona, MN: Anselm Academic/Christian Brothers, 2012.
- Strunk, William, Jr., and E.B. White. *The Elements of Style*, 4th ed. New York: Longman, 1999.
- Vyhmeister, Nancy Jean. *Your Guide to Writing Quality Research Papers: For Students of Religion and Theology*, 2d ed. Grand Rapids, MI: Zondervan, 2008.
- Zinsser, William. *On Writing Well: The Classic Guide to Writing Nonfiction*, 30th anniv. ed. New York: HarperCollins, 2006.

Internet Resources

Your seminary library has access to hundreds of online religion and theology databases that allow you to search for a variety of materials by subject area. Be sure to learn how to access and navigate these resources, because you'll need them to locate journal articles, electronic books, research studies, and other essential materials. These are the different kinds of resources you'll find.

- *Archives.* Resources such as the *American Religion Data Archive* provide research statistics and studies on various aspects of religious life.
- *Concordances.* Online concordances allow you to search by a specific

word to find all verses in the Bible that contain that term (concordances correspond to different Bible translations).

- *Databases.* These provide access to journal articles, monographs, and other documents through resources such as the *ATLA Religion Database with Serials, JSTOR,* or *Humanities Abstracts.*
- *Dictionaries.* There are a number of online dictionaries—such as the *Concise Oxford Dictionary of the Christian Church* or *Dictionary of the Bible*—that provide detailed definitions of key theological terms.
- *Electronic books.* Resources such as *Ebrary* and *Oxford Scholarship Online* offer access to libraries of electronic books that can be read online or downloaded.
- *Encyclopedias.* Resources like the *Encyclopedia of the Enlightenment* or *Routledge Encyclopedia of Philosophy* provide in-depth interpretations of theological concepts.
- *Reference books.* You can find online reference books on topics related to religion and theology through resources like *Blackwell Reference Books in Religion* or *Credo Reference.*

Here are a few general and discipline-specific resources that will be helpful as you begin your research.

Biblical Studies

- *Association for Religious and Intellectual Life (ARIL), Bible and Biblical Studies.* http://www.aril.org/Bible.html. This is a listing of the best resources on the Bible and biblical studies available on the Internet.
- *Early Christian Writings.* http://www.earlychristianwritings.com/. This site offers access to a large selection of early Christian writings—in chronological order—including the New Testament, the Apocrypha, Gnostic texts, writings of the church fathers, and other pagan/Jewish, and Jewish/Christian texts.
- *The Five Gospels Parallels.* http://www.utoronto.ca/religion/synopsis/. Here, you can see how a particular Gospel passage compares to versions in the other Gospels.
- *New Testament Gateway.* http://www.ntgateway.com/. This award-winning directory of Internet resources allows you to search for a variety of topics related to the New Testament and Christian origins.
- *Old Testament Gateway.* http://www.otgateway.com/. This site offers a comprehensive, searchable directory of internet sites that will be useful for students of the Old Testament.
- *Resource Pages for Biblical Studies.* http://torreys.org/bible/. This is an excellent, easy-to-use resource for students exploring the early Christian writings and their social world.
- *Society of Biblical Literature, Educational Resources.* http://www.sbl-

site.org/educational/sitesofinterest.aspx. SBL offers a list of resources useful for students researching biblical literature—covering topics such as ancient languages, the Greco-Roman world, and Jewish/Middle-Eastern studies.

Christian Education and Faith Formation

- *Christian Education Resources Database, Cedarville University.* http://www.cedarville.edu/cf/library/christianed/. This searchable database is designed to help students, professors, and clergy working with children and young adults in a church setting.
- *Faith Formation Learning Exchange.* http://www.faithformationlearning exchange.net/. FFLE offers a searchable collection of materials articles, books, research for faith formation across the whole life span—for instructors, students, and clergy.
- *Religious Education Association.* http://www.religiouseducation.net/about. This organization offers resources, programs, and news for professors, practitioners, and researchers in the field of religious education.

Early Church History and Literature

- *Christian Classics Ethereal Library.* http://www.ccel.org/ccel/schaff/hcc1.html. Classic Christian texts are available on this site, including the writings of the early church fathers, reference books, hymns, creeds, catechisms, liturgies, sermons, and histories.
- *Christian History Institute (CHI), Educational Resources/Church History.* https://www.christianhistoryinstitute.org/study/. This site offers church-history resources and self-study material that focuses on Christian church history, including the early church, medieval, Reformation, and post–Reformation.
- *Early Christianity/Patristics, Yale University Library.* http://guides.library.yale.edu/content.php?pid=129512&sid=1111001. This resource guide helps students find resources in several categories: general reference works, specialized reference works, primary texts, databases, journals, and websites.
- *History of Christianity, Yale University Library.* http://guides.library.yale.edu/content.php?pid=29272&sid=213807. Another resource guide from the Yale University Library, this one offers quick links to a wealth of resources—including journal articles, databases, dictionaries, and encyclopedias—related to early, medieval, and modern Christianity.
- *Internet Christian Library.* http://www.iclnet.org/pub/resources/christian-history.html. This is an excellent resource for early Christian writings, including writings of the apostolic fathers, patristic texts, creeds and canons, and other documents.

- *Internet History Sourcebooks Project, Christian Origins.* http://www.fordham.edu/halsall/. This excellent site offers links to historical texts on Christian origins, including ancient, medieval, and modern documents.

Liturgy, Preaching and Worship

- *Center for Excellence in Preaching, Calvin Seminary.* http://cep.calvinseminary.edu/. This site offers sermon ideas, Bible commentary suggestions, sermon recordings, and recommendations from experienced preachers.
- *Liturgical Studies and Liturgical Music, Internet Theology Resources.* http://www.users.csbsju.edu/~eknuth/itr/ltgy/index.html#LTGY. This site offers a wide selection of hard-to-find links to hymns, liturgies, and missals.
- *Living Web Homiletics Library.* http://www.livingweb.com/library/251.htm. An ecumenical resource, this site offers a library of materials on sermon preparation, delivery, preaching theology, and general homiletics.
- *Pastor's Pointers Christian Sermon, Worship, and Bible Links.* http://www.garyritner.org/ppcss.html. This page offers a substantial list of links to individual sermons and Bible-related sites.
- *The Text This Week.* http://www.textweek.com/. This valuable site offers detailed resources for all lectionary texts, including links to various online Scripture sources, historical references, and Bible commentaries. Also included are helpful preaching aids such as a thematic movie and art index, ideas for holidays and special events, and suggestions for preaching in times of violence, war, terrorism, or natural disaster.
- *The Revised Common Lectionary, Vanderbilt Divinity School Library.* http://lectionary.library.vanderbilt.edu/. This easy-to-use site provides the full text of all three years of the Revised Common Lectionary.
- *Wabash Center for Teaching and Learning in Theology and Religion, Preaching.* http://www.wabashcenter.wabash.edu/resources/result-browse.aspx?topic=697&pid=650. The Wabash Center offers links to a variety of resources related to preaching and homiletics.
- *The Word on the Web.* http://www.kn.sbc.com/wired/fil/pages/listpreachergr.html. A helpful resource for preachers or students, this site provides links to sites on lectionary texts, Bible commentaries, biblical interpretation, and cultural analyses.

Pastoral Care

- *American Association of Pastoral Counselors (AAPC).* http://www.aapc.org/. AAPC promotes the development of pastoral counseling ministry, providing certification and training, educational materials, programs, and events.
- *MennoLink Pastoral Care Resources.* http://pastors.mennolink.org/pcare.html. This site offers links to resources for general pastoral care and

care-giving, as well as materials for spiritual growth, weddings and marriage, birth and adoption, hospital care, dying and grief.
• *Pastoral Ministry, Internet Theology Resources.* http://www.users.csbsju.edu/~eknuth/itr/theorled.html#RLED. This page offers a broad range of topics related to pastoral ministry, including spirituality, discernment, alcoholism, grief, domestic violence, and LBGTQ issues.

Theology and Ethics

• *American Academy of Religion (AAR).* http://www.aarweb.org/publications. AAR publishes print and online materials for the field of religious studies, including journals, academic books, and special-topic publications.
• *Global Digital Library on Theology.* http://www.globethics.net/gtl. This online library offers free access to thousands of articles, journals, books, and other resources related to theology and ethics.
• *Internet Resources for Theological Studies, Fuller Theological Seminary Library.* http://library.fuller.edu/library/Internet_resources.asp. From Fuller Theological Seminary Library, this site offers a comprehensive listing of links by topic—including theology, ethics, religion, missions, and practical theology—as well as useful web search engines and gateways.
• *The NTS Library (Northwestern Theological Seminary).* http://www.onlinetheologylibrary.com/. An online theological library, NTS offers free access to a large collection of reference books, religion resources, research studies, and religious journals.
• *Online Theology-Related Periodicals, Internet Theology Resources.* http://www.users.csbsju.edu/~eknuth/itr/jour.html. This is an excellent list of links to electronic and print journals related to theology and ethics.
• *Systematic Theology, Internet Theology Resources.* http://www.users.csbsju.edu/~eknuth/itr/syst/index.html. Students can find here a collection of documents and articles related to Christology, ecclesiology, theological anthropology, moral theology, and social ethics.
• *Theological Commons, Princeton Theological Seminary.* http://commons.ptsem.edu/. Part of the Princeton Theological Seminary Library, the Theological Commons is an online library of books and journals on theology.
• *Theology Guide, Yale University Library.* http://guides.library.yale.edu/content.php?pid=17512&sid=118992. This online research guide directs students to a wealth of resources, including dictionaries, encyclopedias, books, journals, and other Internet materials.
• *Wabash Center for Teaching and Learning in Theology and Religion, Internet Guide to Religion.* http://www.wabashcenter.wabash.edu/resources/guide-headings.aspx. For students interested in religion and theology, this is a comprehensive guide to online resources, including electronic texts and journals, web sites, bibliographies, reference resources, and software.

World Religions and Ecumenism

- *Association for Religious and Intellectual Life (ARIL), World Religion Resources.* http://www.aril.org/World.html. This is a listing of the best resources on world religion available on the Internet.
- *Association of Religion Data Archives (ARDA).* http://www.thearda.com/Archive/Browse.asp. This organization offers statistical data—surveys, polls, and other information submitted by researchers on various worldwide religions.
- *Church, Denominational, and Ecumenical Resources, Yale University Library.* http://guides.library.yale.edu/content.php?pid=45595&sid=337010. This research guide from Yale University Library offers links to databases, reference tools, journal articles, and online resources related to ecumenism and various Christian denominations.
- *Ecumenical News International (ENI).* http://www.eni.ch/news/. This is a global news service that reports on ecumenical developments, offers news on the worldwide church, and gives religious perspectives on news developments around the world.
- *Internet Sacred Texts Archive.* http://www.sacred-texts.com/stbib.htm. This site offers access to the largest collection of online books about world religions, mythology, folklore, and other sacred traditions.
- *University of Calgary, Religious Studies Web Guide.* http://people.ucalgary.ca/~lipton/biblio.html. This is a comprehensive listing of bibliographies available on the Internet covering Christianity, Judaism, Islam, and other world religions.
- *World Council of Churches (WCC).* http://www.oikoumene.org/en/resources/documents. This organization brings together churches throughout the world in an ecumenical movement designed to promote Christian unity. Their website offers access to a searchable collection of WCC documents.

Appendix C

Style Guides

Be sure to check with your professors to find out which citation and style manual they prefer for written work. Generally, an institution requires all students to conform to one style, making it easier for professors who have to read and evaluate student writing. Depending on the area, however, a professor may ask for a style specific to that field. The following is a list of those most common in seminary. Your library most likely has print versions of these style guides, but you also can access them online.

- *Chicago Style*. The Chicago Manual of Style has two documentation systems, but the humanities style is most common in literature, history, and the arts. Bibliographic information is presented in footnotes and endnotes, as well as in the bibliography.
    - ➢ *Print Guide*. *Chicago Manual of Style: The Essential Guide for Writers, Editors, and Publishers*, 16th ed. Chicago: University of Chicago Press, 2010.
    - ➢ *Online Guide*. The Chicago Style Citation Quick Guide can be found at http://www.chicagomanualofstyle.org/tools_citationguide.html.
- *Turabian Style*. Turabian Style is used quite often in literature, history, and the arts, and it differs from Chicago style only slightly. Bibliographic sources are listed alphabetically at the end of the paper and can be referred to in the paper itself with footnotes or using the in-text style.
    - ➢ *Print Guide*. Turabian, Kate. *A Manual for Writers of Research Papers, Theses, and Dissertations*, 8th ed. Chicago: University of Chicago Press, 2013.
    - ➢ *Online Guide*. The address for the Turabian Quick Guide is http://www.press.uchicago.edu/books/turabian/turabian_citationguide.html.
- *APA (American Psychological Association) Style*. APA Style is used in the fields of psychology and the social sciences; if you are studying pastoral care or the psychology of religion, for example, you may be asked to use this style. It also is sometimes referred to as "Harvard Style."
    - ➢ *Print Guide*. *Publication Manual of the American Psychological Asso-*

ciation, 6th ed. Washington, DC: American Psychological Association, 2010.
- ➢ *Online Guide*. The official APA online guide can be found at http://www.apastyle.org/.
- *MLA (Modern Language Association) Style*. MLA style is most commonly used within the fields of liberal arts and humanities. This style features a bibliography of works cited at the end of the paper and brief parenthetical citations within the body of the paper.
  - ➢ *Print Guide*. *MLA Handbook for Writers of Research Papers*, 7th ed. New York: Modern Language Association, 2009.
  - ➢ *Online Guide*. MLA does not allow access to their online guide without purchasing a copy of the print guide, but you can find an MLA Formatting and Style Guide on the Purdue Online Writing Lab website, http://owl.english.purdue.edu/owl/resource/747/01/.
- *SBL (Society of Biblical Literature) Style*. SBL style is often required for students writing papers related to the study of biblical literature, especially if you're planning to publish your work in an academic journal.
  - ➢ *Print Guide*. Alexander, Patrick H., John F. Kutsko, James D. Ernest, and Shirley Decker-Lucke. *The SBL Handbook of Style: For Ancient Near Eastern, Biblical, and Early Christian Studies*. Peabody, MA: Hendrickson, 2003.
  - ➢ *Online Guide*. You must be a member of SBL to access the handbook online, but a succinct Student Supplement to the SBL Handbook of Style can be downloaded from http://www.sbl-site.org/assets/pdfs/SBLHSrevised2_09.pdf.

APPENDIX D

Recommended Reading for Beginning Seminary Students

Biblical Interpretation

- Anderson, Cheryl B. *Ancient Laws and Contemporary Controversies: The Need for Inclusive Biblical Interpretation.* New York: Oxford University Press, 2009.
- Brown, Michael Joseph. *What They Don't Tell You: A Survivor's Guide to Biblical Studies.* Louisville: Westminster John Knox, 2000.

Christian Education and Faith Formation

- Conde-Frazier, Elizabeth, Steve Kang, Gary A. Parrett. *A Many Colored Kingdom: Multicultural Dynamics for Spiritual Formation.* Grand Rapids, MI: Baker Academic, 2004.
- Tye, Karen B. *Basics of Christian Education.* Atlanta: Chalice, 2000.

Church History

- González, Justo L. *Church History: An Essential Guide.* Nashville: Abingdon, 2010.
- Mullin, Robert B. *A Short World History of Christianity.* Louisville: Westminster John Knox, 2008.
- Noll, Mark A.. *Turning Points: Decisive Moments in the History of Christianity*, 3d ed. Grand Rapids, MI: Baker, 2012.

Congregational Studies

- Bass, Diana Butler. *Christianity for the Rest of Us: How the Neighborhood Church is Transforming the Faith.* New York: HarperCollins, 2006.

Liturgy, Preaching and Worship

- Foster, Richard J. *Prayer: Finding the Heart's True Home*, 10th anniv. ed. New York: HarperCollins, 1992.
- Gilbert, Marlea, Christopher Grundy, Eric T. Myers, and Stephanie Perdew. *The Work of the People: What We Do in Worship and Why*. Herndon, VA: Alban Institute, 2007.
- Tisdale, Leonora Tubbs. *Prophetic Preaching: A Pastoral Approach*. Louisville: Westminster John Knox, 2010.

New Testament

- Levine, Amy-Jill. *The Misunderstood Jew: The Church and the Scandal of the Jewish Jesus*. New York: HarperCollins, 2009.
- Matera, Frank J. *New Testament Theology: Exploring Diversity and Unity*. Louisville: Westminster John Knox, 2007.
- Sanders, E.P. *Paul: A Very Short Introduction*. New York: Oxford University Press, 1991.

Old Testament

- Anderson, Bernhard W., and Steven Bishop. *Contours of Old Testament Theology*. Minneapolis: Fortress, 1999.
- Brueggemann, Walter. *Journey to the Common Good*. Louisville: Westminster John Knox, 2010.
- _____. *Old Testament Theology: An Introduction*. Nashville: Abingdon, 2010.

Pastoral Care

- Dykstra, Robert C. *Images of Pastoral Care: Classic Readings*. Danvers, MA: Chalice, 2005.
- Lartey, Emmanuel Yartekwei. *In Living Color: An Intercultural Approach to Pastoral Care and Counseling*. London: Jessica Kingsley, 2003.
- Patton, John. *Pastoral Care in Context: An Introduction to Pastoral Care*. Louisville: Westminster John Knox, 2005.

Theology and Ethics

- Allen, Diogenes, and Eric O. Springsted. *Philosophy for Understanding Theology*, 2d ed. Louisville: Westminster John Knox, 2007.
- Cox, Harvey. *When Jesus Came to Harvard: Making Moral Choices Today*. New York: Houghton Mifflin, 2004.
- McGrath, Alister E. *Christian Theology: An Introduction*. Malden, MA: John Wiley and Sons, 2011.

- Stone, Howard W., and James O. Duke. *How to Think Theologically*, 3d ed. Minneapolis: Augsburg Fortress, 2013.
- Thielicke, Helmut, trans. Charles L. Taylor. *A Little Exercise for Young Theologians*. Grand Rapids, MI: William B. Eerdmans, 1962.

Theology in Context/Culture

- Chopp, Rebecca S., Mark Lewis Taylor, eds. *Reconstructing Christian Theology*. Minneapolis: Augsburg Fortress, 1994.
- Hopkins, Dwight N. *Being Human: Race, Culture, and Religion*. Minneapolis: Augsburg Fortress, 2005.
- Niebuhr, H. Richard. *Christ and Culture*, 50th anniv. ed. New York: HarperCollins, 1951.
- Pears, Angie. *Doing Contextual Theology*. New York: Routledge, 2009.

World Religions and Ecumenism

- Neusner, Jacob, ed. *World Religions in America*, 4th ed. Louisville: Westminster John Knox, 2009.
- Sharma, Arvind. *Our Religions: The Seven World Religions Introduced by Preeminent Scholars from Each Tradition*. New York: HarperCollins, 2011.
- Smith, Huston. *The World's Religions*, 50th anniv. ed. New York: HarperCollins, 2009.

Chapter Notes

Chapter Two

i. Donald K. McKim, *Westminster Dictionary of Theological Terms* (Louisville: Westminster John Knox, 1996), 98.

ii. John Haralson Hayes and Carl R. Holladay, *Biblical Exegesis: A Beginner's Handbook* (Louisville: Westminster John Knox, 1987), 14–18.

iii. McKim, Westminster Dictionary of Theological Terms, 127.

iv. "The Critical Study of Biblical Literature: Exegesis and Hermeneutics," Encyclopedia Britannica Academic Edition, last modified December 14, 2010, accessed August 13, 2013, http://www.britannica.com/EBchecked/topic/64496/biblical-literature/73485/The-critical-study-of-biblical-literature-exegesis-and-hermeneutics?anchor=toc73485.

v. Michael Joseph Brown, *What They Don't Tell You: A Survivor's Guide to Biblical Studies* (Louisville: Westminster John Knox, 2000), 5.

vi. Richard N. Soulen and R. Kendall Soulen, *Handbook of Biblical Criticism*, 3d ed. (Louisville: Westminster John Knox, 2001), 156–57.

vii. Hayes and Holladay, *Biblical Exegesis*, 29.

Chapter Three

i. "Developing a Central Claim," Thompson Writing Program, Duke University Writing Studio, accessed July 21, 2013, http://twp.duke.edu/uploads/media_items/central-claim.original.pdf.

ii. "Acknowledging, Paraphrasing, and Quoting Sources," in *The Writer's Handbook* (Madison: Writing Center, University of Wisconsin-Madison, 2003), accessed July 19, 2013, http://writing.wisc.edu/Handbook/Acknowledging_Sources.pdf.

iii. "Reading to Write," University of North Carolina at Chapel Hill, Writing Center, accessed July 17, 2013, http://writingcenter.unc.edu/handouts/reading-to-write/.

iv. "Reading to Write," Thompson Writing Program, Duke University Writing Studio, accessed July 17, 2013, http://twp.duke.edu/uploads/media_items/reading-to-write.original.pdf.

v. "Reading to Write," University of North Carolina at Chapel Hill.

Chapter Four

i. "Style," University of North Carolina at Chapel Hill, Writing Center, accessed July 17, 2013, http://writingcenter.unc.edu/handouts/style/.

ii. Ibid.

iii. Ibid.

iv. "The First Person in Academic Writing," Thompson Writing Program, Duke University Writing Studio, accessed July 17, 2013, http://twp.duke.edu/uploads/media_items/first-person.original.pdf.

Chapter Five

i. Shay Craig Robertson, "The Costly Loss of Laughter," Master's Thesis,

Garrett-Evangelical Theological Seminary, Evanston, IL, May 2012.
　ii. Faye Halpern, et al., *A Guide to Writing in Religious Studies* (Cambridge, MA: Harvard University, 2007), 8, accessed June 22, 2013, http://edwardseducationblog.files.wordpress.com/2013/07/religious_studies.pdf.
　iii. "Using Research and Evidence," Purdue Online Writing Lab (OWL), last edited March 11, 2013, accessed July 23, 2013, https://owl.english.purdue.edu/owl/resource/588/02/.
　iv. Halpern, et al., A Guide to Writing in Religious Studies, 19–21.
　v. "Body Paragraphs: Moving from General to Specific Information," Purdue Online Writing Lab (OWL), last modified February 25, 2013, accessed June 22, 2013, http://owl.english.purdue.edu/owl/owlprint/724/.

Chapter Six

　i. Duane Kelderman, "What Makes a Sermon a Good Sermon?" in *Calvin Theological Seminary Forum Magazine* 9, no. 2 (Spring 2002), accessed July 21, 2013, http://www.calvin.edu/library/database/crcpi/fulltext/csf/spring2002.pdf#page=9.
　ii. Marie E. Isaacs, "Exegesis and Homiletics," in *Spirituality and Scripture, The Way Supplement* 72 (1991): 36–37.
　iii. John Dally, "Developing and Preaching the Sermon," class lecture, Garrett-Evangelical Theological Seminary, Evanston, IL, September 15, 2009.
　iv. Peter Mead, "Exegesis Homiletics," *Biblical Preaching*, September 17, 2008, accessed September 1, 2013, http://www.biblicalpreaching.net/2008/09/17/exegesis-homiletics/.
　v. Aaron Damiani, "15 Preaching Best Practices: Tips from Great Preachers that Make a Difference in the Pulpit," *Preaching Today*, August 19, 2013, accessed August 30, 2013, http:www.preachingtoday.com/skills/2013/august/15-preaching-best-practices.html.
　vi. Ibid.
　vii. Kelderman, "What Makes a Sermon a Good Sermon?"
　viii. Dally, "Developing and Preaching the Sermon."
　ix. Isaacs, "Exegesis and Homiletics."
　x. "Writing Transitions," Purdue Online Writing Lab (OWL), last edited March 1, 2013, accessed July 24, 2013, https://owl.english.purdue.edu/owl/resource/574/01/.
　xi. Damiani, "15 Preaching Best Practices."

Chapter Seven

　i. Deborah Core, *The Seminary Student Writes* (St. Louis: Chalice, 2000), 45–46.
　ii. Lucretia B. Yaghjian, Writing Theology Well: A Rhetoric for Theological and Biblical Writers (New York: Continuum, 2008), 303–304.

Bibliography

Brown, Michael Joseph. *What They Don't Tell You: A Survivor's Guide to Biblical Studies*. Louisville: Westminster John Knox, 2000.

Core, Deborah. *The Seminary Student Writes*. St. Louis: Chalice, 2000.

Dally, John. "Developing and Preaching the Sermon." Class lecture, Garrett-Evangelical Theological Seminary, Evanston, IL, September 15, 2009.

Damiani, Aaron. "15 Preaching Best Practices: Tips from Great Preachers that Make a Difference in the Pulpit." *Preaching Today*, August 19, 2013. Accessed August 30, 2013. http:www.preachingtoday.com/skills/2013/august/15-preaching-best-practices.html.

Duke University. "Developing a Central Claim." Thompson Writing Program, Duke University Writing Studio. Accessed July 21, 2013. http://twp.duke.edu/uploads/media_items/central-claim.original.pdf.

———. "The First Person in Academic Writing." Thompson Writing Program, Duke University Writing Studio. Accessed July 17, 2013. http://twp.duke.edu/uploads/media_items/first-person.original.pdf.

———. "Reading to Write." Thompson Writing Program, Duke University Writing Studio. Accessed July 17, 2013. http://twp.duke.edu/uploads/media_items/reading-to-write.original.pdf.

Encyclopedia Britannica Academic Edition. "The Critical Study of Biblical Literature: Exegesis and Hermeneutics." Last modified December 14, 2010. Accessed August 13, 2013. http://www.britannica.com/EBchecked/topic/64496/biblical-literature/73485/The-critical-study-of-biblical-literature-exegesis-and-hermeneutics?anchor=toc73485.

Halpern, Faye, Thomas A. Lewis, Anne Monius, Robert Orsi, and Christopher White. *A Guide to Writing in Religious Studies*. Cambridge, MA: Harvard University, 2007. Accessed June 22, 2013. http://edwardseducationblog.files.wordpress.com/2013/07/religious_studies.pdf.

Hayes, John Haralson, and Carl R. Holladay. *Biblical Exegesis: A Beginner's Handbook*. Louisville: Westminster John Knox, 1987.

Isaacs, Marie E. "Exegesis and Homiletics." *Spirituality and Scripture, The Way Supplement* 72 (1991): 32–47.

Kelderman, Duane. "What Makes a Sermon a Good Sermon?" *Calvin Theological Seminary Forum Magazine* 9, no. 2 (Spring 2002). Accessed July 21, 2013. http://www.calvin.edu/library/database/crcpi/fulltext/csf/spring2002.pdf#page=9.

McKim, Donald K. *Westminster Dictionary of Theological Terms*. Louisville: Westminster John Knox, 1996.

Mead, Peter. "Exegesis Homiletics." *Biblical Preaching*, September 17, 2008. Accessed September 1, 2013. http://www.biblicalpreaching.net/2008/09/17/exegesis-homiletics/.

Purdue University. "Body Paragraphs: Moving from General to Specific Information." Purdue Online Writing Lab (OWL). Last modified February 25, 2013. Accessed June 22, 2013. http://owl.english.purdue.edu/owl/owlprint/724/.

———. "Using Research and Evidence." Purdue Online Writing Lab (OWL). Last edited March 11, 2013. Accessed July 23, 2013. https://owl.english.purdue.edu/owl/resource/588/02/.

———. "Writing Transitions." Purdue Online Writing Lab (OWL). Last edited March 1, 2013. Accessed July 24, 2013. https://owl.english.purdue.edu/owl/resource/574/01/.

Robertson, Shay Craig. "The Costly Loss of Laughter." Master's Thesis. Garrett-Evangelical Theological Seminary, Evanston, IL, May 2012.

Soulen, Richard N., and R. Kendall Soulen. *Handbook of Biblical Criticism*, 3d ed. Louisville: Westminster John Knox, 2001.

University of North Carolina. "Reading to Write." The University of North Carolina at Chapel Hill, Writing Center. Accessed July 17, 2013. http://writingcenter.unc.edu/handouts/reading-to-write/.

———. "Style." University of North Carolina at Chapel Hill, Writing Center. Accessed July 17, 2013. http://writingcenter.unc.edu/handouts/style/.

University of Wisconsin. "Acknowledging, Paraphrasing, and Quoting Sources." *The Writer's Handbook*. Madison: Writing Center, University of Wisconsin-Madison, 2003. Accessed July 19, 2013. http://writing.wisc.edu/Handbook/Acknowledging_Sources.pdf.

Yaghjian, Lucretia B. *Writing Theology Well: A Rhetoric for Theological and Biblical Writers*. New York: Continuum, 2008.

Index

academic jargon 87
academic voice 87, 89–90
acknowledgment of sources 110
active vs. passive voice 87, 112
argument 32–33, 59, 65, 72, 87–90, 102–103, 105, 107–108, 109–110, 111, 183–184
audience 21, 29, 33–34

biblical authorship 21, 24, 33
biblical criticism:
  feminist criticism 25, 27
  form criticism 24, 26
  historical criticism 23–24, 25
  ideological criticism 24–25, 27
  liberationist criticism 24–25, 27
  literary criticism 24, 26
  methods of biblical criticism 22–26
  narrative criticism 24, 26
  political/ideological criticism 24–25, 27
  post-colonial criticism 24–25, 27
  reader-response criticism 24–25, 27
  redaction criticism 24, 26
  rhetorical criticism 24, 26
  social-science criticism 23–24, 25
  socio-economic criticism 24–25, 27
  source criticism 23–24, 25
  tradition criticism 23–24, 25
  womanist criticism 25, 27
  world behind the text 23–24, 25
  world in front of the text 24–25, 27
  world of the text 24, 26
biblical exegesis:
  exegesis for sermon writing 165–167
  exegetical papers 26–36

criticism *see* biblical criticism; feminist criticism; form criticism; historical criticism; ideological criticism; liberationist criticism; literary criticism; narrative criticism; political/ideological criticism; post-colonial criticism; reader-response criticism; redaction criticism; rhetorical criticism; social-science criticism; source criticism; tradition criticism; womanist criticism

editing 111–112
exegesis 20–22
exegetical papers:
  analysis/research 26–31
  elements of exegetical paper 33–34
  guidelines 28–31, 34–36
  sample exegetical papers 36–58
  synthesis 31–34
  unifying theme 32–33

feminist criticism 25, 27
first-hand research 106
first-person perspective 90
form criticism 24, 26
free writing 83, 85–86

gender bias 169–70
genre (biblical) 21, 24, 26, 30, 34, 35

hermeneutics 22–23
historical criticism 23–24, 25

ideological criticism 24–25, 27
inclusive language 169–170

journal articles:
  sample journal articles 184–224
  writing for publication 183–184

language 21, 24, 30, 34, 35
liberationist criticism 24–25, 27
literary criticism 24, 26

masculine images for God 170
methods of biblical criticism 22–26

narrative criticism 24, 26
original source document 59, 61
outlining 107-108

papers *see* exegetical papers; research papers
paraphrasing 71-72, 109
personal voice 87, 89-90
political/ideological criticism 24-25, 27
post-colonial criticism 24-25, 27
primary sources 106-107
proofreading 111-112

reader-response criticism 24-25, 27
reading critically 72-73
redaction criticism 24, 26
reflection papers:
    reflecting 85
    sample reflection papers 91-101
    writing the reflection paper 86
research basics 106-107
research papers:
    analytical/exploratory 103
    argument 109-110
    argumentative 102-103
    introduction, body, conclusion 107-109
    outlining 107-108
    paper topic 103-104
    questions to explore 104
    research basics 106-107
    sample research papers 113-162
revising 111-112
rhetorical criticism 24, 26

secondary sources 59, 107, 108
second-hand research 106-107
sermons:
    exegesis for sermon writing 165-167
    expository sermon 164
    proposition/big idea 167
    qualities of great sermon 168
    sample sermons 171-180
    sermon writing 168-169
    textual sermon 164
    topical sermon 164
social location 24, 28, 33, 35
social-science criticism 23-24, 25
socio-economic criticism 24-25, 27
source criticism 23-24, 25
style guidelines 87-89

theological book reviews:
    critical book review 8
    descriptive book review 8
    sample book reviews 9-11, 12-19
    short version 9, 11
theological essay/summaries:
    chapter review 65
    historical document 61-62
    sample essays/summaries 62-64, 66-68, 69-71
theological reflection 83-86
thesis/thesis statement 8, 9, 33, 35-36, 59-61, 65, 73, 102-103, 104-106, 107-110, 111-113
tradition criticism 23-24, 25

womanist criticism 25, 27